EXPERIENCING BEETHOVEN

The Listener's Companion
Gregg Akkerman, Series Editor

Titles in **The Listener's Companion** provide readers with a deeper understanding of key musical genres and the work of major artists and composers. Aimed at nonspecialists, each volume explains in clear and accessible language how to listen to works from particular artists, composers, and genres. Looking at both the context in which the music first appeared and has since been heard, authors explore with readers the environments in which key musical works were written and performed.

EXPERIENCING BEETHOVEN

A Listener's Companion

Geoffrey Block

ROWMAN & LITTLEFIELD
Lanham • Boulder • New York • London

Published by Rowman & Littlefield
A wholly owned subsidiary of The Rowman & Littlefield Publishing Group,
Inc.
4501 Forbes Boulevard, Suite 200, Lanham, Maryland 20706
www.rowman.com

Unit A, Whitacre Mews, 26-34 Stannary Street, London SE11 4AB

British Library Cataloguing in Publication Information Available

Library of Congress Cataloging-in-Publication Data

Names: Block, Geoffrey Holden, 1948- author.
Title: Experiencing Beethoven : a listener's companion / Geoffrey Block.
Description: Lanham : Rowman & Littlefield, [2017] | Series: The listener's companion | Includes
    bibliographical references and index.
Identifiers: LCCN 2016018116 (print) | LCCN 2016018457 (ebook) | ISBN 9781442245457
    (cloth : alk. paper) | ISBN 9781442245464 (electronic)
Subjects: LCSH: Beethoven, Ludwig van, 1770-1827—Criticism and interpretation
Classification: LCC ML410.B42 B4913 2017 (print) | LCC ML410.B42 (ebook) | DDC 780.92—
    dc23 LC record available at https://lccn.loc.gov/2016018116

Printed in the United States of America

For Andrew—
Treasured colleague
Friend to me and Jacqueline
Honorary uncle to Jessamyn and Eliza

CONTENTS

TIMELINE

1770   Baptized in Bonn on December 17 and most likely born on December 16, the first surviving child of Johann van Beethoven (ca. 1740–1792), a court singer, and Maria Magdalena (1746–1787). Two brothers also survive, Caspar Carl (born 1774) and Johann (born 1776).

1773   Death of Beethoven's grandfather, also named Ludwig, Kapellmeister to the elector Max Friedrich.

1778   First public appearance as a performer.

1779   Christian Gottlob Neefe, Beethoven, major composition teacher, arrives in Bonn. Beethoven begins his studies with Neefe two years later.

1782   First musical publication, the Piano Variations on a March by Dressler, WoO 63.

1783   Publication of the three *Elector* Sonatas for piano, WoO 47.

1784   Death of Elector Max Friedrich and appointment of Elector Maximilian Franz, brother of Emperor Joseph II. Beethoven joins the payroll as court organist.

1785   Composes the three piano quartets, WoO 36.

1787   Travels to Vienna. Meets and hopes to study with Mozart but returns to Bonn to see his dying mother, who dies on July 17.

1789   Plays viola in the court orchestra and petitions Maximilian Franz for half of his father's salary.

1790   Death of Joseph II on February 20. Composes the Cantata on the Death of the Emperor Joseph II, WoO 87, which is not performed.

1791   Publication of the Twenty-Four Variations on Righini's arietta *Venni amore*, WoO 65. Death of Mozart on December 5.

1792   Beethoven leaves Bonn for Vienna in early November "to receive *the spirit of Mozart from the hands of study with Haydn.*" Death of Johann van Beethoven on December 18.

1793   Begins counterpoint studies with Joseph Haydn.

1794   Haydn's second trip to England. In his absence, Beethoven studies with Johann Georg Albrechtsberger until the spring of 1795.

1795   Beethoven's first public performance in Vienna as pianist and composer in March. Haydn returns from England. The publication of the three piano trios, op. 1, in August.

1796   Publishes his piano sonatas, op. 2. Concert tour of Prague, Dresden, Leipzig, and Berlin from February to July and Pressburg and Pest in November. Based on his letter in 1801, the beginning of Beethoven's hearing loss occurs around this time.

1797   Publishes his first cello sonatas, op. 5, and the piano sonata, op. 7.

1798   Beethoven performs his first and second piano concertos in Prague in the fall. Publication of the piano sonatas, op. 10. Begins his lifelong habit of using bound sketchbooks instead of loose sheets of music paper.

1799   Publication of the *Pathétique* Sonata, op. 13.

1800   First Academy concert on April 2 at the Burgtheater. Works performed include the premieres of the septet, op. 20, and the First Symphony, op. 21, and a revised First Piano Concerto, op. 15.

1801   Premiere of the ballet *The Creatures of Prometheus*, op. 43, the composition of the *Moonlight* Sonata, op. 27, no. 2, and the publication of the string quartets, op. 18. First-known acknowledgment of his hearing loss in a letter to his friend, Franz Wegeler.

1802   The Heiligenstadt Testament (October 6 and 10). Composes the *Tempest* Sonata, op. 31, no. 2, and the *Prometheus* Variations for Piano, op. 35 (known as the *Eroica* Variations).

1803   Academy concert on April 5 at the Theater an der Wien. The concert repeats the First Symphony and premieres the Second Symphony, op. 36, the Third Piano Concerto, op. 37, and the oratorio *Christ on the Mount of Olives*, op. 85. First performance of the *Kreutzer* Violin Sonata, op. 47, and the publication of the three violin sonatas, op. 30.
Begins to compose the *Eroica* Symphony.

1804   *Eroica* Symphony receives a private performance in the palace of Prince Lobkowitz in August. Completes the *Waldstein* Sonata, op. 53, and begins to compose *Leonore*, later named *Fidelio*. Napoleon crowns himself emperor.

1805   Completes the *Appassionata* Sonata, op. 57. The first public performance of the *Eroica* at the Theater an der Wien on April 7. *Leonore*, the first version of *Fidelio*, premieres on November 20.

1806   Composes the *Razumovsky* String Quartets, op. 59, the Fourth Symphony, op. 60, and the violin concerto, op. 61. The first performance of the revised *Fidelio* on March 29.

1807   Prince Esterházy commissions the Mass in C.

1808   Academy concert on December 22 at the Theater an der Wien with the premieres of the Fifth Symphony, op. 67, the Sixth (*Pastoral*), op. 68, the Fourth Piano Concerto, op. 58, and the *Choral Fantasy*, op. 80.

1809   Archduke Rudolph, Prince Lobkowitz, and Prince Kinsky agree to give Beethoven a large annuity in exchange for the composer's remaining in Vienna. Napoleon occupies Vienna.

1810   Composes music for Goethe's *Egmont*, op. 84, and Goethe songs, op. 83, the string quartet, op. 95, and the first of dozens of folk-song arrangements for George Thomson.

1811   Composes the *Archduke* Piano Trio, op. 97.

1812   Passionate love letter addressed to the Immortal Beloved. The
        identity of the recipient is unknown but widely thought to be
        Antonie Brentano. Beethoven meets Goethe at Teplitz.
        Begins a diary (*Tagebuch*) that he will continue until 1818.

1813   Premieres of the Seventh Symphony, op. 92, and *Wellington's
        Victory*, op. 91, at a charity concert held in University Hall on
        December 8.

1814   Concert in the Redoutensaal on February 27, which includes
        repeat performances of the Seventh Symphony and
        Wellington's Victory and the premiere of the Eighth
        Symphony, op. 93. Performance of the third and final version
        of *Fidelio* on May 23. Beethoven and his music celebrated at
        the Congress of Vienna. Begins the practice of using pocket
        sketchbooks.

1815   Brother Caspar Carl dies on November 15, and Beethoven
        embarks on a nearly five-year bitter struggle to gain legal
        custody of his nephew Karl from his mother Johanna van
        Beethoven.

1816   Composes the song cycle *An die ferne Geliebte*, op. 98.

1817   The Philharmonic Society of London invites Beethoven to
        compose two new symphonies.

1818   Completes the *Hammerklavier* Sonata, op. 106. The extent of
        Beethoven's hearing loss leads to the practice of using
        conversation books.

1819   Begins work on the *Missa solemnis* and composes twenty-two
        variations of the Thirty-Three Variations on a Waltz by Anton
        Diabelli.

1820   The court rules in favor of Beethoven's guardianship of Karl
        in July. The previous month Johanna had given birth to a
        daughter out of wedlock with the physician Samuel Raics de
        Nagy-Megyer (the wealthy bell founder Johann Kaspar
        Hofbauer acknowledged paternity, however, and provided a
        legal last name). In light of the animosity between Beethoven
        and Johanna, it may come as a surprise to learn that this child
        was named Ludovika, the feminine form of Ludwig. It should

also be noted that, despite the view espoused by director Bernard Rose in the biopic *Immortal Beloved* (1994), Beethoven was not the father of Karl.

1821 Completes the piano sonatas op. 109, 110, and 111.

1822 Prince Galitzin commissions "one, two, or three new quartets" (eventually op. 127, op. 132, and op. 130). Revises but does not publish *Für Elise*, WoO 59.

1823 Completes the *Missa solemnis*, op. 123, and completes and publishes the remaining eleven *Diabelli* Variations, op. 120.

1824 Premiere of the Ninth Symphony, op. 125, on May 7. Completes his last work for piano, the Six Bagatelles, op. 126, and begins the string quartets in Eb Major, op. 127, and A Minor, op. 132. Begins to favor score sketches, especially valuable for drafting string quartets, instead of single-line sketches.

1825 Completes the string quartets op. 127, op. 132, and Bb Major, op. 130, with the *Grosse Fuge* as the finale (the latter published separately as op. 133).

1826 Completes the String Quartet in C# Minor, op. 131, the F Major, op. 135, and a new finale for the Bb quartet. Karl attempts suicide but survives with little injury.

1827 Dies on March 26.

INTRODUCTION

"Why Beethoven?"

In an imaginary conversation between Leonard Bernstein (L.B.) and Lyric Poet (L.P.) in *The Joy of Music* (1959), the issue of "Why Beethoven?" arose during an otherwise uneventful drive in the mountains of New Mexico on the way to Taos. L.P., the unnamed poet Stephen Spender, proclaimed, "These hills are pure Beethoven." L.B. was moved to respond, "I'm not complaining. I'd just like to know why not Bach, Mozart, Mendelssohn, Schumann—"(Bernstein 1959, 22–23). After discussing various musical parameters one by one, L.P. and L.B. concur that Ludwig van Beethoven was fundamentally "a mediocre melodist, a homely harmonist, an itinerant riveter of a rhythmist, an ordinary orchestrator, a commonplace contrapuntist!" (28).

Nevertheless, L.B. goes on to single Beethoven out for possessing a "magic ingredient," the "gift of inevitability": "Beethoven broke all the rules and turned out pieces of breath-taking rightness. Rightness— that's the word! When you get the feeling that whatever note succeeds the last is the only possible note that can rightly happen at that instant, in that context, then chances are you're listening to Beethoven" (28–29). L.B. continues to wax lyrical (to the Lyric Poet) when he goes on to praise Beethoven as the composer who more than any other bestows *something we can trust, that will never let us down* (29). When L.B. is finished, L.P. points out "quietly" that this description "is almost a definition of God" (29). L.B. gets the last word when he replies, "I meant it to be" (29).

For L.P. and L.B. Beethoven is a composer whose musical whole is miraculously greater than its parts and a being endowed with a godlike status. Though they do not discuss this, he also profits from his compelling backstory, the story of a driven creator who managed to transform a composer's greatest nightmare, the emotional suffering brought about by the affliction and shame of deafness, into music that is full of not only anger and pain but also joy, or to use the word Beethoven used at the beginning of the Ninth's finale, Freudenvollere (joyfulness). In addition to his heroic response to life's challenges and his sublime talents and artistic achievements, Beethoven, the man, embodies nineteenth-century (and contemporary) notions of a genius so focused on creative acts that he is oblivious to his surroundings and his physical appearance. He is a social and aesthetic revolutionary who breaks the rules. After their meeting, Luigi Cherubini, at the time a well-known Italian composer working in France, memorably and famously described Beethoven as "an unlicked bear" (Sonneck 1967, 69), that is, unpolished and crude.

This book will take its readers on a guided tour of the music created by this unlicked bear, on a road a little less travelled than some other tours. There are thousands of books on our subject. Some center on a single work such as the Ninth Symphony or a genre such as the string quartets. Others attempt a broader survey encompassing numerous works. In contrast, *Experiencing Beethoven* devotes three chapters to single works (*Fidelio*, the Ninth Symphony, and the C# Minor String Quartet), while six other chapters treat somewhere between four and seven instrumental works, or in the case of a chapter on "Beethoven and Song," eleven songs. Many of the indispensable works, the "usual suspects," are found here, including seven of Beethoven's nine symphonies (First, *Eroica*, Fifth, *Pastoral*, Seventh, Eighth, and Ninth); seven of the thirty-piano sonatas (the so-called *Pathétique, Moonlight, Tempest,* and *Appassionata* sonatas plus three others, op. 10, no. 3, op. 110, and op. 111); three string quartets (the first quartet from the earliest set of six, op. 18, the first *Razumovsky* from the middle op. 59 set of three, and the late C# Minor String Quartet, op. 131); two piano concertos (no. 1 in C Major and no. 4 in G Major); and the *Diabelli* Variations for solo piano. The volume also embraces several fascinating but lesser-known works such as the *Joseph Cantata* Beethoven composed at the age of nineteen in Bonn; a group of songs that includes the historic (and gorgeous) song cycle *An die ferne Geliebte*; the Ninth's overlooked predecessor, the *Choral Fantasy*; the potboiler *Wellington's Victory*; and the piano bagatelle more familiarly known as *Für Elise*.

Experiencing Beethoven will also transport readers to historic concerts where many of these works were first performed. We will attend the private performance of the Third Symphony in 1804 in the home of Prince Lobkowitz at which Beethoven's shocked friend Ferdinand Ries complained about what he thought was a premature horn entrance. We will also witness the unfortunate debut of *Fidelio* in 1805, several days after the French had invaded Vienna, and the private and unofficial Vienna debut of the C# Minor String Quartet, for Franz Schubert, who was on his deathbed in November 1828. In particular, we will share firsthand reports of what occurred at the high-profile public concerts then known as Academies and other public occasions where the following works received their debuts:

1800	First Piano Concerto, First Symphony, and Septet
1808	Fifth and Sixth Symphonies, Fourth Piano Concerto, and *Choral Fantasy*
1813	Seventh Symphony and *Wellington's Victory*
1814	Eighth Symphony and (as encores) the Seventh and *Wellington's Victory*
1824	Ninth Symphony
1825– 1827	String Quartets in Eb Major (op. 127), A Minor (op. 132), and Bb Major (op. 130)

Almost all composers, including Mozart and Schubert, at least occasionally sketched their preliminary ideas. But no major composer sketched nearly as much as Beethoven, a composer for whom sketching became a fundamental component of the compositional process. Surviving sketches form a significant part of the backstory of a composer relentlessly seeking perfection and leaving abundant physical traces of the struggle. It took scholars more than 150 years to reconstruct and inventory Beethoven's nearly seventy-five surviving sketchbooks (about evenly divided between desk and pocket sketchbooks). It may take another generation or more before we realize the full compositional meanings that can be gleaned from the approximately four thousand extant sketch pages (many more have vanished), among them the 650 extant pages for the C# Minor String Quartet, some of which I will discuss in the final chapter.

Beethoven also left several unusual biographical documents that have enhanced our knowledge of the man and added to his mystery. Scholars and general readers have learned much from the nearly two thousand currently extant letters that span his entire adult life, the 171 entries in his *Tagebuch* (diary) from 1812 to 1818, and the 113 extant conversation books that, as his deafness progressed, became necessary in order for Beethoven to communicate with others, starting in 1818. Two letters in particular have generated enormous interest in our attempts to understand Beethoven's private life and loves. One is the unsent letter to his brothers from 1802 known as the Heiligenstadt Testament, in which the troubled composer acknowledges the suffering caused by his deafness and vows to conquer this affliction and live for art. The second is a letter that may have been sent in 1812 to the unnamed woman the world has come to know as the Immortal Beloved, the first woman on record who truly wanted to marry Beethoven. If we accept Maynard Solomon's determination of Antonie Brentano as this beloved woman, as perhaps most but by no means all scholars do, she stands alone as the only woman we know willing to leave her husband and children for the "unlicked bear." For the first and probably only time, it was Beethoven who got cold feet.

* * *

While best known for his incalculable contributions to the orchestral, chamber, and solo literature (piano, violin, and cello), Beethoven left a significant body of work in nearly every genre, including one completed opera and over a hundred songs. Pianists can choose from among thirty-two piano solo sonatas from op. 2 to op. 111, as well as numerous variation sets, smaller pieces, and five fine concertos. Violinists can choose among ten sonatas and one great concerto. Cellists can perform five sonatas ranging from op. 5 to op. 102 as well as a few fun theme-and-variation sets based on themes by Handel and Mozart. Wind players, too, are invited to celebrate at the Beethoven party. Horn players have their sonata, op. 17; and wind players an octet, op. 103, two sextets, opp. 71 and 81b, and especially the perennially popular septet, op. 20, perhaps the most popular work during Beethoven's own lifetime.

Beethoven also composed a number of idiosyncratic works that have ensured his legacy in smaller but telling ways, for example the often-programmed triple concerto for piano, violin, and cello, op. 56, perhaps the only work of its kind in the classical repertoire. Even trombonists have something to play, the admittedly obscure Three Equali, WoO 30.[1] If a mandolin work is needed, Beethoven wrote two sonatinas, an adagio, and a theme and variations for that instrument as well. Young piano students enjoy a large array of finger-friendly piano music to play, including the two short sonatas published as op. 49, the first movement of the *Moonlight*, the second movement of the *Pathétique*, and of course *Für Elise*. More ambitious pianists can sink their fingers into such "monsterpieces" as the *Hammerklavier* Sonata, op. 106, and the *Diabelli* Variations, op. 120, or savor the profundities of the final piano sonata trilogy, opp. 109–11.

Students in my freshman Beethoven seminar, like Bernstein and the Lyric Poet in the imaginary conversation titled "Why Beethoven?" where we began, ponder this and related questions. Why is Beethoven's Ninth Symphony the musical protagonist in the films *A Clockwork Orange* (1971) and *Die Hard* (1988), and why was its *scherzo* the theme song of the *Huntley-Brinkley Report* for fourteen years? Why is the *Ode* performed at every Olympics since 1956? And why, for many years nearly everywhere in Japan, is *Daiku*, "The Big Ninth," heard throughout the Christmas season (see chapter 8)? Why does Schroeder, Charles M. Schulz's *Peanuts* comic-strip character, play only Beethoven on his toy piano in over 250 strips? Why did Chuck Berry demand that Beethoven and not some other composer roll over in his grave in the anthem to the 1956 rock-and-roll hit song "Roll Over Beethoven"? Why did Walter Murphy choose a fifth of Beethoven rather than Mahler for his disco blockbuster hit of 1976, "A Fifth of Beethoven"? Why Beethoven and not Berlioz for the name of the slobbering St. Bernard and his twenty-year-long film franchise (*Beethoven, Beethoven's 2nd, 3rd, 4th, 5th*, etc.)? References to Beethoven in novels, plays, movies, television programs, popular music, classical music, and commercials designed to sell a multitude of products are too numerous to count. Why are we then surprised that the Lyric Poet described the hills of New Mexico as pure Beethoven, and not Bach or Mozart? Tell Tchaikovsky the news that the hills are alive with the sound of Beethoven. Why Beethoven? Who can explain it? Who can tell you why?

Experiencing Beethoven: A Listener's Companion will try to answer the question "Why Beethoven?" Despite his fiction-worthy biography, iconic scowl, and the powerful image of a man raging and shaking his fist against a stormy fate on his deathbed, I am convinced that the answer to "Why Beethoven?" is to be discovered *in his music*. For this reason *Experiencing Beethoven* will look primarily to the music. Acknowledging the limitations of words about music, we will also look at the descriptive utility and accessibility of works—with some additional guidance at the end of the volume from the glossary of musical terms and forms prominent in the classical style. The goal throughout will be to help readers and listeners hear more in Beethoven's timeless music than they did before.

Our fascinating story includes an often-retold prophecy regarding Beethoven's future greatness, allegedly voiced by Mozart after his meeting with the sixteen-year-old composer, a mixed but ultimately fruitful apprenticeship with Haydn when Beethoven was in his twenties, and until his deafness caused him to largely abandon his performing career, adulation as a virtuoso pianist invariably recognized for his extraordinary improvisation skills. During his lifetime Beethoven also enjoyed enormous success as a composer, first with the Viennese aristocracy and eventually with a broader public as his music was published throughout Europe by a rapidly expanding printing industry. Today Beethoven is the embodiment of musical greatness—more than the Lyric Poet's New Mexico hills, a veritable mountain range of distinctive artworks and engaging stories. His compositions remain at the center of the classical musical universe. As prophesied by Count Waldstein, Beethoven indeed inherited the classical style and received *"the spirit of Mozart from the hands of Haydn"* (Lockwood 2003, 50). Without abandoning this great heritage, he created something new and strikingly original. Like his fictional contemporary, Goethe's Faust, Beethoven was a kind of musical alchemist who, in the course of remarkably varied works, converted suffering into joy, a joy that is ours to savor, nourish, and treasure.

I

"THE SPIRIT OF MOZART" (1770–1792)

Dear Beethoven! You are going to Vienna in fulfillment of a wish that has long been frustrated. Mozart's *genius* is still in mourning and weeps for the death of its pupil. It found a refuge with the inexhaustible Haydn but no occupation; through him it wishes to form a union with another. With the help of unceasing diligence you will receive *the spirit of Mozart from the hands of Haydn* (Lockwood 2003, 50).
—Count Waldstein's "prophecy" that Beethoven would inherit the classical style of Mozart and Haydn, entry in the autograph album that Beethoven took on his journey from Bonn to Vienna in November 1792

We begin in Bonn, a small town that could nonetheless boast strong political and cultural connections with the distant Vienna metropolis 450 miles to the southeast. For more than seven hundred years, starting in 1238, Bonn served as the residence of the elector of neighboring Cologne, one of seven electors appointed to choose the next Holy Roman Emperor. In 1784, Maximilian Franz was appointed to this position. Franz was the younger brother of Joseph II, the ruler of what was then the Austro-Hungarian Empire, comprising much of Central and Eastern Europe. Their sister was Marie Antoinette ("Let them eat cake"), the queen of France before she was beheaded in 1793. One year later, Franz, who apparently took his sister's advice to heart (he reportedly weighed 480 pounds), was forced to flee Bonn, pursued by the French army. He died in exile in 1801, and the empire collapsed shortly thereafter in 1806. In 1949, Bonn regained its political glamour when it became the capital of West Germany.

In 1732, the year George Washington was born, Beethoven's grandfather, also named Ludwig (1712–1773), came to Bonn from Belgium as a young man. After beginning his musical career as a bass soloist and chorister, from 1761 to his death in 1773, the senior Ludwig served with distinction as the court Kapellmeister, supervising music for the chapel, concert hall, and theater. Although he barely got a chance to know his grandfather, who died when little Ludwig was three, for the rest of his life Beethoven would keep a large portrait of his namesake on the walls of his many lodgings. Alas, the wife of Kapellmeister Beethoven was reportedly an alcoholic and so certainly was his only son Johann (ca. 1740–1792), our Ludwig's father. Johann spent his career in Bonn as a court tenor before his drinking made him unable to work. In contrast to the treasured memories of his grandfather, with the exception of a single legal document, Beethoven would never speak of his father, or even write down his name.

When Ludwig was about four or five, his father began teaching him the piano and violin. For a short time in 1779 Johann's drinking companion, the actor-musician Tobias Pfeiffer, who also lived with the Beethovens, shared the teaching duties. The central turning point of his youth occurred when, one or two years after arriving in Bonn (also in 1779), the composer and court organist Christian Gottlob Neefe (1748–1798) started teaching the prodigy. Between the years 1782 and 1785, before reaching the age of fifteen, Neefe's student had already demonstrated considerable promise as a composer.

The first work composed under Neefe's guidance, indeed Beethoven's first-known work, was a set of nine variations in C minor on a march by Dressler, WoO 63 (1782). A variation set is a work in which a theme is followed by a series of variations that preserve the theme's formal structure and vary one or more musical elements inherent in the theme, while retaining other elements. Despite signs of immaturity, the variations demonstrate Beethoven's secure grasp of keyboard and compositional technique and even the roots of a personal style. The choice of C minor would also turn out to be the first in a lengthy list of compositions in C minor, including the second movement of the *Eroica* Symphony (also a march), the famous Fifth Symphony more than twenty years later, the final piano sonata op. 111 more than twenty years later, and others in between. For an eleven-year-old, the *Dressler* Variations were an impressive as well as a prophetic start.

THE *ELECTOR* SONATAS, WOO 47 (1782–1783)

The *Dressler* Variations were soon followed by a set of three piano sonatas (WoO 47) dedicated to the proximate royal relative, Maximilian Friedrich, the elector of Cologne. The set was considered good enough to be published in 1783 when Beethoven was twelve (keep in mind that his birthday was not until December). Although later published as sonatas by publisher Tobias Haslinger, presumably after some consultation with the composer in the first edition of all Beethoven's sonatas published from 1828 to 1829, they only rarely stand alongside the standard thirty-two. But although the *Elector* Sonatas, as they have come to be known, may tend to imitate his contemporaries, they also convey considerable craft and understanding of the classical sonata form. Additionally, in some places, especially in the surprising slow introduction to the first movement of the second sonata in F minor, we can recognize the future composer of the *Pathétique* of 1798 and of even later works.

Sonatas were multimovement works in three or four movements. (See the glossary under Musical Forms for a discussion of Sonata Form and Other Movements in a Multimovement Work).[1] Composers began with a first movement in sonata form (exposition, development, recapitulation, and increasingly, a coda), usually in a fast tempo. Next came usually a slow movement in a variety of forms such as A-B-A, theme and variations, or "slow-movement" form (i.e., a sonata form without development). In a four-movement sonata, the third movement was usually a minuet or *scherzo* and trio. In a three-movement sonata, the third movement was typically a rondo or a sonata rondo, but it could also use other forms. Other than a minuet or *scherzo* movement, any movement could also be a theme and variations. Sonatas can be dramatic, a drama in which the protagonist invariably triumphs as thematic material from the second key area reappears and appropriates the secondary thematic material satisfyingly in the original tonic, the central key in tonal music (see tonality in the glossary). Musical tension generally builds during the approach to the secondary material and especially in anticipation of its return in the recapitulations. The complex, variable form offers con-

siderable opportunities for variety and flexibility. Even in the early sonata in which Beethoven is imitating contemporary classical models, he
often offers something out of the ordinary—something structurally novel. For example, at the recapitulation of the third *Elector* Sonata in D
major, Beethoven abandons the main theme after a single measure,
instead following a few measures later with the original second theme
(thus reducing what was originally a sixteen-measure first theme group
to only four measures, only the first of which is an actual return).

In the second sonata in F minor, however, we recognize the Beethoven of the future. In contrast to most solo sonatas of the era, rather than
introducing a central theme in a fast tempo, it begins with a nine-
measure slow introduction in F minor that builds tension for several
measures before subsiding into a soft resolution. The following *Allegro
assai* (very fast), still in F minor, has struck many Beethoven commentators as prophetic of the energy, mood, and even thematic content of
the *Pathétique* (piano) Sonata in C Minor, op. 13 (1798).[2] It also shares
its key with Beethoven's first published sonata, op. 2, no. 1 (1795).
Additionally, like many of Beethoven's future works in the minor mode
(see scales and modes in the glossary), the first movement of the F
Minor *Elector* Sonata exhibits greater concentration and brevity than in
most of his works in the major mode (see scales and modes in the
glossary). With a minimum of fuss or transition, Beethoven follows a
statement of the first theme in F minor with a second theme in the
relative major to complete the exposition only twenty-seven measures
after it began. After an extremely brief development section (ten measures), Beethoven again anticipates the *Pathétique* when he takes the
unusual step of returning to the material of the slow introduction. Since
Beethoven presents the return of the introduction in the subdominant
(a chord on the fourth degree of the scale; see triads in the glossary)
minor rather than the tonic minor, it perhaps makes better sense to
think of this passage as part of the development, but it certainly *sounds*
like a new return rather than a point of closure. After four measures the
slow introduction return departs from its predecessor to take the listener to the recapitulation of the opening fast part, this time entirely in F
minor and for exactly the same number of measures as the exposition.

Shortly before the *Elector* Sonatas were published, Neefe, writing in
a music magazine in 1783, noted that Beethoven possessed a "most
promising talent" (Lockwood 2003, 34), that he played "chiefly *The*

Well-Tempered Clavier of Sebastian Bach" (34), had been taught fig-
ured bass (the foundation of music theory and practice for nearly a
century), and had already composed and published Ernst Christoph
Dressler's nine variations for the piano. The "youthful genius" (34),
wrote Neefe, deserved financial support so that he could travel and
become better known (34). Neefe predicted that Beethoven "would
surely become a second Wolfgang Amadeus Mozart if he progresses as
he has begun," a resounding endorsement (34). Neefe was a mentor in
deeds as well as words. In addition to exposing young Ludwig to Bach,
he arranged for the publication of Beethoven's first-known compositions, the *Dressler* Variations and the three *Elector* Sonatas, when Beethoven was eleven and twelve respectively. Concerning Beethoven's age
it should be noted that since Beethoven was baptized on December 17,
and presumably born the day before, in most cases he is one full year
younger than any given calendar year suggests. This is especially significant during the Bonn years when he had composed all the works discussed in this chapter between the ages of eleven and twenty.

Neefe's prediction remained unfulfilled. Beethoven never became a
second Mozart. Despite the demonstrable competence of the Bonn
works, the vast majority of Beethoven's Mozart-influenced works remained unpublished until after Beethoven's death and remain virtually
unknown. Meanwhile, Maximilian Franz, who had met Mozart on several occasions and perhaps nearly hired him as Kapellmeister of Bonn,
made Mozart a centerpiece of Bonn's musical life. While Mozart's great
contemporary Haydn was not entirely neglected during Franz's reign,
Mozart received special attention with frequent instrumental and operatic performances.

Over the next fifteen years Beethoven would use specific Mozart
works as a starting point. Although it would take Beethoven at least
until the beginning of his second stylistic period in the early 1800s to
fully assert his own musical personality, as early as fourteen he had
begun to show how he could establish his musical identity while following the lead of his famous predecessor. In 1787 Franz sponsored Beethoven's first journey to Vienna. Unfortunately, after meeting with Mozart, perhaps only once, Beethoven was called back to Bonn to see his
dying mother. By the time he was able to receive the necessary financial
support to return in November 1792, Mozart, though only fourteen
years older than Beethoven, had been dead for nearly a year.

THE THREE QUARTETS FOR PIANO AND STRINGS, WOO 36 (1785)

We tend to think of Mozart as *the* precocious composer, and he was. But though far less prolific, Beethoven's early efforts have not received the admiration and the performances they deserve. The largest group of instrumental works from the Bonn years appeared when Beethoven was only fourteen, most likely at the encouragement of Neefe. These are the three ambitious quartets for piano and strings (WoO 36), composed in 1785 and published posthumously in 1828 in the order Eb, D, and C major, the order used here (although the surviving autograph indicates a C, Eb, and D major ordering). Not surprisingly, Beethoven did not publicly acknowledge specific debts to Mozart, but scholars have identified to varying degrees particular sonatas for violin and piano from the larger group of Mozart sonatas published as op. 2 in 1781 as a source for each quartet: Mozart's sonatas in G (K. 379), Eb (K. 380), and C (K. 296), for Beethoven's Eb, D, and C quartets, respectively. Some of the resemblances between Beethoven's quartets and their Mozartean models are readily audible; most are not. The reason is that Beethoven successfully managed to assimilate, rather than slavishly imitate, the master. But if you have listened well to works by both, it is still likely the piano quartets will sound more than a little like Mozart, albeit with persuasive touches of the Beethoven yet to be.

Ironically, perhaps the most overt indebtedness to Mozart in Beethoven's Eb quartet turns out to demonstrate the greatest independence. This is how borrowing and influence often work in classical music, although we should note that the theme in Beethoven's slow introduction also bears some melodic similarities with Mozart. As in Mozart's Sonata in G Major, Beethoven follows a long, slow introductory movement with a fast movement in the parallel minor, Eb major to minor in Beethoven's piece. At that time and for a long time to come, Eb minor, with its busy key signature of six flats, would be considered an unusual key choice. Interestingly, some prominent melodic notes of the initial harmonies, and that unusual choice of key, are likely traceable to the Eb minor prelude in book 1 of Bach's *Well-Tempered Clavier*, a set of twenty-four preludes and fugues in every possible key (a fugue is a form based on the working out of a single main theme usually with three or more simultaneous independent melodic lines). Beethoven knew Bach's work well from his studies with Neefe. As with the F Minor *Elector* Sonata, the rhythmic energy of the Beethoven's Eb minor first movement clearly foreshadows the future composer, and its second theme (as with the *Pathétique* and *Tempest* sonatas to follow) is placed unusually in the dominant (the chord on the fifth degree of the scale; see tonality in the glossary) minor instead of the customary relative major. The theme also noticeably anticipates the second theme of the *Pathétique*, and another four-measure passage reappears in a slightly later work, the first movement of Beethoven's Piano Trio op. 1, no. 3, in C Minor.

The other quartets are less recognizably derived from Mozart's violin sonatas, although the C Major Piano Quartet, in the same key as the work by Mozart on which it is modeled, borrows isolated thematic material. For example, Beethoven takes the rhythm presented in the first two measures of Mozart's left-hand part and uses it pervasively throughout his quartet. More subtly (and less audibly), the first movement of Beethoven's C Major Piano Quartet contains almost the *identical* number of total measures, an unusual feature that seems to go beyond coincidence (153 in Mozart, 157 in Beethoven). In particular, the expositions are only one measure apart in length (sixty-eight in Mozart, sixty-seven in Beethoven), and despite some proportional differences, the total number of measures in the developments and recapitulations are nearly the same. Beethoven departs from Mozart by including an expanded development (forty-three measures to Mozart's twenty-seven), using some of the additional space to further vary Mozart's opening left-hand rhythm. Perhaps Beethoven's major departure is a "false" recapitulation of the opening theme in the *subdominant* (the chord on the fourth degree of the scale; see tonality in the glossary) that appears only a few measures after the beginning of the development. Beethoven also foreshortens the recapitulation (forty-seven to Mozart's fifty-eight), although, like his model, the acolyte offers a recapitulation considerably shorter than the exposition.

Unlike the *Dressler* Variations and the *Elector* Sonatas, the piano quartets were not published. Instead they became a musical quarry that Beethoven could mine in subsequent works, either for main ideas or as "filler" material. An example from the latter is the reuse of nine measures from the second movement of the Eb Major Quartet in the third piano trio of Beethoven's opus 1. More substantially, Beethoven was able to use a distinctive minor mode theme from the latter part of the C Major Quartet's first-movement exposition as the central second theme in the C Major Piano Sonata (op. 2, no. 3) in the exposition of the first movement. He was also able to adopt other material from the quartet, including the transition to this second theme (see Musical Forms: Sonata Form in the glossary). In fact, the sketches for the piano sonata drafted years later clearly reveal that the starting point for the first movement was the original first theme of the C Major Quartet.

The opening theme of the slow second movement of Beethoven's F Minor Sonata, op. 2, no. 1 (in F major), borrows still more substantially from the C Major Piano Quartet. Of the theme's eight measures, the first five measures and the last are unchanged in the decade between the piano quartet and the sonata, while the new sixth and seventh measures depart from the original and more conventional ending. The second phrase (a unit of musical syntax, analogous to a sentence in spoken or written language) of the sonata also borrows from the quartet's opening, but only as a starting point. After that the sonata replaces the quartet's B section, which starts in the tonic with a dramatic contrasting B section in the relative minor (D minor). Both works return to their first sections to create an A-B-A form. Also in both works Beethoven follows the A material with a coda, the final section of a sonata-form movement (ten measures in the quartet and fourteen measures in the sonata). In the latter work Beethoven uses the opening of the second phrase, which appears in both works, to bring the movement to its close.

In addition to the connections between the quartets and the published piano sonatas, Beethoven used the opening theme of the Eb Major Quartet as the starting point for a possible Symphony in C Minor. Most scholars think Beethoven entered this 112-measure "Sinfonia" sketch in the late 1780s, while he was still a teenager but several years after he had completed the quartets. Beethoven also designates a tempo marking, *proesto*, a seemingly idiosyncratic alternative spelling to *presto* that Beethoven used on several other early manuscripts. The thematic resemblance between the symphony and the second movement of the quartet, the most symphonic-sounding movement of the three quartets, is unmistakable. The "Sinfonia" sketch also bears a recognizable familial melodic resemblance to the much later C minor *scherzo* of the Fifth Symphony (see Musical Forms: Other Movements in a Multimovement Work in the glossary). Since Beethoven wrote the sketch in piano notation (right hand in one staff, left hand in another), it is possible to play this promising work even though the composer left the movement in an undeveloped state (you can hear the movement so realized on YouTube). It would take Beethoven more than another decade and numerous sketches for an unfinished symphony in C major before he was able to complete his first symphony in 1800, the Symphony no. 1 in C Major, op. 21. Still, it is worth noting that Beethoven had made an important effort to compose a first symphony while still in his teens and that his starting point was a piano quartet composed before he had turned fifteen.

THE *JOSEPH CANTATA*, WOO 87 (1790)

Following the early compositional flurry between the ages of eleven and fourteen, in particular the publication of the three *Elector* Sonatas of 1783 and the composition of the three piano quartets of 1785, for reasons that remained unexplained Beethoven seemed to have ceased composing and publishing. In fact, it has been conjectured that he may have abandoned composition altogether for most of the next five years. In any event, the compositional record yields no works that can be placed with any certainty between 1786 and 1789. The composition trail resumes during Beethoven's final years in Bonn between 1790 and 1792, during which time he wrote about two-thirds of the known total of about fifty Bonn works. Among these later Bonn compositions, one work in particular stands out, the Cantata on the Death of Emperor Joseph II, WoO87, not only for its length (about forty minutes), but also for its quality, achievement, and historical importance in Beethoven's work. Moreover, as with the piano quartets, but still more meaningfully, Beethoven reused passages of his *Joseph Cantata* for two of the most powerful and important moments of his opera *Fidelio* in 1805 to 1806, and 1814.

In Beethoven's time a cantata was a multimovement work for soloists, chorus, and orchestra based on a quasi-dramatic text. The impetus behind the creation of this cantata was the death of the Emperor Joseph II on February 20, 1790. Joseph coruled with his mother the Empress Theresa beginning in 1765 and alone after Theresa's death in 1780.

Known during his reign as an "Enlightened Despot," Joseph imple-
mented some educational, legal, health, social, and religious reforms.
He was also, indeed, despotic as well as having a head filled with dangerous Enlightenment ideas—a paradoxical combination. He abolished
serfdom, emancipated Jews, and increased religious freedom somewhat
in his Catholic domains. He also labored mightily to centralize power in
the empire in his persona and in Vienna via a vast bureaucracy, usurp-
ing many local dignitaries in the process. Joseph's policies and practices
proved riotously unpopular with various groups, for example, dissolving
hundreds of Catholic monasteries, making German the official language
of Hungary, and replacing wooden coffins with sack burials in mass
graves to save natural resources and to speed the decomposition process. It was because of this imperial green initiative, not due to poverty,
that Mozart, and nearly everyone else, was buried in an unmarked mass
grave (the so-called pauper's funeral). Joseph's ideas concerning burial
practices were criticized during his reign and reversed not long after his
death—not soon enough for Mozart, who died in 1791, but in time for
Beethoven's massive public burial in 1827. In contrast to his lack of
popularity during his rule, in the decades after his death, and especially
in light of the Napoleonic Wars and the repression that followed the
Congress of Vienna (1814–1815), Joseph would become increasingly
regarded as the symbolic leader of an imagined golden age in Vienna. It
was Beethoven's nostalgia for this Golden Age that led to the hopeful
vision for a better world envisioned in his Ninth Symphony, a future
based on a return to the past glories of Joseph II. Clearly Joseph's death
was a momentous occasion for the nineteen-year-old musician, one that
called for an appropriate memorial.

Although less popular in Vienna, especially among conservatives,
Joseph's reforms were widely celebrated among liberal intellectuals in
other parts of Austria and what became (in 1870) Germany. To review,
because Joseph's brother Maximilian Franz had become the elector of
Cologne in 1784, Joseph's presence was particularly strong in neighboring Bonn, one of the most intellectually progressive cities in the empire
despite its distance from the capital. No doubt Joseph's personal relationship with the composer contributed to Mozart's popularity and acclaim in Bonn, a view amply shared by Beethoven.

Shortly after Bonn heard the news of the emperor's death, a theolo-
gy student, Severin Averdonk, wrote a text to commemorate the event.

Although known primarily as a performing musician in the court and opera ensembles, with no significant choral music compositions to his credit, Beethoven nevertheless received the commission to compose the work. He completed the cantata a few weeks later, but the minutes of the Literary Society reported that "for various reasons the proposed cantata cannot be performed" (Forbes 1964, 119), and the projected performance never took place. In their memoirs Beethoven's friends Franz Wegeler and Ferdinand Ries recalled that another performance of the cantata scheduled in nearby Mergentheim the following year was also cancelled because "several sections were so difficult for the wind instruments that some musicians declared they could not possibly play them" (Wegeler 1987, 22).

In contrast to masses and requiems, cantatas tend to be designed to commemorate unique and unrepeatable events and situations. A funeral cantata dedicated to a particular figure, even one as distinguished as Joseph II, was destined for oblivion, no matter how good it was or how well received. It took nearly a century, in 1884, before the *Joseph Cantata* was acquired at an auction and performed in Vienna. After examining the manuscript, the composer Johannes Brahms became the first luminary to extol the work's virtues, writing the following in a letter to the critic Eduard Hanslick: "Even if there were no name on the title page, none other could be conjectured—it is Beethoven through and through! The beautiful and noble pathos, sublime in its feeling and imagination, the intensity, perhaps violent in its expression, moreover, the voice-leading and declamation, and in the two outside sections all the characteristics which we may observe and associate with his later works!" (Forbes 1964, 120).

Like bookends, the opening and closing choruses share similar music and texts. The opening of each chorus creates a stirring musical drama that surpassed anything Beethoven had composed prior to this point, displaying a compositional power and maturity that arguably would not be matched until the "heroic" period fifteen years later. The orchestra begins with a ten-measure introduction that emphasizes C minor, the key of the *Dressler* Variations. But first the opening measure sounds a single soft and deep unharmonized C spread out over several octaves in the strings below a *fermata* (a symbol with a curved line above a dot to indicate a hold of an indefinite length). In the second measure the winds state a C minor chord, the third returns to the unadorned C in the strings, and the fourth measure states a dissonant diminished-seventh chord (a four-note chord in which each note is a minor third apart) again in the winds. In the next two measures the winds alone continue the plaintive lament. After that, the strings replace the winds for the next three measures.

When the process repeats with a return to the opening C in the strings, it is clear we are hearing a death trope—that the repeated C, sounding over and over, is a richly reimagined version of a muffled church bell tolling at a funeral. The chorus now joins the winds in the two chords that follow the solitary C note in the strings, C minor and the diminished seventh, each time on the word Todt (dead). The crucial component of this opening will return to introduce Florestan's aria (the Italian word for song) at the beginning of *Fidelio*'s act 2. Beethoven sets off the final two words of the concluding lines, "Joseph the great is dead," frequently and in numerous ways in the second half of the chorus. Gradually, but inexorably, the lament moves from the pain and terror of dying to the comparative peace of death itself in the relative major with three statements of Todt, the last of which is prolonged, seemingly, into musical infinity (although in actual fact only six measures of music).

Shortly before Joseph began to share the throne with his mother, the philosopher Voltaire expressed an optimism not found in his novella *Candide*: "Year by year the fanaticism that overspread the earth is receding in its detestable usurpations" (Swafford 2014, 23). In the bass recitative (sung speech) and aria that follows this startlingly original opening chorus lamenting Joseph's death, Averdonk's words speak of Joseph as a tireless opponent of fanaticism of all sorts. The recitative describes a situation in which "a monster, Fanaticism by name, arose from the depths of hell, stretched itself twixt earth and sun, and night fell," while the aria speaks of Joseph slaying this fanatical monster: "Then came Joseph, with the strength of God, tore the raging monster forth, forth from between earth and heaven, and trampled on its head." Two soprano arias separated by a short recitative with full orchestra consider Joseph's Christlike capacity for bringing light to God's word. Like Christ, Joseph was "the great sufferer who on this earth plucked no rose without pain" and who "bore to his life's end with pain the cares of mankind."

The first of the two soprano arias focuses on Licht (light) and Joseph as an en*lightened* ruler bringing his subjects to a better "well-lit" place. The music for "Da stiegen die Menschen" (Then Mankind Climbed into the Light) will be familiar to anyone who can recall the climactic moment of *Fidelio* when Florestan is freed of his shackles by his faithful wife, Leonore. This well-known, memorable, and distinctive melody, which begins with successive rising fourths before a scalar descent back to its starting note, returns almost unchanged to mark the most significant moment of Beethoven's only opera. Also as in the opera Beethoven precedes the soprano entrance with an instrumental statement of this melody featuring the oboe, an instrument that will represent Leonore in Florestan's dreams as a prisoner as well as when he is freed. Finally, as in the opera, the full chorus repeats the soprano's music. We have observed Beethoven's practice of recycling material directly from the piano quartet to the piano trios and sonata a decade later and an earlier foreshadowing of the *Pathétique* Sonata in the F Minor *Elector* Sonata that Beethoven composed at the age of twelve, but his dramatic use of the opening of the cantata and the soprano aria "Da stiegen die Menschen" is truly extraordinary. Beethoven's cantata, composed at the age of nineteen, is indeed a prophetic work, pointing the way to *Fidelio*.

The soprano's "slumber" aria, "Hier schlummert seinen stillen Frieden" (Here Slumbers in His Quiet Peace) stays mainly in Eb major, the relative major that marked Joseph's eventual resting place in his journey from C minor to Eb major in the opening chorus. It is notable for its restfulness and lack of tension. *Adagio* throughout its more than eight minutes, the aria opens its leisurely introduction (twenty-one measures) with a distinctive melody whose opening intervals are a rising fourth and a falling leap of a sixth. When the soprano eventually enters, her melody lags behind the orchestra's return of the introductory material, but after that, the vocal melody matches the orchestra closely.

Although the final chorus repeats the opening chorus largely unchanged, it does alter the original ending significantly. In the first chorus the death chant on C minor moves to and concludes with a peaceful Eb major chord. The final Todt in the concluding chorus ends in grief, not release, on a prolonged C minor chord, and the somber winds (including the oboe) mourn Joseph's demise.

Later in 1790 Beethoven was asked to write the music to mark the coronation of Joseph's brother and successor, Leopold II, crowned in

October. Like the *Joseph Cantata* the *Leopold Cantata* was written but not performed. The *Leopold Cantata*, about half the length of its successor, naturally removed the chorus of mourning that framed the earlier work. Instead it focused almost exclusively on the soloists: first a soprano recitative with chorus; then a virtuosic and operatic aria for soprano with flute and cello obbligato (i.e., the term for obligatory countermelodies); a bass recitative; a trio for soprano, tenor, and bass; and ending with a choral movement with solo quartet, the latter interestingly set to a text, "Stürzet nieder, Millionenen" that would return in the "Ode to Joy" many years later. Although the *Leopold Cantata* begins in a subdued mood that reflects the text, "He slumbers . . . slumbers! Let the great Prince rest in peace!" the mood soon shifts to one of the most triumphant passages Beethoven ever wrote to mark the arrival of the new prince, Leopold II. The *Leopold Cantata* may not possess the originality, range, and power of the *Joseph Cantata*, but it nevertheless further demonstrates that two years before Beethoven left Bonn for Vienna he was already an accomplished and promising composer.

RIGHINI VARIATIONS, WOO 65 (1790)

During his final years in Bonn, Beethoven composed a considerable number of competent works for wind and string ensembles, most notably the Wind Octet, op. 103, and the String Trio, op. 3. One work stands out for its precocious maturity, the variations for piano on an operatic aria by Vincenzo Righini, *Venni amore*, which itself served as the basis for five vocal variations. During the same trip to nearby Mergentheim where he hoped (in vain) to arrange a performance of the *Joseph Cantata*, Beethoven played the twenty-four piano variations on Righini's little theme at a gathering. According to the memoirs of Wegeler and Ries, Beethoven was challenged by the virtuoso pianist Abbé Sterkel, who like Righini worked for the elector of Mainz. Sterkel did not believe Beethoven could play the difficult work he had composed. Beethoven rose to Sterkel's challenge as reported by Wegeler:

> Sterkel's playing was very light, highly pleasing, and, as the elder Ries put it, somewhat ladylike. Beethoven stood beside him concentrating intensely. Then he was asked to play but only complied when Sterkel intimated that he doubted whether even the composer of the Varia-

tions could play them all the way through. Beethoven played not only these variations, as far as he could remember them (Sterkel could not find the music), but also a number of others no less difficult and, to the amazement of his listeners, he played everything in precisely the same pleasant manner with which Sterkel had impressed him. That is how easy it was for him to adapt his style of playing to someone else's (Wegeler and Ries 1987, 23).

On this same Mergentheim excursion, the composer and writer Carl Ludwig Junker heard a private piano performance in which he was invited to provide a theme for Beethoven to vary. Junker is the first of numerous writers over the next several decades to single out Beethoven's powers of improvisation. This is what Junker wrote in a published letter that appeared the same year: "The greatness of this amiable, light-hearted man, as a virtuoso, may in my opinion be safely estimated from his almost inexhaustible wealth of ideas, the altogether characteristic style of expression in his playing, and the great execution which he displays. I know, therefore, no one thing which he lacks, that conduces to the greatness of an artist" (Forbes 1964, 105). Junker goes on to compare Beethoven favorably with one of the major pianists of the day: "Bethofen [sic], in addition to the execution, has greater clearness and weight of idea, and more expression—in short, he is more for the heart—equally great, therefore, as an *adagio* or *allegro* player. . . . His style of treating his instrument is so different from that usually adopted, that it impresses one with the idea, that by a path of his own discovery he has attained that height of excellence whereon he now stands" (105).

Further testimonials by virtuoso Joseph Gelinek, written soon after Beethoven's arrival in Vienna in 1792, Václav Tomásek in 1798, and Muzio Clementi in 1807, as well as descriptions after the fact by Beethoven's student Carl Czerny, give us tantalizing clues to what Beethoven's improvisation sounded like. Perhaps some of the quasi-improvisational ideas in the published variations and the improvisational nature of works such as the *Choral Fantasy*, op. 80 (1808), and the Fantasia in G Minor, op. 77 (1810), offer more tangible evidence. The *Righini* Variations, a work that can stand beside the *Joseph Cantata* as a harbinger of the composer's maturity, offers particularly striking evidence of Beethoven's potential prowess as an improviser.

The piece, composed in 1790, was in fact so precocious that until the first edition of 1791 (dedicated to the highly regarded pianist Countess

Hatzfeld) was discovered in the 1980s, it was often assumed that Beethoven, who continued to play these variations well into his Vienna years, must have extensively revised the work when he republished it in 1802. Earlier surviving sketches for what would become variations 7, 6, 5, 4, 15, 16, 10, and 9 (in this order), demonstrably from the Bonn years, clearly indicate that a number of variation ideas were well developed long before Beethoven left for Vienna. The recent appearance of the 1791 edition confirms that the variations were not revised. After Beethoven's death, Czerny, who took lessons from Beethoven from 1801 to 1803 during the time the variations were republished, informed Mozart's biographer Otto Jahn that his teacher continued to play them during this period. Indeed, it wasn't until the publication in 1803 of the Six Variations on an Original Theme in F Major, op. 34, and the *Prometheus* Variations that a set of Beethoven piano variations rivaled the *Righini* for complexity, ingenuity, virtuosity, and imagination. In fact, recognizable *Righini* footprints are traceable thirty years later in the *Diabelli* Variations.

Long before we arrive to this distant future, we will have ample opportunities to perceive the fulfillment in Count Waldstein's prophecy that stands as the epigraph to the present chapter, as well as the perspicacity of Mozart's alleged prophecy upon meeting the sixteen-year-old Beethoven on his abbreviated first trip to the big city: "Keep your eyes on him—someday he will give the world something to talk about" (Lockwood 2003, 46).

2

"FROM THE HANDS OF HAYDN"
(1792–1801)

THE ACADEMY CONCERT OF 1800

During his first years in Vienna, Beethoven was recognized as one of the finest pianists in the city. Starting in 1795 with the publication of the three op. 1 piano trios, closely followed by the three impressive piano sonatas published as op. 2 one year later, Beethoven also began to emerge as one of the most promising composers of his era. He was on his way to fulfilling Count Waldstein's widely quoted prophecy of November 1792: "With the help of unceasing diligence your will receive *the spirit of Mozart from the hands of Haydn*" (Lockwood 2003, 50).

Between 1793 and 1800, Beethoven composed thirteen of his thirty-two piano sonatas, five string trios, four piano trios, three violin sonatas, and two cello sonatas, among other works. He also made a good start on his first six quartets published as a set, op. 18, in 1801. With the exception of his Piano Sonata in C Minor, op. 13 (*Pathétique*), his best-known works were still to come, especially in the first decade of the 1800s. Still, before Beethoven was thirty he had established himself as the unmistakable heir to his glorious predecessors, Mozart who died in 1791, and Haydn. Although in his sixties, Haydn remained at his peak during the 1790s, composing the twelve *London* Symphonies, dozens of his finest string quartets, and in the vocal realm, his best-known masses and monumental oratorios, *The Creation* (1798) and *The Seasons* (1801).

Perhaps the greatest sign of Beethoven's public arrival occurred on April 2, 1800, an event announced a few days earlier in the *Wiener Zeitung*, Vienna's largest daily newspaper. This historic concert was the first to feature the music of the twenty-nine-year-old composer and pianist, who had been gaining stature on both fronts since his arrival in Vienna. A handbill posted on the day of the event preserved by the widow of Beethoven's nephew Karl describes the program contents, albeit incompletely. It begins: "Today, Wednesday the 2nd of April 1800, in the Imperial-Royal Theater beside the Burg, Herr Ludwig van Beethoven will have the honor of giving a grand musical Academy for his benefit. The pieces to be heard are the following" (Heartz 2009, 762). The handbill then lists seven numbered items, four of which featured the evening's star (items 3–4 and 6–7). For at least one night in Vienna, Beethoven was the toast of the town.

The concert opened with an unspecified "grand symphony by the late Kapellmeister Mozart" (Heartz 2009, 762). The source of the second number and fifth numbers was Haydn's new oratorio, *The Creation*, an aria (no. 2) and a duet (no. 5). No doubt it did not escape notice that Beethoven was sharing the stage with the revered Mozart, Beethoven's lifelong inspiration whom he met briefly when only sixteen, and his former teacher, Haydn, widely acknowledged since Mozart's death as the greatest living composer. Although biographers often emphasize the personal tensions between teacher and student and Haydn's lack of diligence in marking his student's exercises, most scholars acknowledge that Beethoven received an invaluable musical education, both from Haydn's teaching and of course the example of his music. Since *The Creation* was still new and fresh, it made great sense to offer selections sung by the popular bass Herr Saal (the original Raphael and Adam) and his teenage daughter Therese (who replaced the original soprano in the dual roles of Gabriel and Eve in 1799). Quite likely Haydn, then sixty-eight, would have been present on this historic and auspicious occasion.

Public concerts, especially those offering orchestral music, were rare events at this time, usually reserved for the Lenten season when operas and other theatrical performances were prohibited. In fact, as we will observe in future chapters, even with his growing fame Beethoven would only be able to organize two other public concerts, or Academies, over the next eight years, in 1803 and 1808. But although the red tape and expense of putting on such a concert was daunting, at least in contrast to charity concerts, such as the one in which Beethoven performed a piano concerto (see Musical Forms: Concerto-Sonata Form in the glossary) in 1795, a composer who survived the obstacle course facing the mounting of these events could reap considerable financial benefits if the concert managed to fill one of the larger halls such as the Imperial-Royal Theater (also known as the Kärntnerthor Theater) that could hold audiences greater than one thousand. Despite complaints about the overuse of winds in Beethoven's symphony and "the faults of the orchestra," which were "all the more striking since B's [Beethoven's] compositions are difficult to execute," the summary verdict of this concert was that it "was probably the most interesting public concert for a long time" (Senner 1999, 162, 163).

The Beethoven component of this generously long evening that started at 6:30 p.m. began with item 3 on the program, described on the handbill as "a grand concerto for the Piano-Forte, played and composed by Herr Ludwig van Beethoven" (Heartz 2009, 762). Since the description does not identify the concerto's key, no one knows for sure whether audiences heard his earlier Concerto in Bb Major, the future no. 2 published as op. 19 in 1801, or his more recent Concerto in C Major, the future no. 1 published as op. 15 a few months later that year.

Beethoven had been playing various versions of the Bb concerto as early as his Bonn years and in continuously evolving versions in Vienna (1793–1795) and Prague (1798). The evidence also suggests he played an earlier version of his later C Major, both in Vienna (1795) and on the same Prague trip. Nevertheless, cadenza sketch material (a cadenza is the place late in the first movement of a concerto where the soloist plays alone and has the opportunity to show off his or her improvisational skill and virtuosity) that can be reasonably traced to 1800 as well as Beethoven's higher opinion of the second completed piano concerto of his young maturity—no one even considers that he would have played his immature student concerto effort of 1784—have led a consensus of Beethoven scholars to conclude that he performed the C Major at his Academy debut. The still-unfinished Third Piano Concerto in C Minor received its debut at the 1803 Academy.

The other Beethoven works on the program are more certain, starting with the fourth item on the concert, the septet in Eb, published in 1802 as op. 20, unusually scored "for four stringed [violin, viola, cello, and double bass] and three wind instruments [clarinet, bassoon, and horn]" (Heartz 2009, 762). The penultimate portion of the program (no. 6) consisted of Beethoven's improvisation at the piano, a skill for which Beethoven was invariably singled out for praise in numerous accounts. The final item (no. 7), "a new grand Symphony with full orchestra" (762), could only have been the First in C Major, published in 1801 as op. 21. Much to his chagrin, the septet, a work designed for "the rabble," became arguably the most popular work of Beethoven's lifetime. In fact, when his musical manuscripts were sold, the lowly septet autograph sold for more than twice the price of the lofty *Missa solemnis*. A few years earlier Charles Neate recorded Beethoven's response to the well scored but conventional septet's continued popularity in London: "That's damned stuff! I wish it were burned!" (Forbes 1964, 620).

FIRST PIANO CONCERTO IN C MAJOR, OP. 15

The classical concerto as developed by Mozart, Beethoven's central model, is a hybrid of baroque and classical forms and approaches. It retains the formal outline of the concertos in three movements (fast-slow-fast) of Vivaldi and Bach, in which orchestra sections (called ritornellos) alternate with solo sections, often sharing musical material but maintaining a certain degree of autonomy even as the soloist or soloists play unobtrusively along in the orchestra sections. Classical concertos greatly expand this format. The first movements follow a concerto-sonata form (see Musical Forms: Concerto-Sonata Form in the glossary), in which expanded solo sections correspond to the exposition, development, and recapitulations found in classical sonata form. The first solo sections contain the most extensive opening nonmodulating ritornellos. Shorter orchestra ritornellos are interspersed throughout the remainder of the movement.

At a climactic moment at the end of the recapitulation, the penultimate orchestra ritornello stops on a suspenseful chord (technically known as the I 6/4 chord, the tonic in second inversion), after which Mozart and later Beethoven improvised a cadenza before allowing the orchestra to resolve the chord with a cadence (a harmonic point of arrival) and concluding ritornello. Shortly before the end of the decade, Beethoven, who by then knew his days as a soloist were numbered, wrote out cadenzas for his first four concertos, including three separate, quite different cadenzas for the C Major Concerto alone. These manuscripts give us great insight into Beethoven the famous improviser.

First Movement: *Allegro con Brio*

In the Mozartean classical concerto model, an extensive ritornello at the outset of the first movement allows the orchestra to introduce a central theme and a second theme. Customarily, both of these themes will return in the piano exposition. Beethoven subverts the model in two ways. First, he refuses to share the opening theme when the soloist enters in the piano exposition. The theme in question begins with an octave statement of the rhythm LONG-short-short-short (later simply LONG-short-short), followed by a rapid, ascending, seven-note stepwise scale and a restatement of the entire theme one pitch higher. The second subversion occurs about halfway through the opening ritornello when Beethoven does the unthinkable (at least in a classical concerto). Instead of staying in the tonic, as he should, he modulates (changes key), and he does so with great dramatic flair. He then follows the dramatic modulation with another surprise when he states the first four measures of what will become the second theme in the exposition in the remote key of Eb major, followed by two additional statements of the second theme opening, one in F minor and one in G minor. After a brief contrapuntal return of the main theme, the ritornello concludes with a tuneful closing theme in C major, a tune that would not be out of place in Mozart's *Marriage of Figaro*. The piano is now ready for its entrance and its close-up. The reader is greatly encouraged to listen along with a recording to hear what happens next.

As in several Mozart concertos, Beethoven introduces his exposition with a brand-new theme, a theme that will never be heard from again. As the piano continues to demonstrate its virtuoso nature with *arpeggios* (sounding a chord successively rather than simultaneously, derived from the Italian word for harp, *arpa*) and scales, the orchestra occasionally inserts the four-note (LONG-short-short-short) theme that opened the concerto. The piano leads the modulatory transition to the second theme in the dominant as expected in a classical concerto in the major mode. In contrast to the trifold statement of the first phrase of this second theme, however, first the orchestra and then the soloist complete a second phrase, after which both the orchestra and the soloist complete the exposition with the same march-like Mozartean closing theme that closed the opening ritornello. After the soloist takes charge over a firm close on the dominant, a short contrapuntal ritornello returns with a LONG-short-short descending scale and three statements of unadorned LONG-short-short that take the music to its unusual development.

With so many themes to choose from, Beethoven limits his choices to the opening orchestral gesture (LONG-short-short) and the descending scale associated with the second measure of the second theme. Within a few measures Beethoven even abandons the scales, leaving the LONG, now followed by all three shorts. In future developments Beethoven might confine his choice to a single idea from the exposition (e.g., in the Piano Sonata, op. 110), but the development of the C Major Concerto inaugurates a new standard of musical economy. Another striking feature of this understated development is its soft dynamic range. After one *fortissimo* orchestral outburst of the LONG-short-short-short motive early on, the piano enters with a *piano* dynamic that will continue until the music moves to the dominant and a *pianissimo* dynamic for the retransition that prepares for the recapitulation. Only the final two measures in the piano part are *fortissimo*, a dynamic that will continue for the first eight measures of the recapitulation.

Beethoven offers another harmonic surprise when the piano enters with *arpeggio* figuration in another remote key, the *same* remote Eb major that Beethoven introduced against the rules in the opening ritornello. Soon we hear the LONG-short-short-short motive that will continue as the music moves from Eb major to F minor (significantly following the same progression of the opening ritornello) before Beethoven replaces the G minor of the ritornello with G *major*, the dominant of the C major tonic. In the final mysterious *pianissimo* passage of the development (the retransition), the two horns, an octave apart, sound the opening LONG-short-short-short. Now, for the first time, the piano declares a series of ambiguous and tense diminished sevenths and repeats the opening rhythm starting on the orchestra's final "short." After three statements of this orchestral-piano dialogue, the horns state only the first two "shorts" (without the LONG) no less than four times before the *fortissimo* descending scale takes the music back to the main theme and the final large formal section, the recapitulation.

Second Movement: *Largo*

The second movement in Ab major is an unwaveringly lyrical movement in the simplest slow movement form, A–B–A. Although the themes are new, Beethoven offers subtle connections with the first movement at the outset. The A theme, first presented by the piano, incorporates the rhythm of the first movement's second theme in the right hand while the left hand (along with the strings) accompanies the theme with the LONG-short-short motive from the first movement, replacing the third short with a LONG. The B section begins in Eb major, the dominant of Ab, thus creating a harmonic link with the first movement, also in Eb.

Third Movement: Rondo: *Allegro Scherzando*

The *Allegro* finale is a rondo, characterized by the presence of self-contained and memorable tunes organized into clear-cut sections: A–B–A–C–A–B coda with a transition theme linking the A and B sections and the C and final A sections. The A sections are in the tonic. The first B section begins in the dominant as if it were a second theme in a sonata-form movement. The second B starts in the tonic as it would in a sonata-form recapitulation. The C theme is in the relative minor (the key a minor third lower than the tonic with the same number of flats or sharps, in this case A minor). Recent research by Theodore Albrecht (2007) reveals that Beethoven sketched a recognizable version of the main A theme as early as 1793—although he would not complete a performable draft of the concerto until 1795—and that this theme bears a demonstrable resemblance to the overture to Antonio Salieri's opera *Les Danaïdes*, a full score of which was found in Beethoven's estate at the time of his death. Salieri, Mozart's rival and falsely accused poisoner, made infamous in the play and film *Amadeus*, was an early supporter of Beethoven and served as his occasional teacher during the years encompassed in this chapter.

The piano then introduces a rhythmically regular first theme that is answered by the full orchestra. Reversing this process, the orchestra introduces the second theme, answered by the piano and characterized by *sforzando* (a sudden, strong emphasis) accents on the final eighth note in each of the first three measures and by a string of syncopations (irregular accentuations) when the piano completes its statement of the theme in G major. In another harmonic surprise, Beethoven suddenly swerves to Eb major for a piano restatement of the second theme. This constitutes yet another return of the surprisingly remote key of Eb, three flats away from C (the relative major, the key a minor third higher than the tonic with the same number of flats or sharps, in this case C *minor*) that has marked major moments in the first two movements. The A minor theme in the C section, which belongs exclusively to the piano, has reminded some commentators of the popular tune *Tico-Tico* by the Brazilian composer Zequinha de Abreu, a tune made still more popular by Carmen Miranda in the 1947 movie *Copacabana*.

FIRST SYMPHONY IN C MAJOR, OP. 21

The reviewer in the weekly *Allgemeine musikalische Zeitung* (*General Music Newspaper*), Germany's main musical periodical since its inception in 1798, remarked that in Beethoven's First Symphony "there was more music for wind instruments than for a full orchestra" (Senner 1999, 163). The review also praised the work for containing "very much art, novelty, and a wealth of ideas" (163). Within a few years the lesser-known *Historisches Taschenbuch* (*Historical Pocket-book*), in its only known review of a Beethoven work, praised the symphony as "a master-piece that does equal honor to his [Beethoven's] inventiveness and his musical knowledge" with "such a rich, but at the same time never weari-some, instrumentation that this symphony can justly be placed next to Mozart's and Haydn's" (164). Although the status of Beethoven's first foray into the symphony has suffered in comparison with the works enthusiasts know will follow, it should not be forgotten that, from a contemporary perspective, that Beethoven had arrived by 1800.

First Movement: *Adagio Molto—Allegro con Brio*

Audiences and commentators then and now have noticed Beethoven's abundant use of the winds in his First Symphony, with pairs of flutes, oboes, clarinets, bassoons, horns, and trumpets joining timpani and of course strings. Although not unprecedented, Beethoven begins the symphony with a slow introduction that strikingly features the winds against *pizzicato* (an indication to pluck) strings in three successive cadences, all resolving outside of the central key: a dominant of F major resolving to F (the subdominant); the dominant of C major resolving "deceptively" to A minor; and the dominant of G resolving to G major, the first step on the way to confirming the dominant (G) of the tonic C major. The main note of the melody, and heard above all the other sounds in the introduction, is played by the flute (with a doubled *pizzicato* in the first violins). This high note is invariably a leading tone, the note of the scale that pulls up to its upper note, one half step above (first E to F, then B to C, and finally F# to G). The leading tone appears somewhere in every dominant seventh chord (the fifth degree of the scale with an added seventh; see functional harmony in the glossary) resolution, but when it appears as the highest note in the chord, the resolution is particularly noticeable and powerful. This is what happens in the first three pairs of chords in the flutes and the oboes and first violins one octave lower (although the second dominant seventh deceptively resolves to an A minor triad instead of the expected C major).

Few motives are as memorable and powerful as the short-short-short-LONG rhythm that pervades Beethoven's Fifth Symphony, a work first heard at his third Academy in 1808. After starting with a major third and then a minor third, the primary rhythm of the Fifth can be heard in the foreground or background ubiquitously in the first movement and at key moments (often supported by entrances of the brass) in subsequent movements. On a smaller scale and utilizing the smallest interval in tonal music, the half step, Beethoven's use of the leading tone, introduced three times at the outset of the First Symphony, offers an early example that embodies the same principle. The motive may be less memorable than the famous Fifth Symphony motive and it may not occur as often as the Fifth's primary motive, but its presence can nonetheless be heard almost everywhere. For starters, the first theme of the *Allegro con brio* in the first violins that follows the slow introduction features the leading tone on the downbeat in each of its five measures.

Immediately after the opening violin phrase, the winds offer another dominant seventh to tonic progression with the leading note audibly high in the flute part. This time the new temporary tonic is D, one whole step higher than C, where the first violins repeat the opening melody with another string of melodic leading tones. Throughout the second theme in the dominant, which begins with a dialogue between the oboe and the flute, the leading tones of the introduction and first theme appear prominently, albeit in the accompaniment. The closing theme too begins with the leading tone, after which the leading tone resolves to the downbeat no less than four times in the six measures that conclude the exposition. The first phrase of the main theme with all its leading tones pervades the first part of the development as well. During the second part of this section, Beethoven reduces the theme to its first three notes, the second and third of which contain the leading tone and its resolution. The theorist Carl Schachter has persuasively argued on behalf of a **[Au: Please provide closing quotation mark.]**"network of resemblances" (1991) between Mozart's C major symphony, K. 551 and Beethoven's C major Op. 21 in the essay "Mozart's Last and Beethoven's First," including a closely detailed and presumably Mozartean model for Beethoven's tonal plan in the first-movement development.

Even in his evolutionary rather than revolutionary so-called first stylistic period, the years encompassed in this chapter, Beethoven sought new ways to link one movement to another, for example, the strategic reuse of an unusual key (Eb) in all the movements of the C Major Concerto. In the First Symphony the leading tone continues to appear prominently in the second, third, and fourth movements. Although it plays a lesser role in the second movement, it can be heard after a few seconds in both the main melody (first by the second violins and then by the firsts) and again in the opening of the second theme, also introduced by the second violins. At the beginning of the development section the music moves to the tonic minor before swerving without warning a half step higher to Db to create a harmonic realization of the melodic leading tone idea.

Third Movement: Menuetto: *Allegro Molto e Vivace*

Beethoven labeled the third movement *Menuetto*, but this label has not fooled anyone from noticing that he has in fact created a *scherzo* that will become standard for most of his remaining symphonies. The key difference is the tempo. In fact, it might be stated that a *scherzo* (in this case the imprecisely labeled *Menuetto*) is fundamentally a fast minuet (the dance movement in triple meter found in most symphonies, usually the third movement) with one beat to the bar instead of three beats to the bar. The leading tone continues to be heard prominently in both the first part of this form ||:A:||:BA:|| and the trio ||:C||:DC:||, but the latter section contains a particularly imaginative use of this simple idea. Probably not coincidently, on the same pitch that begins the symphony (an E), the first oboe sounds this note no less than *seventeen* times (including in three continuous measures) before resolving the leading tone up to an F.

Fourth Movement: Finale: *Adagio*

In the final two movements Beethoven returns to another simple musical idea first heard in the last measure of the slow introduction, a simple ascending scale. The principal melody of the *Menuetto* is a straightforward version of this idea. In the trio (a contrasting B section of the minuet movement), the string answer to the oboes is only a slightly fancier version of the scale idea. In the finale Beethoven stretches out the dominant scale of the introduction to comic proportions. First we hear the first three opening notes of the scale and then the first four notes (which include a leading tone and its resolution), the first five notes, the first six, and the first seven, all in an excruciating and teasing *adagio* tempo before Beethoven cuts loose with all eight notes from G to G with the *allegro molto e vivace* tempo for the rest of the movement.

Scales in both directions are everywhere in this movement, especially in the development, which consists of little else. Now the previously ubiquitous leading tones are reserved for prominence only in the closing theme of the exposition and recapitulation. Following the second statement of this theme, Beethoven adds an extensive coda, at sixty-six measures and nearly one-quarter of the movement's total. The coda's first part consists of four statements of the seven-note scale and the octave that once again leads to another recapitulation of the complete major theme. To launch the final forty measures, all in the tonic, Beethoven introduces a march-like new theme in the oboes and horns, supported by a continuous stream of ascending C major scales and concluding with a descending C major triad and two firm dominant to tonic cadences with the leading tone moving to the tonic.

STRING QUARTET IN B-FLAT MAJOR, OP. 18, NO. 6

Two years before Beethoven made his public Viennese debut with his C Major Concerto and Symphony and his septet, he embarked on the most ambitious project of the early Vienna years: a set of six quartets. Commissioned by Prince Lobkowitz, one of Beethoven's most consistently loyal patrons from 1796 until his death in 1815, the six quartets, composed in the order 3, 1, 2, 5, 4, and 6, were completed in the summer of 1800 and published the following year. Prior to the quartets Beethoven had composed five string trios and a string quintet, the latter a reworking of his wind octet, but the string quartet had been under the artistic ownership of his former teacher and now competitor Haydn, who had composed no less than fourteen of his greatest quartets since Beethoven arrived in Vienna, the six combined quartets of op. 71 and op. 74 (1793), the six quartets of op. 76 (1797), and the first two of the six quartets also commissioned by Prince Lobkowitz, the op. 77 quartets begun in 1799 and published in 1802. No doubt Haydn's musical shadow loomed large over Beethoven as he created his first quartets in this important genre.

The first quartet published in the set was the F major, the largest and most ambitious of the quartets, which includes Beethoven's perhaps most rigorous treatment of a single motive (a short melody or melodic fragment) so far in the first movement and the most impassioned second movement in D minor, which was preceded by verbal notations in the sketches that indicate a literary inspiration, Shakespeare's tomb scene in *Romeo and Juliet*. The F Major Quartet also offers a rare example in Beethoven's output of two complete extant versions in the composer's own hand, the first a copy lent to Beethoven's friend Karl Amenda in 1799. Fortunately Amenda heeded Beethoven's request two years later to "not lend your quartet to anybody because I have greatly changed it, having just learned how to write quartets properly, as you will observe when you receive them" (Forbes 1964, 282). The set of six quartets include the customary inclusion of one quartet in a minor key, the fourth quartet in C minor, and another quartet, no. 5 in A major, clearly modeled on a quartet by Mozart in the same key, K. 464, one of two Mozart quartets that Beethoven copied out by hand as preparation before beginning his six-quartet pack but with many subtle transformations and reinterpretations that only musical connoisseurs would fully perceive. Although Mozart continued to play a major role in Beethoven's compositional development, by the time he composed the A Major Quartet, op. 18, no. 5, in 1800, it is evident that the former acolyte had fully received Mozart's spirit from the hands of Haydn.

The journey of the final quartet in Beethoven's first and largest set of quartets is one from lightness in the first movement to simple and unadorned lyricism in the second, playfulness and humor in the third, and the darkness of *La Malinconia* ("Melancholy"), the introduction to a fourth movement that eventually emerges (after two smaller bursts of melancholy) into the bright lightness of *prestissimo* (very fast).

First Movement: *Allegro con Brio*

The spirited first movement opens with an unwavering pulse of quarter notes in the viola and then in the cello and eighth notes in the second violin and later the viola. The main melody in the first violin, answered by the cello, contains strong, dotted half-note downbeats on the tonic. The fourth beats on alternate measures present a rapid turning figure of four sixteenth notes that introduce a melody that outlines a Bb triad but with special emphasis on the final two notes, a descending major third (D–Bb). As with the leading tone in the First Symphony, the descending major third is ubiquitous in this movement and will return in conspicuous places in future movements. In the first phrase, the third, like the turn, moves from the fourth beat (the upbeat) to an accented and elongated *fp* (*forte piano* or loud soft) on the downbeat, but when the cello answers the phrase a few measures later, the first note of the third (still the D) sounds on the downbeat.

Whether as an upbeat or a downbeat, the D–Bb third sounds ten times in the first thirty measures. Aside from the four-sixteenth-note turning figure, which sounds no less than *sixteen* times in the first minute of the movement (all but once on the fourth beat of the measure), the descending third sets the tone for the entire movement, including the closing theme of the exposition and recapitulation and the development. After a short transition the music moves to a more static and confined second theme that begins with an ascending major sixth, as in the future main finale theme, followed by five notes on the same pitches. The first statement of the theme is in F major, the second in F minor, and a first whiff of the *Malinconia* follows in the finale.

The development begins with a restatement of the opening theme in F major where the exposition left off, but now all four parts play the opening quarter notes and conclude with a strongly accented downbeat after the descending third. The first violin then plays the opening phrase alone, and three upper parts hone in on the turn figure, usually supported by the eighth-note pulse in the cello. This section lasts twenty measures. The central section in the development that follows for the next twenty-six measures is derived from the scalar figure in the bridge but now invariably concluding with the descending third on various pitches. By now, the music has returned to the dominant where it prepares for the return of the tonic for no less than thirty-six measures. The recapitulation parallels the exposition closely, and in the absence of a coda and the relative brevity of the movement, Beethoven, for only the second time in the cycle (the other quartet is the similarly coda-less A major), inserts the repeat sign for the development and recapitulation.

Second Movement: *Adagio ma non Troppo*

The lyrical slow movement in A–B–A form begins with a melody that outlines the tonic triad Eb major but that also manages to include a descending major third to conclude the second measure of the theme. Significantly, this third is the same D–Bb third that appeared so ubiquitously in the first movement. The B section offers the second hint of the darker tones of the *Malinconia* when it opens in Eb minor, the parallel or tonic minor (the key featured in the first movement of the Eb Piano Quartet). Again Beethoven emphasizes the descending major third, which he gives to the second violin below the filigree of the first violin. At the return of the A section, the melody in the first violin is accompanied by rapid four-note sixty-fourth notes that recall the turn figure from the first movement. A coda begins with the B theme; and its opening is a descending major third, now in unison, in C minor (the relative minor of Eb) and *pianissimo*. Two measures later the two-measure phrase repeats in C *major* with *sforzando* accents on the up-beats.

Third Movement: *Scherzo: Allegro*

The *scherzo* movement (minuet-trio form) is probably Beethoven's most rhythmically intricate movement of any in this quartet cycle, per-haps of any movement during his early Vienna years. The meter (the organization of musical time into measured units) is three-quarter time, but it doesn't sound like three-quarter until the following trio section. Instead the groups of six eighth notes throughout the *scherzo* section have the rhythmic feel of six-eighths time, while the *sforzandos* that appear on the six eighth notes no less than five times in the first section of the *scherzo*, all tied to the downbeat, create a dizzying rhythmic ambiguity. The first part of the *scherzo*'s second section adds more *sforzandos* and other less heavy accents on weak beats and other unex-pected places. If one were able to isolate the cello part for the first section and most of the second, the meter would appear to be in two-fourths time. The trio features the first violin throughout in a melody with an unwavering, steady dactyl rhythm (LONG-short-short, in this case an eighth note followed by two sixteenths), a clear triple meter for the first time in the movement, and a simple accompaniment in quarter notes. The first section in both the *scherzo* and the trio remain firmly in the tonic.

Fourth Movement: *La Malinconia: Allegretto Quasi Allegro*

Beethoven marked the slow introduction to *La Malinconia*, the slow introduction to the final movement, "Questo pezzo si deve trattare colla più gran delicatezza" (This piece is to be played with the greatest pos-sible delicacy). This unusual introduction, almost a movement in itself, is widely regarded as one of the most forward-looking passages before the "late" style of his final years. The movement is complex and full of nuances difficult to convey in words. I will try.

The movement starts with the upper three instruments playing in rhythmic unison four times on the same chord, not unlike the homo-rhythmic (all the parts stating the same rhythm) second theme of the first movement. The rhythm itself revisits the dactyl rhythm heard throughout the trio (now a quarter note followed two eighth notes). At the fourth and final measure of the phrase, the violins play a three-note turn figure (reminiscent of the prominent turn figure in the first movement) that surrounds the concluding note, but starting one note lower and finishing one note higher. The key is the tonic Bb. The phrase repeats, still in Bb, now with the lower three parts. The third time through Beethoven repeats the original first four notes, but now the *Malinconia* melody, played by the entire quartet, is harmonized with a diminished seventh on Ab and then a G major triad. So far the dynamics (levels of softness and loudness) have been *sempre* (always) *pianissimo* (very soft). After a brief *crescendo* (getting louder) on the first measure of the third statement, the music *decrescendos* (gets softer) down to *pianissimo*. The measure demonstrates considerable escalating intensity as it begins its move to an unanticipated resolution of the G chord to the remote B minor instead of the expected C. The next four measures consist of four successive diminished sevenths, each with a different root. The dynamic level changes dramatically each measure as well, alternating between *forte* (loud) and *piano* (soft). At the fifth diminished seventh (on C), Beethoven returns to the original four-measure phrases, this time on B major, the major version of the B minor chord that preceded the diminished sevenths.

In the next part of the introduction, Beethoven changes the texture from homorhythm to a passage of imitative counterpoint (the technique of combining two or more independent, although often similar, melodic lines simultaneously), more precisely a *fugato* (a less developed fugue within a movement) shared by all members of the quartet in staggered entrances. The principal melody of the fugato bears a melodic resemblance to the B theme of the first *Adagio*, and the rising minor sixth interval in two entrances foreshadows the sixths that open the *Allegretto* theme that will soon follow. At the end of the final fugato, the harmony closes on C minor, thus resolving the dangling G major harmony from seventeen measures earlier. Now Beethoven states the turn in *all* the instruments *forte* on the first beats of the next three measures and *piano* on the second beats in the upper three instruments with only the first violin taking the turn. The melody moves upward by half steps on each beat in the first violin for six pitches, A–Bb–B–C–C#–D, after which the first violin states the opening fugato theme one last time.

The bass line answers the chromatic ascent (moving up by half steps) of the first violin with a chromatic ascent of its own in the cello starting with D and moving up to D#–E–F–F#–G–Ab, and then stopping on an A that coincides with a *crescendo* from *pianissimo* to *fortissimo*. Starting with the third note of the ascent, E, the key of the first fugato, the three-note turns resume as well. Throughout the chromatic cello ascent from E to A, each note is answered by the violins and viola on the second beats, but after the final *fortissimo* A (still in the cello), the entire quartet erupts with a diminished-seventh chord, *fortissimo* and *sforzando*, before resolving to the dominant of the *Allegretto* finale. This melody begins with a *major* sixth (in the fugato the sixth was minor), followed by a descending third that fills in the ubiquitous major third from the earlier movements, most recently the main theme of *Malinconia*. The melodic unity of the passage is nothing short of staggering.

The fast part of the finale has been described as a *Deutscher* (German) dance in a fast triple (one beat per measure) with its three-note upbeats and *sforzando* accent on the second beat. The form consists of two themes, the first in the tonic Bb and the second in the dominant F, after which the two themes are restated in the tonic. In the absence of a development the movement, although fast, would be described paradoxically as "slow movement form" (i.e., a modified sonata form without development found in many slow movements), also known as sonatina form.

At the end of the recapitulation Beethoven offers a surprise abbreviated return of the *Malinconia* (ten measures versus forty-four measures in the original statement). The first four measures are identical to its predecessor, but the second four bars, again stated by the lower three parts, offer a new and unexpected harmony, a dominant seventh on the fourth degree of the scale. Instead of resolving this chord, however, Beethoven swerves to a G major triad and then a dominant seventh *on* G, which also fails to resolve to C. The harmonic ambiguity is as acute as anything in Beethoven's early Vienna years. The final three measures of the *Malinconia* present additional statements of the turn figure. The last of these rests on E major, the dominant of A minor where Beethoven introduces a brief statement of the *Deutscher* dance before abruptly cutting it off.

Malinconia returns once more, this time for only two measures and one statement of the dactyl rhythm on a single pitch. The chord supporting the last note is a dominant seventh of G major, one of the keys heard in the previous *Malinconia* reprise. A statement of the opening of the *Deutscher* tune in G major starts an upward climb of ascending fifths (G major, C minor, F major, and Bb major). The fourth key catches up to the key of the movement and the quartet as a whole. Once reestablished Beethoven will remain in the tonic, albeit with one final surprise, a statement of the first two phrases of the tune, now *poco adagio*, followed by a concluding statement of the *Deutscher Prestissimo*, without the offbeat accents. The quartet ends with a final unison flourish in all four parts and all cylinders *fortissimo* before a final unequivocal cadence.

PIANO SONATAS IN D MAJOR, OP. 10, NO. 3, AND C MINOR, OP. 13 (*PATHÉTIQUE*), OP. 13

We noted at the outset of this chapter that Beethoven composed nearly half of his total number of piano sonatas, thirteen of his eventual thirty-two, during his early Vienna years between 1793 and 1800.

Sonatas (op. nos. and keys)	Composition	Publication
Op. 2, nos. 1–3 (F minor, A major, C major)	1793–1795	1796
Op. 49, nos. 1–2 (G minor, G major)	1795–1797	1805?
Op. 7 (Eb major)	1796–1797	1797
Op. 10, nos. 1–3 (C minor, F Major, D major)	1795–1798	1798
Op. 13 (C minor [*Pathétique*])	1797–1798	1799
Op.14, nos. 1–2 (E major, G major)	1798–1799	1799
Op. 22 (Bb major)	1800	1802

This group of sonatas represents the largest and perhaps the most varied early body of Beethoven's compositional activity during these years. They also demonstrate maturity and a consistently high level of accomplishment. The present chapter will take a closer look at two of these sonatas, the Piano Sonata no. 7 in D Major, op. 10, no. 3, perhaps the most ambitious of the early sonatas, and the most widely known work in any genre composed before 1800, the Piano Sonata no. 8 in C Minor, *Pathétique*, op. 13.

Piano Sonata No. 7 in D Major, Op. 10, No. 3

As with the preceding sonatas op. 2, nos. 1–3, and op. 7 and op. 22 to follow, the D Major Sonata, op. 10, no. 3, contains four movements, in this case, unusually, all in D, including a *Presto* first movement in sonata form in D major, a passionate *Largo e mesto* in *da capo* or A–B–A form in D minor with an extensive coda, a *Menuetto* trio in D major, and a Rondo: *Allegro* also in D major.

First Movement: Presto

The *Presto* opens with a fourteen-note theme all in quarter notes, first in single and then in double octaves. Throughout the movement Beethoven will focus on the first four, a four-note scale that starts with an upbeat on the tonic. The double octaves in the first phrase conclude with an A (the dominant) underneath a *fermata*. In the next two phrases the four-note motive is answered with a two-note motive: a short upbeat and long downbeat, the first in a high range and the second in the bass. The two-note motive recalls a duet in the opening scene of *The Marriage of Figaro*, which premiered just twelve years earlier. In this second act 1 duet, "Se a caso madama" ("If at Night My Lady"), Susanna and Figaro, in song, imitate the sound of the service bells rung by the Countess (*din-din*) and the Count (*don-don*) they work for. A return of the fourteen-note theme (with a six-note extension), in which each upper note of the melody answers the lower note on the upbeat, concludes with another long note underneath a fermata. The transition that follows introduces a distinctive new theme in B minor. As with all the material of the opening measures, each phrase begins with an upbeat.

We have observed Beethoven's predilection for reusing his basic thematic material in later sections of the exposition, including portions of the second theme area. Before he composed the D major sonata he was not as yet incorporating ideas from the first theme into the *second* theme. This time Beethoven uses the same four-note descending scale that opened the fourteen-note first theme as the starting point for the second. Although its use of eighth notes instead of quarters and its placement in the second part rather than the first part of the measure might make it easy to miss, Beethoven gives listeners a chance to make the connection by repeating the four-note phrase two more times in the next two measures. Then after four measures of a new *staccato* (detached) idea, he repeats the four notes another three times in the minor mode. Although not yet a truly distinctive melody, the three-note rhythmic figure accompanying the four-note opening of the main theme will return as the *rhythmic* foundation of the main theme in the fourth movement.

As the second subject area continues, Beethoven brings back the four-note theme with its original first-theme quarter notes and metric placement as the starting point for a passage that features considerable contrapuntal imitation. Also in this continuation of the second theme Beethoven brings back the *din-din* motive from the second phrase of the movement. The closing theme takes the original fourteen notes in their original rhythm (but with new pitches) and states this new transformation of the main theme another three times. After a brief choral-like respite in half-note values, Beethoven states the rhythm of the first theme alternating between the left hand and the right no less than ten times before the repeat sign that formally ends the exposition yet another four times, now alternating between the right and left hands and in D minor.

The first, central gesture of the development is the return of all fourteen notes of the first theme in a *crescendo* that moves from *piano* to *fortissimo* (very loud) in D minor. As in the opening statement, the final note (A) is held underneath a fermata. The next chord is the greatest harmonic surprise in the movement and one of the great harmonic surprises in "early" Beethoven, a sudden swerve up a half step to Bb major to the chord known as the flat submediant or bVI (a chord on the lowered sixth degree of the scale; see triads in the glossary), a particularly intense deceptive cadence (a cadence in which a dominant is followed by a chord other than the tonic; see functional harmony in the glossary). One does not need to know the chord name to feel the impact of this astonishing swerve. As we will discover, Beethoven employed this same harmonic change frequently in his final period, most consistently in the Ninth Symphony where every movement starts in D minor or Bb major and alternates between these two key areas with three of the four movements. The fourteen-note melody supported by a relentless eighth-note accompaniment will occupy the main stage of the development, via another seven complete statements in all, moving harmonically from Bb major to G minor and Eb major. After a recapitulation that follows the exposition closely, Beethoven concludes with a rousing coda based once again on the first four descending notes and concluding with a new version of the four-note motive, in major and in minor, a motive not unlike the opening of "How Dry I Am" in its major form.

Second and Third Movements: Largo e Mesto and Menuetto: Allegro

The *Largo e mesto* (Broad and mournful) begins with a theme whose second through fourth notes in each of the first two measures incorporates as it transforms the fifth through seventh notes of the first-movement main theme (now in the minor mode). The first four notes of the third measure is a downward scale in the minor mode that transforms the opening four-note motive of the first movement into a truly mournful lament. Both the first and last A sections in D minor (twenty-nine and twenty-one measures respectively) and the shorter middle B section in relative major, F major (fourteen measures) feature tense and ambiguous diminished sevenths, often sounding in both hands to produce dense chords consisting of eight notes each. The B section also prominently displays the submediant Bb, the surprise harmony introduced near the outset of the first-movement development. The final section, a coda second only to the first A section in length, returns to the first measure of the main theme, now in the lowest regions of the piano. Soon the bass line begins its long ascent, two notes per measure until the fifth and final measure (up an octave from an A to an A). The final twelve measures return to the first three notes of the theme, which contains a rising half step, an interval that pervades the mournful close of this deeply penetrating movement. The main theme of the *Menuetto* also encompasses the descending four-note motive but convincingly disguises this recycled idea into a memorable new tune. Against a steady triplet accompaniment the trio that follows returns to the two-note motive introduced and emphasized in the second phase of the first movement.

Fourth Movement: Rondo: Allegro

The rondo finale is both a tour de force and wickedly comic in the way it sets up and thwarts expectations. In keeping with Beethoven's growing desire for unity, its central idea is the three-note rhythmic figure that accompanied the second theme in the first movement. The pitches that go with this rhythm are also the same as the fifth through seventh notes of the main theme (in major) heard in the minor mode as the second through fourth notes of the main *Largo e mesto* theme. But instead of offering the three-note motive in the tonic at the outset, Beethoven begins the finale in G major (the subdominant of the tonic D). Beethoven then lingers in this "wrong key" for the first eight measures, in this context a long time. On the sixth measure he presents a dominant seventh that *should* resolve to the tonic but instead swerves to B minor (another deceptive cadence). This is the same key that marked the transition theme of the first movement, a decision that demonstrates Beethoven's increasing attention to harmonic as well as thematic and rhythmic unity. After stating the dominant seventh a second time, Beethoven relents and allows the music to come to a close on the tonic. We are now in the first B episode of the rondo form (A–B–A–C –A–B–A–coda). Most rondo B sections (e.g., op. 15) will be in the dominant key. This one is in the tonic, the tonic that Beethoven managed to avoid throughout the entire A section.

Another dominant seventh of D returns to the subdominant G instead of the expected tonic. This time Beethoven wastes no time in offering his deceptive cadence to B minor, although when he returns to the dominant for the expected resolution to the tonic, he moves instead to the same flat submediant (Bb) that marked the startling harmonic deceptive swerve in the first-movement development. After stopping the music short on an Eb, Beethoven offers a "false" recapitulation starting with the main theme on Bb and stopping once again with a *fermata* on the dominant seventh of D. Once again the dominant resolves to the subdominant for a genuine but abbreviated return of the main theme. After the deceptive cadence to B minor and a cadence to

D major, the B section roughly follows its counterpart earlier in the movement. Once again a dominant on a fermata fails to resolve to the tonic but instead resolves to the subdominant.

Following the by-now-expected deceptive cadence on B minor and the resolution to the tonic D major, we arrive at a coda firmly on the tonic. Still, after yet another dominant seventh and another fermata, this time with a one-measure cadenza known as an *Eingang* (entrance), Beethoven delays the inevitable with yet another resolution to the subdominant G major followed by G minor. A few measures later Beethoven arrives at a dominant seventh one last time. Finally, Beethoven concedes the inevitable and concludes with eight measures of tonic pedal (a tone held for several measures) underneath ascending and descending chromatic scales and *arpeggios* combined with no less than twelve statements of the opening rhythm.

Piano Sonata No. 8 in C Minor (*Pathétique*), Op. 13

Perhaps no Beethoven work in any genre has received as much recognition, popularity, and lasting acclaim as his eighth piano sonata. Published at the end of Mozart and Haydn's century in December 1799, this famous work clearly anticipates the spirit of the future. Although Beethoven had already created works of enormous passion, subtlety, imagination, variety, and even wit and humor, including the D major sonata of op. 10, no other work from his early years, and few since then, has generated the kind of buzz surrounding Beethoven's *Pathétique*.

How does this sonata stand out from its contemporaries? We might start with the sobriquet *Pathétique*, or pathetic in English, as in the word pathos, a quality that inspires pity, sadness, or compassion. *Pathétique* is the first of several of Beethoven's piano sonatas and works in other genres whose acquired names correspond to perceived qualities in the compositions they label. For some works the names can be traced to Beethoven himself, works such as the two sonatas published as op. 27, each described by Beethoven as a *Sonata quasi una fantasia* (see chapter 3). The second work in this opus was additionally dubbed the *Moonlight* but not by its composer. Beethoven also bestowed the title *Pastoral* on his Sixth Symphony and *Les Adieux* or *Lebewohl* (Farewell) on the Piano Sonata op. 81a. On the other hand, the *Pastoral* Sonata, op. 28; the *Tempest*, op. 31, no. 2; the *Waldstein*, op. 53; the *Appassio-*

nata, op. 57; and the *Hammerklavier*, op. 106, were titles added later by others. The *Pathétique* was thus the first of only two Beethoven sonatas with an authentic title that appeared as early as the title page when first published: the *Grande Sonata Pathétique*. Although the title does not suggest a story (or "program"), it does convey and encompass a wide range of moods and emotions during the course of its journey that might suggest or inspire a pathetic character.

The *Pathétique* is also Beethoven's first published piano sonata to begin with a slow introduction, which he marked *Grave* (i.e., grave or solemn). Slow introductions, relatively common in symphonies (1, 2, 4, and 7), are rare in the piano sonatas. In fact, after the *Pathétique* only *Les Adieux* and the final sonata, op. 111, like op. 13 also in C minor, contain substantial slow introductions (the sonata op. 78 begins with a four-measure introduction, and the *Moonlight* begins with a slow *movement*). Still more unusual than a weighty introduction is the fact that Beethoven brings a portion of it back later in the movement, twice. Perhaps the earliest, if not the only, example of this idea belongs to Beethoven himself in the second *Elector* Sonata in F minor published in 1783, WoO 47, no. 2, in which he answers an eight-measure introduction to the *Allegro assai* with nine introductory measures, albeit beginning in the minor subdominant, immediately prior to the recapitulation. Interestingly, both the introduction and the main theme of the F minor sonata share several additional melodic and textural features as well as a similarity of tone with his *Pathétique*. In the latter, Beethoven brings back four measures from the introduction, now in the dominant minor, and then another four measures derived from the introduction, to prepare for a short coda based on the opening of the *Allegro*. The *Grave* introduction and its partial reappearance contribute greatly to establishing an intense (and pathetic) quality to this movement.

Although as a rule Beethoven's works in the minor mode such as the Fifth Symphony and *Pathétique* seem to receive greater attention and notoriety than works in the major, the minor is far less common in the works of Haydn, Mozart, and Beethoven. Including the F minor *Elector* Sonata, Beethoven composed only twenty-seven instrumental works in the minor over the course of his career. Significantly, ten of these works are in C minor, most famously, the Fifth Symphony. Beethoven demonstrated a predilection for C minor as early as his *Dressler* piano variations of 1782 and the opening and closing movements of the *Joseph*

Cantata. Before the *Pathétique* Beethoven had already published three large instrumental works in C minor: the third piano trio of op. 1, the third string trio of op. 9, and the Piano Sonata op. 10, no. 1. Not only was C minor widely perceived as a "pathetic" key during Beethoven's youth, but also the frequency with which he turned to this key suggests that it carried special meaning for him.

First Movement: Grave-Allegro di Molto e con Brio

When composing in C minor, Beethoven favored tense and ambiguous chords called diminished sevenths, chords comprised of nothing but stacked minor thirds. The *Grave* is filled with these chords that first appear immediately after the deep and thick C minor triad that opens the work. The first chords in each of the next three measures are also heavily accented diminished sevenths that contribute to an increasingly intense mood. The opening melodic line of the first four measures consists of the first three notes of a minor scale with the third sounding a second time before resolving down by a half step, a descent that for the previous two hundred years connoted grief and sadness.

After the third consecutive measure to begin with a resounding diminished seventh, the harmony modulates to the relative major (Eb major). Soon the melody reverts back to minor, and the final note of each phrase invariably concludes with the dolorous half-step descent. In the eighth measure the descending half steps change to ascending half steps, which increase the musical intensity still further. Beethoven intensifies the traditional return to the tonic by employing a rapidly descending chromatic scale that encompasses no less than three octaves in a single measure.

Finally the *Allegro* and its main theme arrive, a theme supported by what was in the late eighteenth century already an old-fashioned, broken-octave eighth-note figuration known as a "murky" bass. Most measures, especially the active ones, conclude with a rising half step, the interval that briefly marked the *Grave*. The second theme arrives first in Eb *minor* instead of the conventional Eb major and later, still more unusually, in Db major (bVII) before eventually arriving at Eb major for the closing theme. A major melodic component of the second theme is the same three notes that followed the opening chord, the 1–2–3 part of a melody, but now with a new preparatory note, 5–1–2–3. Although it takes far less time to hear than to explain, once given the hint, most listeners can hear the melodic resemblance between the second theme of the exposition and the central melodic figure of the *Grave*. In any event, the 1–2–3 melody with its half-step descent back to the second degree returns prominently, both in the return of the *Grave* and the beginning of the development, and we will soon observe that Beethoven will return to this idea as the basis for the main theme of the finale.

The attempt to link so many parts of an individual movement with subsequent movements was not new. We can find a number of examples in Haydn and Mozart. What seems new was Beethoven's desire to make the recurrences and altered versions of common material as well as the unprecedented intensity of his musical language memorable and audible, including the uncommon retention of the minor mode throughout the recapitulation. In the exposition Beethoven had offered the second theme in two keys (Eb minor and Db major) before the closing theme entered in Eb major. After reestablishing the C minor tonic following an excruciating twenty-eight measures of dominant preparation, Beethoven states the second theme of the recapitulation minor subdominant (F minor) before repeating it in the tonic C minor, where the music will remain for the closing theme and coda.

Second Movement: Adagio Cantabile

The second movement features a beautiful, memorable, songlike melody that has become one of Beethoven's most famous inspirations. It has even inspired two popular song hits, Ken Dodd's "More than Love" (1966) and Billy Joel's "This Night" (1984). The tempo is appropriately labeled *Adagio cantabile* (slow and songlike) and the form is a simple A (sixteen measures)–B (twelve measures)–A (eight measures)–C (fourteen measures)–A (sixteen measures) rondo followed by a coda lasting seven measures. During the opening A section in Ab major (the submediant of C minor), the symmetrical eight-bar tune is repeated up an octave with a pulsating sixteenth-note accompaniment throughout that becomes increasingly full during the repeat. The short and less symmetrical B section maintains the sixteenth-note pulse, as either chords or melodic lines. It starts in F minor (the submediant) for seven measures and then moves to the dominant (Eb major) before returning to the Ab tonic.

The return of the A section repeats the first eight measures of the first A without change. The section, marked *pianissimo* but with some *crescendos* and three *sforzandi*, shifts to Ab minor, the parallel minor of the A tune. Halfway through this section, Beethoven modulates to the remote key of E major (enharmonic of Fb, an alternate spelling of the same pitch), an expressive move to the flat submediant (bVI) he favored in later works, including the third movement of the Ninth Symphony (Eb to Cb) and with the identical keys (Ab to E) in the recapitulation of the Ab Piano Sonata, op. 110, to mention two works discussed in future chapters. The C section also introduces an intensified accompaniment from eight sixteenth notes per measure to twelve sixteenth-note triplets, an accompaniment that Beethoven will retain in the final A section and coda.

Third Movement: Rondo: Allegro

We have noted that the finale, like the *Adagio cantabile* a rondo but now formally labeled as such by Beethoven, takes as its point of melodic departure the second theme of the first movement (5–1–2–3), which was in turn based on the opening *Grave* theme. The finale's form and key scheme is as follows:

A^1	C minor
B^1	Eb major (two themes)
A^2	C minor
C	Ab major
Retransition	Dominant of C minor
A^3	C minor
B^2	C major and minor (two themes)
A^4	C minor
Coda	C major and minor, Ab major, and C minor

In contrast to the first movement, the two second themes are in the relative major in the first B, and in the return of B Beethoven states both of these themes in C *major*. Interestingly, a move to C major is something Beethoven was also prone to do in most of his C minor works. The contrasting lyrical C section appears after the first return of the A section. The dominant retransition to the third A section returns to the key (Ab), keyboard placement, and the mood of the second

movement. The movement and the sonata end with a conclusive return
of the descending C minor scale that earlier preceded the return of the
A sections and also suggests the chromatic scalar close of the original
Grave introduction to the first movement.

An early positive review in the *Allgemeine musikalische Zeitung*
from February 1800 praises the return of the "vigorous agitation" (Senner 1999, 147) of the first movement in the rondo. For this reviewer, by
reawakening the "fiery Allegro theme" in the closing movement, "the
chief emotion forming the basis of the sonata is carried out; by this
means the sonata itself gains unity and inner life and thus real aesthetic
value" (147). The anonymous reviewer continues with words that ring
true to this day: "To be able to say something like that about a sonata—
assuming, as is the case here, that every other requisite of musical art
has not been left unfilled—is obviously proof of its beauty" (147).

3

THE "HEROIC" STYLE (1802–1806)

It's a pity that I do not understand the art of war as well as I do the art of music. I would conquer him!
—Beethoven to Wenzel Krumpholz upon learning of Napoleon's victory at Jena, quoted in *Thayer's Life of Beethoven*, revised and edited by Elliot Forbes (1964, 403)

Following the success of the Academy concert of April 2, 1800, Beethoven focused on completing the op. 18 quartets. Two years later he managed to organize and mount another Academy concert on April 5, 1803, a concert that featured the debuts of the Second Symphony, the Third Piano Concerto, the oratorio *Christ on the Mount of Olives*, and a repeat performance of the First Symphony. Between these milestones Beethoven achieved yet another with the debut of his first ballet and first public stage success in Vienna, *The Creatures of Prometheus*. *Prometheus* was performed fourteen times the year of its debut in 1801 and on nine additional occasions in 1802 and served as the musical foundation for the *Eroica* Symphony two years later.

Two of these works, the oratorio *Christ on the Mount of Olives* and the ballet *The Creatures of Prometheus* feature heroic figures, in the first the Christian god who suffered for the sins of mankind, and in the second the Greek mythological figure who teaches mankind about the arts and knowledge (in the ballet) and even more famously gave humans the gift of fire (not in the ballet). Within the next few years, music associated with *Prometheus*, the theme and variations for piano op. 35, the work Beethoven referred to as the *Prometheus* Variations, provided

musical source material for a work initially conceived to honor a modern hero, Napoleon, just as the *Joseph Cantata* honored a hero from
Beethoven's youth, Joseph II. The Ab minor "Marcia funebre sulla
morte d'un Eroe" ("Funeral march on the death of a hero") from the
Piano Sonata in Ab Major op. 26, another work on a heroic subject, also
dates from this period (composed 1800–1801; published 1802). *Fidelio*,
the first version of which was performed only few months after the
public debut of the *Eroica*, also features the idea of heroism, embodied
in the heroic actions of Fidelio's faithful wife, Leonore.

Since at least Beethoven's bicentennial in 1970, scholars have referred to a "heroic phase" to describe the early years of the composer's
middle period. More recently, biographers have used the term "heroic
style," a term much more difficult to define. Beyond its heroic theme, a
work such as the *Eroica* may be considered heroic for its ability to
resolve musical obstacles, problems, ambiguities, and tensions, and its
consequent extension of musical forms. It is not always clear as to which
works fit this style. Ironically, most of the works based on heroic subjects mentioned in the previous paragraph do not. In *Beethoven Hero*
(1995) Scott Burnham notes that the heroic style is "a style to which
only a handful of his works can lay unequivocal claim: two symphonies,
two piano sonatas, several overtures, a piano concerto" (xiii), but beyond the Third and Fifth Symphonies, he does not identify the other
works or explain why they fit his definition of the style. Carl Dahlhaus,
who speaks of the "Beethoven myth" rather than to a heroic style, states
in *Nineteenth-Century Music* (1989) that the works "on which the Beethoven myth thrives represent a narrow selection from his complete
output" (76). Dahlhaus's "handful" includes the Ninth Symphony (in
addition to the *Eroica* and Fifth heroic symphonies at the center of
Burnham's heroic list), the *Pathétique* along with the *Appassionata* (the
latter presumably one of Burnham's "two piano sonatas"), *Fidelio*, and
the music to *Egmont*.

No matter how defined, it is worthwhile emphasizing the basic
agreement among scholars that Beethoven's "heroic" works represent
only a small, albeit significant, portion of his extraordinary compositional range. In this chapter we will explore two works invariably acknowledged as "heroic," the *Eroica* Symphony and the *Appassionata* Sonata.
In chapter 5 we will look at the "heroic" Fifth Symphony, a work that
perhaps more than any other embodies the hard-won (and heroic) mu-

sical and psychological progression from adversity and despair to victory and triumph that so many listeners have heard and singled out for praise in these examples of Beethoven's heroic style.

THE *MOONLIGHT* SONATA, OP. 27, NO. 2

Between 1801 and 1803, in addition to completing the new symphony (op. 36), the new concerto (op. 37), the *Mount of Olives* oratorio (op. 85), a string quintet (op. 29), five sonatas for violin and piano (opp. 23, 24, and 30/1–3), and two original sets of variations for piano solo (op. 34 and the *Prometheus* Variations op. 35, the latter known generally known today as the *Eroica* Variations), Beethoven composed eight piano sonatas (opp. 22, 26, 27/1–2, 28, and 31/1–3). With the exception of op. 22 and op. 28, four movements each, the sonatas linked to these opus numbers contain three movements and are smaller in scale, albeit rich in innovation.

The so-called *Moonlight* Sonata, op. 27, no. 2, composed in 1801, soon became, and has remained, one of Beethoven's best-known and loved works. In his book on the performance of the sonatas published in 1842, Beethoven's student Carl Czerny described the first movement as "a nocturnal scene, in which a mournful ghostly voice sounds from the distance" (Jones 1999, 43). The first documented association between moonlight and Beethoven's sonata stems from an 1824 novel by the poet Ludwig Rellstab in which a character describes the first movement of the *Moonlight* Sonata as a portrayal of moonlight over a lake. Contributing to its romantic associations is the fact that Beethoven dedicated the work to his young piano student Countess Julie (Giulietta) Guicciardi. Beethoven's original intention was to dedicate the Rondo in G, op. 51, no. 2, to the countess, but after realizing he needed to give this work to the wife of Count Lichnowsky, the *Moonlight* was available, Guicciardi received the dedication, and the seeds of an indelible association between art and love were sown.

Beethoven himself designated each op. 27 sonata as a "sonata quasi una fantasia," roughly translated as "in the manner of an improvisation." A fantasia was also its own genre, a sectional work employing a variety of piano figurations and played without a break. Fantasias were clearly intended to convey the idea of improvisation, even if the so-called improvisations were carefully worked out on paper. In keeping with this fantasia ideal, none of the movements in op. 27, no. 1, adopts sonata form. Beethoven's instructions to join each of the movements, *attacca subito* (attack immediately), further contribute to the fantasia quality as does the return of ten measures taken from the *Adagio* movement. The overall goal in a fantasia, in contrast to a conventional sonata, is to create the auditory illusion of one long improvisation, encompassing contrasting sections with the formal freedom, looser thematic and formal structure, and free modulations. In the *Moonlight*, op. 27, no. 2, Beethoven follows the famous five-minute long quasi-fantasia-like introductory C# minor dirge with a conventional *Allegretto* in minuet-trio form in Db major (the parallel major and enharmonic of C# minor) that temporarily lightens the mood of this fabulously moody sonata for just over two minutes. The *Presto agitato* finale returns to C# minor with the first and only sonata-form movement in either *fantasia* sonata for an intense seven minutes.

First Movement: *Adagio Sostenuto*

With its haunting *Adagio* melody supported by the continuous triplet accompaniment of broken chords, the *Moonlight*'s universally recognized opening movement is unprecedented in the sonata literature. After deep bass octaves mark an unusual chord progression emphasizing a lowered seventh step of the scale (unusual in minor-mode music of Beethoven's day but common in liturgical modal chants), a melody in the top line emerges in mainly long-note values beginning with the insistent repletion of a single note. According to recent scholarship, the melody, which possesses the narrow range associated with much chant, may be based on a chant found in Mozart's Masonic Funeral Music and Requiem, the latter work known intimately to Beethoven, and another chant associated with the *Lamentations of Jeremiah* and used in Haydn's *Lamentatione* Symphony no. 26 in D Minor (Jones 1999, 78–79). In addition to its mournful, prayerful character, Beethoven instructs the piano to play *pianissimo* and without dampers (*senza sordini*), that is, *with* pedal. Also at the outset he adds the instruction, "Si deve suonare tutto questo pezzo delicatissimamente e senza sordino" (This whole movement must be played very delicately and with pedal).

The added resonance of a modern piano makes it difficult, perhaps impossible, to hold the damper pedal down throughout without causing excessive blurring, but on most Viennese-style pianos at the time, notes died away more rapidly, and holding up the dampers throughout the movement contributed to the mood, character, and distinctive sound quality. Interestingly, Beethoven came to prefer pianos with more resonance, and as his hearing worsened in later years he inclined toward more heavily strung English Broadwood pianos. For those interested in how to perform the third triplet in the accompaniment against the dotted-eighth sixteenth-note figures that occur regularly on the upbeat of a phrase, we recall Czerny's testimony transmitted from Beethoven that the sixteenth note *follows* the last note of the triplet; it is not played *with* the last note of the triplet. Beethoven's alleged preference is known in performance practice circles as non-assimilated triplets.

Second Movement: *Allegretto*

The second movement clearly offers a respite from the brooding first movement and the manic finale. Within its conventional minuet-trio-minuet outline and dance-like character, however, Beethoven does insert some notable elements. For starters, he established a clear Db tonic in the first part only at the end of the first eight-bar phrase, and instead of repeating these eight bars he offers a syncopated variant. Syncopation then becomes a major feature of the movement, absent only during the first half of the second section. In the trio the bass line presents mostly dotted half notes, but every measure in the right hand is syncopated, with each phrase of the first part marked by *sforzando* accents.

Third Movement: *Presto Agitato*

The finale transforms the fundamental material of the first movement into a ferociously passionate outburst. Nevertheless, despite its immense kinetic energy that seems to exceed classical boundaries, the movement is clearly in sonata form. Beethoven's adherence to traditional musical forms, albeit in marvelously stretched and inventive ways, is what makes him a precursor, rather than an avatar, of an emerging Romantic musical style. For the sonata movement's main theme, the slow broken chords within a narrow middle range of the first movement are transformed into erupting, fiery cascades rising over three octaves before exploding into a ferocious and repeated C# minor chord on the last beat of a measure, normally a weak beat. In the second phrase we hear a pair of dominant chords (G# major) and then another pair of C# minor chords, all on the last beat. The meditative mood of the opening chords in the *Adagio* has metamorphosed into the unprecedented manic violence of the *Presto* finale, after which Beethoven adopts a chordal variant of the main theme to transition to the second key.

The *Adagio* went to the relative major (E major) and touched on several other keys before the coda concluded the movement in the original key. In the finale, as in most Beethoven works in minor keys (other than C minor), the composer rejects the relative major for its second theme in favor of the dominant minor, G# minor. Beethoven then adds two distinctive second G# minor themes as closing themes, the second of which shares the repeated notes of the opening melody of the *Adagio*, another audible connection between the first and last movements.

To start his development Beethoven repeats the main theme, now in the tonic major (C# major). He then returns to the second theme, in F# minor (the subdominant), up a half step to G major and back to F# minor, and finally moves to the dominant (G#) to take us back to the tonic. The economical recapitulation undermines our sense of narrative by omitting the transition and instead proceeds directly from the main theme to the second theme, now in C# minor.

A coda restates the ferocious opening phrase, then slows, sounding *ten* diminished-seventh chords that alternate between right and left hands with a fermata after each group of five chords. Beethoven then repeats the second theme twice *fortissimo* in C# minor before proceeding with eight measures of continuous descending and ascending *arpeggios*, two measures of an ascending chromatic scale covering four octaves, a dominant seventh chord under a trill (an ornament that consists of a rapid alternation between a note and the note above) and cadenza-like figuration, and a firm resolution to the tonic minor. A final statement of the second closing theme reiterates the repeated G#s in the top line that echo and prolong the G#s of the opening measures of the sonata. Beethoven completes the transformation from tranquility to turbulence with two *fortissimo* C# minor triads in both hands, the second chord an octave lower than the first.

So expressive are the first and last movements of the *Moonlight* that even in the absence of a program or title such as *Pathétique*, some commentators cannot resist assigning "extra-musical" meanings to the second *fantasia* sonata, meanings that go beyond a love song in the moonlight. Indeed, it is tempting (and might not be capricious) to consider the possibility that the unprecedentedly soft dynamic level and low range throughout most of the *Adagio sostenuto* and its turbulent transformation in the *Presto agitato* may have something to do with Beethoven's response to his by-now-impaired auditory world. By the time he wrote his *Moonlight*, Beethoven had divulged his hearing disability to two close friends in moving letters, and he would soon express his resolve to endure and triumph over this affliction in the unsent letter he wrote at Heiligenstadt to his brothers in the summer of 1802 to be read upon his death.

"JUST READ SHAKESPEARE'S *TEMPEST*": THE *TEMPEST* SONATA, OP. 31, NO. 2

"Just read Shakespeare's *Tempest*" was Beethoven's alleged response when Anton Schindler inquired about the meaning of the Piano Sonata in D Minor, Op. 31, no. 2 (Schindler 1966, 406). Although most scholars dismiss Schindler's recollection, nearly everyone continues to refer to Beethoven's Sonata no. 17 as the *Tempest* Sonata just as we cannot seem to stop referring to his Sonata no. 14 as the *Moonlight*. Beethoven's only piano sonata in D minor was composed in 1802 in response to a commission by the Zurich publisher Nägeli and published the following year as the second sonata in the first of what Nägeli hoped would be two pairs of sonatas. When the fourth sonata was not forthcoming, the third sonata became the final sonata of op. 31 in 1804. Although it has not surpassed the *Pathétique* or *Moonlight* in popularity, in its own way Beethoven's *Tempest* is as remarkable as any Beethoven work composed before the *Eroica* Symphony. In contrast to the *Eroica*, the first *Razumovsky* quartet, and the *Appassionata* Sonata, the *Tempest* offers an alternative smaller-scaled work, a road less travelled on the way to the "heroic" style. After exploring daring and new musical avenues in piano sonatas such as the *Moonlight* and *Tempest*, works with radical ideas but modest formal proportions, Beethoven will turn to a more conventional multimovement plan, but a plan with a greatly expanded scope.

First Movement: *Largo-Allegro*

At every turn, the *Tempest* stands conventional sonata form on its head. Ambiguities begin at the starting gun of the first movement with a rolled chord followed by an arpeggiated triad on a weak dominant that ends underneath a fermata. The anticipation that this will be the beginning of a slow introduction along the lines of the *Pathétique* are thwarted by the sudden presence of four *Allegro* measures on a scalar idea in eighth notes ending with a turn, according to *The New Harvard Dictionary of Music* (Randel 1986), "an ornament that 'turns around' the main note" (885). Although the dominant resolves to the tonic, the resolution is so fleeting it is barely perceptible.

It is a challenge for listeners to grasp the significance of this unusual opening. Have we heard the main theme of the sonata or simply an isolated *arpeggio*, a melodic fragment based on a series of descending scales, and a turn? Perhaps we are experiencing a new species of introduction. Whatever it might be, it is not over, because instead of resolving the dominant to the main tonic, Beethoven starts the process all over with another arpeggiated dominant, this time the dominant of F major, the relative major. Again, after the *arpeggio*, the fast music in eighth notes returns, but no longer as a scalar melody, Beethoven offers only a single fleeting resolution to F major before ambiguous diminished-seventh chords take the music to the first firm dominant-tonic resolution of the movement. After considerable uncertainty and suspense the music arrives unequivocally at D minor. Finally, we are ready to hear the main theme.

The trick is that we will discover in retrospect that the opening *Largo-Allegro*, which sounded like an elaborate introduction, was the *main* theme after all. Moreover, what now clearly sounds like the main theme is actually the beginning of the formal *transition* between the main theme and the second theme. Against a continuous triplet accompaniment in the inner part, this transition theme, which *sounds* like a main theme, brings back the opening, rising *arpeggio* in the bass with its LONG-short-short-LONG rhythm, now in D minor, and then answers it with a more deliberate version (and on the same pitches) as the turn idea that concluded the opening scalar motive. What was once an *ornament* (the turn) is now a central component of the *theme*.

The turn that answers the *arpeggio* disappears after two statements, but the *arpeggios* in the bass continue throughout the transition, each followed by a one-note answer in the treble and with rising harmonic tension as the music modulates to a new key. As with the *Moonlight* and most works in the minor mode, Beethoven's retains the minor mode quality of the exposition by placing the second key in the minor dominant rather than the relative major. It is not known whether Beethoven was familiar with Haydn's Symphony no. 92 (*Oxford*), but his second theme followed Haydn's predilection in that symphony to begin themes on a dominant rather than a tonic. But while Haydn quickly resolves to the tonic, Beethoven does not, at least not in a clear and unambiguous manner. In fact, it is not until the end of the exposition that Beethoven unequivocally resolves to the minor dominant. This is only the second firm harmonic resolution heard so far. The first was the dominant-tonic cadence we heard at the end of the "introduction," immediately prior to the transition theme.

As with virtually all the material of this first movement, the new second theme is made up of a new variant of the turn idea (in the left hand) and a theme that incorporates the scalar rhythm of the opening *Allegro* (in the right hand). Within a few measures, the turn idea, now in a distinctive syncopated rhythm that accents its highest note, creates a seemingly new "turn" on the turn theme, first in the left hand and then in the right. This new use of the turn leads to a closing theme in which one hand sounds a four-note scale and the other a theme based on the *arpeggio*.

At the outset of the development Beethoven returns to the first idea of the introduction, the ascending slow *arpeggio*, three times and three chords in all, each ending with a fermata on a long-held note (tonic major, a diminished seventh, and the remote key of F# major). Instead of the scalar *Allegro*, Beethoven emphasizes the distinct transition theme and LONG-short-short-short (the final short note is now a staccato, replacing what was earlier a LONG rhythm in the bass). The varied LONG-short-short-short is answered, first by the elongated turn figure in the right hand and then with one-note replies. This transition-theme-as-development section starts in the equally remote F# minor before moving through a series of tense chords and culminating in eighteen measures of a dominant harmony (almost as long as the *entire* development) that prepares for the return of the tonic.

The music may prepare for the tonic, but the tonic is nowhere to be found. In fact, in contrast to the vast majority of his works, Beethoven almost completely manages to avoid the tonic at the beginning of a recapitulation. He also nearly removes the transition theme. What happens instead is a return to the *Largo-Allegro* introduction that opened the movement. Rather than resolving the dominant chord and proceeding to the *Allegro*, however, Beethoven interrupts the action with a right-hand melody in the style of an operatic recitative, a passage not unlike the beginning of the Ninth Symphony finale. After the *Allegro* enters to resolve the turn and the *Largo* restates the C major broken chord, Beethoven offers a second passage in recitative style. To put it another way, wandering, improvisational, unaccompanied melodies twice fade away without resolving. Over a gradually ascending chromatic bass line, the tension increases until the dominant (A) resolves to the D minor tonic with one last *arpeggio* pattern underneath an unambiguous D minor triad. The exposition resolved to the tonic only twice, the first time at the beginning of the transition theme to the dominant and the second time at the end of the exposition. The recapitulation similarly avoids a firm return of the tonic until the last possible moment, after which Beethoven concludes with an arpeggiated *pianissimo* rumble in the lowest region of Beethoven's piano. The movement concludes with two quiet, final chords, as T. S. Eliot concluded "The Hollow Men": "Not with a bang but a whimper."

Second Movement: *Adagio*

The second movement, like the first, begins with a rolled arpeggiated chord. Its form is the familiar slow-movement form (also known as sonatina or cavatina form), a sonata form without a development. Significantly, when Beethoven arrives at the recapitulation he ornaments much of the original theme with a healthy dose of rapid *arpeggios* in the left hand thus reinforcing this crucial link with the first movement. Another striking feature that adds a slow martial character to the movement is a recurring thirty-second-note triplet figure that outlines an octave and gives the impression of a drum roll. The figure appears prominently in both the first and second theme sections and the first part of the coda, occasionally sounding high in the treble like a tinkling triangle.

Third Movement: *Allegretto*

The third movement returns to sonata-allegro form, although it can also sound like a rondo form, alternating between a returning section, A, and varied contrasting sections. Aside from two rhythmic breaks in the main theme action filled in with descending chromatic scales in the exposition and a third break in the coda (the recapitulation does not offer a break in the motion), the movement is a *perpetuum mobile* (perpetual motion) with unceasing sixteenth notes that either participate in or support a main melody and a secondary melody. The frequent use of arpeggiated melodies and *arpeggio* accompaniments in both hands, but especially the left, further reinforce the link between the finale and its predecessors. After the third break in the coda the music concludes with four successive dominant-tonic cadences and *arpeggios* in both hands. The final *arpeggio* covers a three-octave span in the final two measures and brings the perpetual motion to a stop on two fully arpeggiated D minor triads before concluding quietly and nonheroically on the lowest note available on Beethoven's piano, conveniently enough, a D.

THE *EROICA* SYMPHONY, OP. 55

Beethoven's Third Symphony began to take shape as he worked through several earlier compositions: a collection of dances, a ballet score, and a set of variations for solo piano. At the beginning of the finale to *The Creatures of Prometheus*, Beethoven inserted two *contredanses*. The next year Beethoven assigned these dances numbers 7 and 11 in his Twelve Contredanses for Orchestra (WoO 14). Since the manuscript evidence for the dances and *Creatures* place both in 1800 to 1801, it is not possible to determine which came first, despite the earlier performance date of the ballet. One year later Beethoven decided to make the seventh contredanse the main theme for a massive set of fifteen variations and a fugue (see Musical Forms: Theme and Variations and Fugue in the glossary). These are the variations on *Prometheus* themes mainly known today as the *Eroica* Variations in Eb major, published in 1803 as Fifteen Variations with a Fugue, op. 35. In contrast to most variations that begin with a statement of the theme, the *Eroica* Variations begin with a theme and variations on the *bass* of the theme, which happens to be identical to the bass that introduces both the *Creatures* finale and the seventh contredanse of WoO 14. Beethoven labels this theme and variations within a theme and variations in Italian as "Introduzione col Basso del Tema" (Introduction with the bass of the theme). To understand the finale of the *Eroica*, we need to distinguish between the contredanse melody (the *Tema*) and its thematic harmonic underpinning, the *Basso del Tema* or bass of the theme. After three variations on the *Basso del Tema* alone, the remaining variations will combine these two complementary parts, *Basso del Tema* and *Tema*.

In the absence of the contredanse theme, the *Basso del Tema*, which begins in isolation, sounds rather comical, especially in the second eight-measure section that begins with a measure of silence followed by three *fortissimo* eighth notes on Bb (the first two eight-measure units were *pianissimo* throughout). Beethoven follows these *fortissimo* notes with another measure of silence and a chord on Bb played *piano* underneath a fermata. The *Basso del Tema* itself begins with a simple outline of an Eb triad (first the root Eb, up a fifth to Bb, down an octave to the lower fifth Bb, and up a fourth to return to the root, 1–5–5–1), after which the music quickly closes on the dominant. After repeating this process Beethoven goes on to present three variations on the *Basso del Tema*, the first in two melodic parts, the second in three, and the third in four (appropriately labeled *A due*, *A tre*, and *A quatro*). Beethoven is now ready to present the contredanse as his *Tema* while using the *Basso del Tema* as harmony. Beethoven displays the *Basso del Tema* prominently and in different registers throughout the variations, and its first four notes will eventually serve as the foundation for the fugue subject as well.

Scholars have noticed that toward the end of the sketches of the *Eroica* Variations from 1802 Beethoven drafted a preliminary outline of the first three movements of a new work (Lockwood 1992, 134–50). A scholarly consensus espouses the view that this new work would evolve into the *Eroica* Symphony, mainly composed in 1803 and finished in 1804. Paradoxically, the *absence* of a finale in the symphony draft led scholars to conclude that upon completing the *Eroica* Variations, Beethoven realized he could create another large work based on the *Basso del Tema* and its contredanse, thus making it unnecessary to reveal a plan for the symphony finale. The larger implications of this hypothesis are that the finale of the *Eroica* was the *starting point* rather than the end point of the process. If this plausible hypothesis is correct, it sheds light on a network of intricate connections, not only between the *Eroica* Variations and the *Eroica* Symphony finale but also between the finale and its first movement. As with the *Eroica* Variations, the *Eroica* Symphony finale is preceded by the *Basso del Tema* in isolation and two variations prior to the appearance of the contredanse, followed by six variations on the contredanse theme (and its *Basso*), and a coda.

Nearly every Beethoven biography and program annotator of the *Eroica* Symphony relates the story of the composer's original dedication to Napoleon Bonaparte followed by the composer's dramatic withdrawal and defacing of the dedication page when his former hero crowned himself emperor in May 1804. When Beethoven began the *Eroica* in October 1803, public opinion regarding Napoleon as a liberator and reformer was high and his French army not considered a major threat to Vienna's Imperial Court. Beethoven clearly regarded Napoleon as an inspiring champion of freedom and wanted to dedicate his new symphony to this very model of a modern major general. One year after the coronation, however, Napoleon became persona non grata in Vienna as French troops had arrived to overrun the city. Some of these soldiers were present among the sparse audience to witness the first performances of *Fidelio*.

The same month that Napoleon declared himself emperor, August 1804, the words "Intitulata Bonaparte" were erased from the title page of the composer's autograph, although Beethoven wrote to his publisher explaining that "the title of the symphony is really *Bonaparte*." He also added the words "Geschrieben auf Bonaparte" in pencil in his own hand at the bottom of the autograph. When the score was published, in parts, the work was dedicated to Prince Lobkowitz (his backup dedicatee in 1803) with the description "to celebrate the memory of a great man." Although the word "hero" was not invoked, as it was in the *Marcia funebre sulla morte d'un eroe* (Funeral march for the death of a hero), the third movement of the Piano Sonata op. 26, the second movement of the *Eroica*, also designated as a funeral march, is precisely the kind of movement we might expect in a symphony that goes by the name *Eroica*. Beethoven rarely offered specific programs about a work, but the inclination to interpret this symphony as a biographical portrait of a hero, or even an autobiographical one, has proved irresistible, perhaps not without basis. In short, the musical obstacles (and their overcoming) and the grand scale of the first movement create a musical parallel with a great hero and his successful efforts to conquer adversity of all types, including musical adversity. Not surprisingly, the *Eroica* has served as the archetype for Beethoven's so-called heroic style, which has become his modern brand, for better or worse. The second movement, the funeral march, captures a hero's death; the third, his godlike resurrection; and the fourth, a musical apotheosis that parallels the finale of the *Creatures of Prometheus*, in which Prometheus brings two statues to life and introduces them to an artistic civilization on Parnassus.

First Movement: *Allegro con Brio*

The first movement begins, literally strikingly, with a brutally short introduction made up of two crisp, but rich, Eb major triads played by the full orchestra (including not two but three horns). The main theme that immediately follows consists of a melodic working out of the opening triad revolving around the tonic Eb (Eb–G–Eb–[low] Bb–Eb–G–[high] Bb–Eb or 1–3–1–lower 5–1–3–5–1). So far the theme is as conventional as a classical theme can be. In fact, until recently it was popularly traced to the overture to *Bastien et Bastienne*, an opera Mozart composed at the age of twelve, published long after Beethoven's death. Although it is unlikely Beethoven knew Mozart's youthful work, recent research suggests that both Mozart and Beethoven derived their respective tunes from a *common* source, a *Deutsche* dance that appeared in print in 1790s and was potentially known to both composers prior to that date. In any event, the similarities among these three tunes soon dissolve when Beethoven's version concludes with a descending chromatic scale that moves down by half steps from Eb (the last "1" above) to a D and then to a surprising C#, a note that negates the possibility of closure.

The *Tempest* Sonata managed to create and sustain tension by limiting dominant-tonic resolution. The opening of the *Eroica* raises the ante on unresolved dominant-tonic cadences, while setting up musical problems, what Joseph Kerman in *The Beethoven Quartets* (1967) described as "sore" notes, unexpected and ambiguous notes that require long-term resolution. When supported by a harmony, the "sore" C# at the end of the first theme will gain in musical significance as the movement progresses, and the movement will remain unresolved until Beethoven removes the ambiguity created by this note. However, this will not happen for more than six hundred measures. Another aspect of the heroic style, although not invariably, is its heroic proportions—the *Eroica* is far longer than any symphony of Haydn or Mozart.

The sore C# is only the first of many musical obstacles Beethoven will need to overcome before the first movement can reach resolution and closure. Since the overcoming of obstacles on such an unprecedentedly grand scale corresponds to the obstacles heroes need to battle and conquer, the relatively few works that were both inaugurated by the *Eroica* Symphony and composed throughout the decade and occasionally beyond, are widely referred to as the "heroic style." Nevertheless, some principles associated with the heroic style, such as the extended delay in resolving long-range obstacles, ambiguities, and tensions, may also be found in other large and usually more lyrical works not customarily placed in the heroic column, for example, the first *Razumovsky* quartet, which possesses the heroic formal dimensions of the *Eroica*, explored later in this chapter.

Moving at great speed, the musically packed first movement offers the longest symphonic first movement composed by anyone up to that point, a size not to be equaled until the Ninth, the only Beethoven symphony to surpass the *Eroica* in overall length and scope. Two formal expansions make this possible. The first is the expansion of the development, 244 measures, to a size greater than the total length of most previous first movements. The second formal expansion is the coda, which at 141 measures nearly equals the length of the exposition and recapitulation (each 153 measures).

To achieve this greatly expanded length Beethoven presents musical obstacles that take considerable space to overcome. The first obstacle is the surprising C#, which creates immediate ambiguity and tension that will require many measures to overcome. Throughout the long exposition with its three transition themes, a second theme, and three closing themes, the only firm harmonic resolution is the move to the dominant about halfway through, a move to a contrasting second theme that creates a rare momentary respite from the preceding relentless rhythmic momentum.

The development begins with small parts of the first transition theme, after which Beethoven returns to the first five notes of the main theme, now in the minor mode. For the next minute we will hear these opening five notes no less than six times, first in C minor, then C# minor (significantly the key based on the "sore" note from the opening of the main theme), and followed by D minor, E minor, G minor, and A minor. None of these five-note statements are answered by a dominant chord that would definitively establish any of these harmonies as key areas. The final statement erupts into the third transition theme followed by a fugato based on the first transition theme. The irregular accentuation that marked several places in the exposition now places *sforzando* accents mainly on the weak second beats of three-quarter time (1–**2**–3) and then 1 and 3. The music grows excruciatingly tense before the next modulation, this time to E minor, arguably as far from the orbit of the central Eb tonality as it is possible to travel.

Beethoven was not the first classical composer to introduce a distinctive new theme in the middle of a development, but the theme's melodic distinctiveness, as well as its remote key, is remarkable. The tune is short, lasting only eight measures, the second four measures duplicating the first four with a firmer close. The theme *sounds* new, but knowing Beethoven's habit of connecting every musical snippet into an organic whole, one of the most influential features of Beethoven's middle period works, heroic or not, we should take a closer look. Indeed, imbedded in this E minor theme, repeated in A minor, is the future *Basso del Tema*, a *Tema* not heard again in its original state until the opening of the finale. Beethoven has offered other intimations of the *Basso del Tema* throughout the exposition, especially of course the main theme, but the E minor theme in the middle of the development is Beethoven's most startling and imaginative manifestation of this bass foundation so far.

After the two statements of the "new" theme, Beethoven returns to a more conventional developmental material—a slightly longer segment of the main theme, four measures, first in C major and then in C minor.

Then he states the new theme a third time, now in Eb minor, the parallel minor of the symphony's tonic Eb major. Soon the bassoon introduces a new form of the main theme in which the final notes remain on the high note of the phrase, the fifth of its triad, instead of returning to the root as before. In the recapitulation and coda, this new, uplifting close to the main theme will be the most frequently sounding version. As with most retransitions to the recapitulation that lead to the inevitable and often triumphant return of the main theme in the main key, Beethoven offers an ample amount of the dominant seventh chord that pulls to the tonic. He also adds an unexpected and highly unusual departure from his convention: he asks the second horn to enter with the opening of the main theme in the tonic *against* the dominant seventh of the strings, several bars before the full orchestra arrives to clarify the tonic resolution.

In his autobiographical memoirs published in 1838, Ferdinand Ries recalled the first time he heard the horn entry at a run-through of the symphony at Prince Lobkowitz's palace on June 9, 1804. This rehearsal, conducted by Beethoven, was the first of several run-throughs that preceded the public premiere of the symphony on April 7, 1805. Ries reported that in the syncopated passage preceding the "new" theme, Beethoven "threw the whole orchestra out of rhythm. . . [and] that they had to start all over again from the beginning" (Wegeler 1987, 68–69). Most famously, Ries recalled that when the second horn entered what appeared to be prematurely (but in fact correctly), he said to Beethoven, "That damned horn player! Can't he count?" (69), a comment that made Beethoven so angry he nearly boxed Ries on the ears, after which he didn't forgive his future chronicler for a long time. The early horn entry, which sketches show was an early and unwavering idea in the compositional process of the work, does not sound so radical today, especially since the dominant seventh chord in the violins is both soft and incomplete, but for years publishers and printers thought this extremely effective touch was an error and consequently contradicted the composer's intention by correcting it.

Although Beethoven firmly reestablishes the tonic Eb along with the main theme, the theme itself continues its descent another half step lower than C#. The horns in F major and then the flutes in Db major (the enharmonic of C#) display the "heroic" version of the first four measures of the theme, which rises and remains on the high fifth. After these departures, the recapitulation follows the exposition closely until Beethoven again reaches the expected Eb major.

Despite the apparent closure, by the time he reaches the end of the recapitulation Beethoven still has a number of loose ends to resolve. This is what the enormous coda will accomplish. The first issue to resolve is the C# and its matching enharmonic Db. This happens right away. After six measures of a prolonged Eb pedal point underneath two statements of the first five notes of the main theme, instead of completing the chromatic descent to C#, Beethoven simply moves the harmony one whole step lower from Eb to Db major for another statement of the first five notes of the main theme. Beethoven then restates the main theme a third time, on C major, one half step lower than Db, after which he offers two additional statements of the main theme's first five notes, still on C. On the third statement, however, he stops the melody after four notes and states the first notes of the theme on the dominant.

The confirmation of the tonic of the main theme by its dominant is a convention that Beethoven has studiously neglected to observe in this expansive first movement. But since the tonic the dominant is confirming is the *wrong* tonic, C major instead of Eb major, the journey toward resolution and closure needs to continue, thus expanding the coda to its necessarily enlarged proportions. Before he arrives at Eb Beethoven states the first four notes of the main theme in yet another new key, F minor, where he remains as the music restates the "new" theme from the development (the theme based on the *Basso del Tema*). From F minor, Beethoven moves down by a step (just as he had just done with the main theme, Eb–Db–C major) and restates the development theme in Eb minor.

Since Eb minor is the same tonic as the main key of the work, Eb major, we may not know it yet, but we are almost home. All Beethoven needs to do now is cancel out all these "wrong" keys and fully *prepare* for the inevitable. Clearly the "heroic" style remains fundamentally the *classical* style. All it takes to accomplish this is to state twenty-eight measures of the correct tonic Bb, the dominant of Eb. This is a considerable amount of preparation, but Beethoven needs it in order to banish the many earlier ambiguities. Can we blame him for wanting to establish a tonic resolution beyond a reasonable (or even an unreasonable) doubt? The resulting establishment of the tonic by its dominant, the most powerful cadence of the movement so far (and we are now in measure 631 out of the 691), is matched by a statement of the first four measures of the main theme, starting with the horns, and with the triumphant ending upward to the fifth, the highest note of the phrase. The four measures of tonic are answered by four measures of dominant, the first time in the movement that the tonic harmony of the main theme has been so firmly established.

Beethoven makes the most of this long-delayed climactic moment by stating it four times, four measures of tonics followed by four measures of dominants. At the first statement he also adds a counter line in the violins that the winds will take up at the fourth statement over a new syncopated figure in the violins. The music also gradually rises to a crashing *fortissimo* after the fourth pair of tonic-dominant statements of the main theme—no more C#s, and no more Db's.

With twenty measures to go Beethoven ties one final loose end. It is easy to escape notice in the flurry of activity and the many themes presented in the exposition that one short theme lasting only eight measures, the second transition theme, invariably concluded with a dissonance (a diminished-seventh chord), when it appeared in the exposition and again in the recapitulation. Although Beethoven uses the first and third transition themes extensively in the development, he avoids this second transition theme, saving it for its close-up in the final seconds of the movement. The sketches reveal that the idea of prolonging the resolution of this theme was, like the "early" horn entrance, an early and unwavering part of the compositional process. Now Beethoven is ready to resolve this final unresolved theme to the dominant, a dominant prolonged for no less than eight measures (the first three with second beat accents throughout the entire orchestra). The movement concludes with three final short tonic chords on the main downbeats, sounding as bookends to the two tonic chords that introduced the movement, to close the movement with a vociferous *fortissimo*.

Second Movement: *Marcia Funebre, Adagio Assai*

The second movement, *Marcia funebre*, is in C minor, the minor key so often favored by Beethoven throughout his career. The form is simple but powerful: a large first section in C minor (A-B-A), with the A sections supported by martial rhythms followed by a contrasting B section in C major that Beethoven labeled *Maggiore* (major). The return of the first section is incomplete but also expanded with fugal sections and expansions, including a harmonic swerve to Ab major, the submediant, an intense passage supported by continuous triplet motion. Instead of returning to the C major section, Beethoven returns to a shortened recapitulation of the first section in C minor, still supported by continuous triplet underpinning. Instead of resolving to C minor, the coda reasserts Ab major with a new theme. After a brief touch of Db (enharmonic to the "sore" note C# from the first movement), Beethoven returns to C minor and a fragmented and eventual dissolution of the original heroic theme, as if the hero has died in front of our ears.

Third Movement: *Scherzo: Allegro Vivace*

The third movement, in *scherzo*-trio form, returns to the Eb major tonic. Originally trios were called trios because they often featured three instruments. In this respect the *Eroica* trio is a real trio because it features three horns throughout. The return of the *scherzo* portion includes a surprise when Beethoven interrupts the relentless fast triple (so fast it must be counted "in 1"), with four measures of duple in "cut time" before continuing with the pervasive triple. In the final measures, which Beethoven himself labels "Coda," Beethoven starts with a return to Db and two statements of a distinctive *rising* chromatic line consisting of three notes, Db–D–Eb, a precise inversion of the same chromatically *descending* three notes that conclude the opening phrase of the first movement (Eb–D–C#). Even though he now spells C# as Db, the aural connection between the closing moments of the *scherzo* and the opening moments of the first movement is unmistakable. After the second statement of Db–D–Eb, Beethoven brings the music to a rapid and emphatic close in the tonic Eb.

Fourth Movement: *Finale: Allegro Molto*

The *Eroica* finale continues to develop the *Basso del Tema* and the contredanse from the *Eroica* Variations for Piano, op. 35, into a complex symphonic finale. After a short orchestral flourish in G minor, Beethoven states the *Basso del Tema* much as he did in the piano work. He then presents "*A tre*" and "*A quattro*" variations on the *Basso del Tema* that differ from the "*A tre*" and "*A quattro*" variations in the

Eroica Variations. Again, as in the *Eroica* Variations, Beethoven follows the *Basso del Tema* variations with the contredanse, the *Tema* (theme). Interestingly, the contredanse *Tema* begins with the same three notes as the opening theme of the *Eroica*, Eb–G–Eb. But since this is a tune rather than a melodically and harmonically open-ended motive, the second phrase of the contredanse presents the dominant chord (Bb) before returning to the tonic. Here too the music corresponds precisely to the primary melodic material of the first movement, especially the pivotal moment in the coda when Beethoven for the first time in the work follows the tonic with the dominant, arguably the most significant and culminating harmonic moment of the entire first movement (and repeated another three times). What took 631 measures of the first movement is over in a four-measure instant in the finale.

Beethoven follows the complete thematic statement of the contredanse tune with a short transition and the first of two *fugati*, both of which are based on the first four notes of the *Basso del Tema*. This is also the first of six variations. The second variation, which returns to the contredanse tune, moves from B minor to D major and features the flute. Variation 3 in G minor is a fast march with a melody that transforms the somber mood of the second movement *Marcia funebre* into a march-like dance of triumph. Variation 4 returns to the contredanse tune in the flute and first violin in C major and then C minor in the second violins, another reference to the C major and minor contrasts of the *Marcia funebre*. Variation 5 doubles as a second fugato in the movement's central key of Eb major. This time Beethoven presents a double fugato, in which one theme is an ornamental version of the main theme filled with sixteenth notes, the other based on the inversion of the first four notes of the *Basso del Tema*. The original four notes are Eb, up a fifth to Bb, down an octave to Bb, and up a fourth back to Eb. In inversion also starts on Eb and then goes *down* a *fourth* to Bb, *up* an octave to Bb, and *down* a *fifth* (the fourth and fifth being inversions of each other).

The final variation 6, *Poco Andante*, returns to the contredanse clearly, first in the winds, with the oboe taking the melodic lead and without the flute that was featured so prominently in variations 2 and 4, then answered in the strings. The theme is slower and reharmonized but unmistakable. The variation culminates with a complete *fortissimo* statement of the contredanse in the cellos and basses. Having restored the tonic key and the contredanse, Beethoven digresses harmonically and melodically in a short passage in Ab major that takes the music back to G minor, the key that opened the movement and the key of the March variation (no. 4). The *Presto* coda begins with a return to the G minor flourish that opened the movement but quickly returns to Eb major with a *Presto* that features thematic fragments of the contredanse to conclude the symphony with a blaze of triumph and optimism.

THE *RAZUMOVSKY* STRING QUARTET IN F MAJOR, OP. 59, NO. I

The *Eroica* marks the beginning of Beethoven's large-scale works in the heroic style. Before we discuss another heroic work (the so-called *Appassionata* Sonata), however, this chapter will look at a work of heroic *proportions* but one usually excluded from the heroic label: the String Quartet in F Major, op. 59, no. 1. This is first of the three *Razumovsky* quartets composed relatively quickly between April and November 1806 (the autograph of the F major is inscribed "Begun on 26 May"). The quartets were published in 1808. Although the work's pervasive lyricism seems to have disqualified it as a heroic work, with its four large-scale sonata-form movements, including an exceptionally grand *scherzo* movement, the F major *Razumovsky* compares in size and scope with the Third Symphony. When compared with other Beethoven quartets, only the three late quartets with five, six, and seven movements, respectively op. 132, op. 130, and op. 131, surpass the first *Razumovsky* in length.

The impetus behind the op. 59 quartets was a commission from Count Razumovsky, since 1792 the Russian ambassador to the Austrian court, a loyal Beethoven patron from the composer's early years in Vienna, and a major supporter and participant of chamber music in aristocratic circles. As a tribute to the count's Russian origins, and perhaps a stipulation of the commission, at least two of the quartets (nos. 1 and 2) incorporate Russian musical themes, the finale of no. 1 and the trio of the third movement of no. 2 (the latter theme also used prominently by Modest Musorgsky decades later in the "Coronation" scene for his opera *Boris Godunov*). Recent research has also revealed that in the second movement of the third quartet Beethoven adapted a preex-isting *arrangement* of a Russian folk song (Ferraguto 2014).

First Movement: *Allegro*

As with the *Eroica* Symphony, the *Allegro* movement of op. 59, no. 1, begins with the cello; albeit in contrast to its predecessor, the cello in the *Razumovsky* plays a long, lyrical, stepwise tune. Beethoven may prolong the harmonic resolution of this tune just a bit during the course of a gradual *crescendo*, but unlike the symphony he completes a *fortissimo* full chordal arrival on the tonic F major at the conclusion of a long phrase within the first thirty seconds of the piece. This is much more what one would normally expect in a sonata-form movement before Beethoven. This assertive tonic arrival also introduces the first chord in which the root of the chord sounds in the lowest sounding part (i.e., the root of the chord is played by the cello *only* at this final cadence). A few measures later the transition theme also offers four measures of a tonic triad in root position. Between these two points of resolution, Beetho-ven inserts a disjunct and harmonically ambiguous theme that features a short-short-LONG rhythm (five times in the next seven measures). More lyrical second and closing themes on the dominant C major bring the exposition to its nonheroic close.

This takes us to the first of two major formal surprises. In nearly every first movement in sonata form, including expositions as long as the *Eroica* (153 measures), expositions are framed by repeat signs, signs observed by most performers. The exposition of the first *Razumovsky*, 102 measures long, is not so marked. Nevertheless, a listener without a score would not be aware that the quartet had not taken a repeat, because Beethoven fools us by beginning the development (about three minutes into the piece) with a *literal* repeat of the first four measures of the exposition, the same measures we would be hearing if Beethoven had instructed the performers to repeat the exposition. What happens a few seconds later shatters any possible complacency that we will enjoy another opportunity to savor the exposition when Beethoven interrupts the imagined exposition repeat with an unexpected "sore" note Gb and holds this seemingly misplaced pitch what seems like a long time (but only three measures in the score). Another enormous development has begun, one that "measures" about 238 measures, more than twice as long as the exposition. Before the end of this imposing development section, comparable in proportions to that of the first movement of the *Eroica* Symphony, we have heard an enormous variety of musical developments, including a *false* recapitulation and a double fugato (as in the *Eroica* finale a fugato with two subjects). One theme is loosely based on the jumpy short-short-LONG theme that appeared after the first major cadence twenty measures into the work. Another is based on the cadential theme of the exposition.

The second major formal surprise occurs when we reach the conclusion of the development. In the vast majority of sonata movements Beethoven combines the return of the central tonality with a return of the main theme. In op. 59, no. 1, Beethoven offers the jumpy "pretransition" (short-short-LONG) theme instead of the main theme. Harmonically, Beethoven supports the "wrong" theme with a tonic F major chord but weakens this resolution by not allowing the bass to sound the root of the chord. After extending the pretransition theme further than he did in the exposition, Beethoven returns to the original main theme. But unlike its first statement at the outset of the movement, he does not resolve the theme with a firm F major cadence in the bass. Instead he returns again to the "sore" Gb, the same Gb that interrupted the "false" repeat of the exposition. Midway through the recapitulation, only slightly longer than the exposition, Beethoven eventually establishes F major firmly with an F root when he arrives at the second theme. This belated arrival constitutes the first clear cadence to the tonic in the recapitulation so far.

In the coda (fifty-two measures) Beethoven makes amends for his extended tonal reticence when he gives the melody to the violin and provides full support from the other quartet members for each note of the melody's rhythm for its entire twelve-note phrase. The music is *fortissimo*, all but one of the cello's repeated tonic F's are supported with open fifths above, and in the first measure the weak beats (two and four) are each marked with a *sforzando*. Having finally established the tonic, Beethoven continues to allow the cello to assert the tonic in its lower register until the end of the movement.

Second Movement: *Allegretto Vivace e Sempre Scherzando*

The second movement, *Allegretto vivace e sempre scherzando*, combines a *scherzo*-trio form (not labeled as such) with sonata form:

- *Scherzo*/Exposition

    Main theme in Bb major

- Trio/Exposition

    Second theme in F minor

- Development-*Scherzo*/Recapitulation

    Main theme, Gb major—eventually Bb major

- Trio/Recapitulation

    Second theme in Bb minor

- *Scherzo*/Coda

    Bb major

The movement opens in an unorthodox, somewhat eccentric manner with the cello playing a distinctive rhythm on fifteen successive Bb's, an opening that apparently so offended the cellist Bernhard Romberg, an acquaintance from the composer's Bonn years, that he tried to destroy his part. The movement is saturated with this quirky rhythm, often played by the entire foursome, as well as other quirky harmonic shifts and startling contrasts of dynamics and mood. At nearly five hundred measures, the *scherzo* is also enormous (the longest *scherzo* up to that time) and takes about as long to play as the first movement.

Third Movement: *Adagio Molto e Mesto*

The third movement includes the word *mesto* (mournful) in its tempo designation, a verbal direction Beethoven previously used to describe the D minor slow movement of the piano sonata in D major, op. 10, no. 3. The present movement in F minor, which like the first two movements incorporates sonata form with a coda, is the longest slow movement Beethoven had composed since the *Eroica's Marcia Funebre*. At the end of the development, begun in the relative major, Ab, after a second theme and closing material in C minor, Beethoven presents a ravishingly lyrical, even ethereal theme in the first violin aptly marked *molto cantabile* (with much singing) in Db major above pulsating inner voices in the viola and second violin and a short imitative passage between the viola and cello.

Fourth Movement: *Allegro*

In the finale Beethoven sets the long-anticipated Russian tune, which translates in English as "Ah, Whether It's My Luck, Such Luck." Beethoven alters his source considerably. Not only does he change the tempo of the song from moderate to fast and the opening modal character from minor to major, but also he transforms its fundamental nature when he converts the simple tune into a repository of countersubjects (subjects that appear concurrently with the main subject) and other sophisticated counterpoint. Ingeniously, in the coda Beethoven takes a fragment from the latter part of the tune and transforms it into a new melody, which allows still further contrapuntal reworking. Shortly before he arrives at the end of the movement, Beethoven slows the tempo down to *adagio ma non troppo* for the last statement of the first six measures of "My Luck" before concluding with a torrential *presto* and *fortissimo* outburst.

THE *APPASSIONATA* SONATA, OP. 57

The *Appassionata* label associated with the F Minor Sonata, op. 57, first appeared in connection with a four-hand arrangement published nine years after Beethoven's death. The label seemed to fit the music and soon become indelibly linked with the work. The sonata, composed between 1804 and 1805, served as a minor-mode counterpart to the comparably epic Sonata in C Major dedicated to Count Waldstein, known today as the *Waldstein* Sonata, completed shortly before the *Appassionata* was begun. Sandwiched between these heroic monoliths is a two-movement sonata, the Piano Sonata in F Major, op. 54, in which the first movement was an unusual minuet and trio and the second a *perpetuum mobile*, as is the finale of the *Appassionata*.

First Movement: *Allegro Assai*

In the *Appassionata*, the opening *pianissimo* phrase with its falling and rising minor tonic *arpeggio* concludes on an unresolved dominant chord (C), the first of many. Next we hear the first of many dramatic silences. Beethoven follows the first moment of silence, not with a return to the tonic F, but with an ascent up a half step from F minor to Gb major, the harmony known as the Neapolitan, and repeats the musical material of the opening phrase. The second phrase ends on *its* dominant followed by more silence. Next we hear the first of three statements of the three shorts and a long motive that will soon pervade the Fifth Symphony. The pitches, three Db's and a C, emphasize the same half-step movement that separated the first and second phrase, now with a descending rather than an ascending half step. After five measures of a tense diminished-seventh chord and more dramatic silences, a weak cadence leads to a return of the original *arpeggio* melody, first on the tonic, *fortissimo*, and then resting on yet another dominant that will never resolve. In fact, a central idea of this first movement is Beethoven's ability to sustain the suspense until *after* the recapitulation and to withhold a firm dominant-tonic resolution excruciatingly until the eleventh hour, the final measures of the movement.

As with a number of other Beethoven works in the minor mode, the first movement of the *Appassionata* is compact. It is also formally egalitarian in that its longest section, the seventy measures of development, is only eleven measures longer than the shortest section, the coda. Consequently, the music moves rapidly with only a few measures separating the second theme in Ab major, a theme that shares the *arpeggio* and rhythmic ideas from the first theme. The exposition concludes with a turbulent closing theme in Ab *minor*, yet another theme that emphasizes *arpeggio* movement.

The development presents the first and second theme in a range of keys, including Db major, before dwelling on a long, tense passage of diminished sevenths also on Db, the same Db that Beethoven emphasized on the three shorts and a long rhythm early in the movement. This time Beethoven sounds the four-note rhythmic motive three times on Db alone and then five times from Db to C. The fifth time Beethoven arrives at C, the dominant of the central F minor tonality, he repeats this note on a steady eighth-note rhythm no less than *sixty-six times*.

Above the first two measures of these powerful and obsessive Cs, Beethoven returns to the main theme in F minor. Although the Cs belong to the F minor triad, the fact that the C is in the bass, a pedal point, makes it sound as though the tonic in the right hand is harmonized by the dominant rather than the tonic.

Beethoven supports the Gb major repetition of the theme with a Db pedal point and then returns to a C pedal. This takes the music back to the second return of the main theme, this time in F *major*. After the second theme, also in F major, the closing theme returns to the tonic minor. In the coda Beethoven offers another variation on a theme that seems to combine elements of both the first and second themes, first in F minor and then in Db major. Once again Beethoven moves the harmony from Db to C, the home dominant, in fact eight measures that focus on this central pitch.

The last five repetitions of the note C are introduced by Db's in the three shorts and a long rhythm as the music slows down and becomes increasingly soft. The final statement, *adagio* and *pianissimo*, concludes with a dominant seventh on C below a fermata. The three shorts, all on a richly chorded dominant seventh *fortissimo*, finally succumb to the inevitable, a full tonic chord on the tonic F minor. This is followed by a variation of the second theme that leads the music to a continuous series of cadences from the dominant to the tonic *sempre più forte* (always louder), after which Beethoven presents a final surprise, a soft landing from a *piano diminuendo* to the unusual *ppp* or *pianississimo* (very, very soft), a fitting close to the *pp* or *pianissimo* (very soft) that opened the movement.

Second Movement: *Andante con Moto*

The second movement is based on a hymnlike theme and its variations in Db major, a key that has been emphasized both harmonically and melodically throughout the first movement. Beethoven achieves a state of serenity throughout the theme through simple chords and rhythms, a low register, and a melodic line that barely moves. The first variation remains largely subdued in the low range; the second and third variations offer increasing rhythmic movement and rising registers. The final variation returns to the hymnlike theme, mixing low, high, and middle registers, and closes on two broken diminished-seventh chords, the first *pianissimo* and the second *fortissimo*, each under a fermata.

Third Movement: *Allegro ma non Troppo*

After *twelve* diminished-seventh chords in rhythmic unison and an elaborate sixteenth-note flourish, first in the right hand and then in both hands, the music resolves to the tonic after each of five repetitions of the main theme, all within a *pianissimo* dynamic level. As in the first movement Beethoven follows the first F minor statement with another in the Neapolitan, Gb major, before the second of the five cadences returns to F minor. At the end of the first musical unit, which never truly leaves F minor to establish a clear second theme, Beethoven closes with a diminished-seventh chord on the Neapolitan Gb rather than the tonic, dominant, or relative major.

Unusually, Beethoven expressly asks the performer to repeat the *second* section (*la seconda parte due volte*). Unlike a conventional sonata development, the second section remains harmonically static with thirty-two measures of the minor subdominant followed by forty-four measures of preparation for the return to the tonic and the recapitulation. Beethoven marks the final measures of this preparation with frequent moments of silence and a withdrawal from the perpetual and unceasing sixteenth-note treadmill.

The recapitulation returns to the *perpetuum mobile* until the second ending where Beethoven moves to a binary *presto* passage in which the first two notes of each section consist of two *fortissimo* chords, the second with a *sforzando*, followed a series of eighth notes *piano*, five measures in the first section, and seven in the second. The flurry of sixteenth notes returns with the original central melody in the right hand and an arpeggiated left hand that stops for the second beat on a *sforzando*. After sixteen measures the accents shift to the *sforzandi* on the first beat, albeit every other measure. After one final outburst in which the right and left hands play *fortissimo* F minor *arpeggios* in opposite directions, the sonata comes to a boisterous close.

The composition of the *Appassionata* finale inspired an often-repeated anecdote that appeared in Ferdinand Ries's biographical notes. The reminiscence was inspired by a long walk that brought Beethoven and Ries back to the composer's lodgings about 8:00 p.m. Ries writes,

The entire way he had hummed, or sometimes even howled, to him-self—up and down, up and down, without singing any definite notes. When I asked what this was, he replied: "A theme for the last Allegro of the sonata has occurred to me" (in F minor, Opus 57). When we entered the room he rushed to the piano without taking off his hat. I took a seat in the corner and he soon forgot all about me. He stormed on for at least an hour with the new finale of this sonata, which is so beautiful. Finally he got up, was surprised to see me still there, and said: "I cannot give you a lesson today. I still have work to do." (Wegeler 1987, 87)

4

FIDELIO: BEETHOVEN'S ONE AND ONLY OPERA (1805–1806 AND 1814)

The music is among the most beautiful and perfect one could hope
to hear; the subject is interesting because it concerns the liberation
of a prisoner through the loyalty and courage of his wife. But nevertheless, probably nothing has caused so much aggravation for Beethoven as this work, whose worth will come to be fully appreciated
only in the future (Wegeler 1987, 58).
—Stephan von Breuning, librettist of the 1806 revision, to his sister
Eleonore and her husband Franz Wegeler, June 2, 1806

When the conductor Leonard Bernstein chose to perform Beethoven's Ninth Symphony on Christmas 1989 to celebrate the recent fall of
the Berlin Wall, he made the historically suspect but politically effective
decision to change the word Freude (joy), wherever it occurs, to Freiheit, the German word for freedom. No such liberty was necessary
when, on the previous October 7, at a performance to mark the fortieth
anniversary of the DDR (East Germany), audiences erupted into wild
applause after the Prisoner's Chorus during a performance of *Fidelio* by
Dresden's Semperoper in which the prisoners appeared in street
clothes at the end of the evening. One month later on November 9,
East Germany, and soon thereafter the wall itself, came tumbling down.
The finale of *Fidelio* certainly anticipates the Ninth's "Ode to Joy," but
the idea of Freiheit is at the opera's core. The word Freiheit itself also
serves as a mantra, repeated and emphasized musically throughout *Fidelio*, especially in the Prisoner's Chorus at the end of act 1 and at the

beginning of act 2 when audiences witness Florestan's vision of Freiheit at the hands of his courageous wife Leonore, disguised as Fidelio.

Fidelio, Beethoven's one and only completed opera, occupies a unique and significant position in the composer's output and in the history of German opera. If one regards Carl Maria von Weber's *Der Freischütz* (*The Free Shooter*) of 1821 as more nationalistic than universal, *Fidelio* might be the only German opera to have gained a secure place in the international repertoire between Mozart's *Die Zauberflöte* (*The Magic Flute*) of 1791 and Wagner's *Der Fliegende Holländer* (*The Flying Dutchman*) of 1843. Perhaps even more than Claude Debussy's *Pelléas et Mélisande* (1902) or George Gershwin's *Porgy and Bess* (1935), Beethoven first (and only) opera has, with a few lingering reservations, achieved a rarefied and even exalted place in the history of opera and Beethoven's career. *Freiheit* may be the governing concept in *Fidelio*, but the opera is also about love, especially marital love, and fidelity, the latter not only the essence but also even the dictionary definition of the title character's name. In fact, at its first performance in 1805, the work was titled *Fidelio, oder: Die eheliche Liebe* (*or: The Conjugal Love*). Indeed, a major component of *Fidelio*'s meaning as well as its plot is the love between Leonore and Florestan, a wife's heroic efforts to save her husband from tyranny and certain death, and Florestan's heroic efforts to endure unimaginable hardship and suffering, an ordeal made possible only by the love of his "angel" Leonore.

Fidelio, like *The Magic Flute*, is a *Singspiel*, a genre in which spoken dialogue replaces the sung recitative familiar from both serious and comic Italian opera. Beethoven's opera also exemplifies the once-popular subgenre known as a "rescue opera," so called because the rescue of a hero or heroine from prison, capture, or threat of bodily harm constitutes a central component of the plot. To overcome rejection by the censors, Beethoven's setting was altered from the French Revolution to sixteenth-century Spain, although the references to political oppression and the release of political prisoners no doubt evoked the recent past for the audience that consisted of a few remaining Austrian citizens and the occupying French soldiers. Beethoven borrowed from a number of operatic models, including librettos by Jean-Nicolas Bouilly, who supplied the text for Luigi Cherubini's rescue opera *Les deux journées* (*The Two Days*) in 1800, and the original source for *Fidelio*, *Léonore*, first set to music by Pierre Gaveaux in French and produced in Paris in 1798, and later *Leonora* by Ferdinando Paer in Italian for a Dresden production in 1804.

Reliable evidence suggests that both Beethoven and his first librettist Joseph von Sonnleithner were familiar with the rescue operas of Gaveaux and Paer and learned something from them (Beethoven apparently owned a score of the Paer). Clearly Mozart's example also paved the way for Beethoven's first effort as an opera composer. Prior to beginning his work on *Fidelio*, Beethoven's stage works had been limited to the popular ballet *The Creatures of Prometheus* in 1801 and the oratorio *Christ on the Mount of Olives*; the latter work featured in the composer's second Academy in April 1803. Two months later Beethoven received a commission from Emanuel Schikaneder, the librettist for *The Magic Flute* as well as the first Papageno and now the artistic director of the Theater an der Wien, to set his opera text for *Vestas Feuer* (*The Vestal Flame*). After completing most of the *Eroica*, Beethoven began serious work on Schikaneder's opera. Before he abandoned the opera the following January, Beethoven drafted the eighty-one pages of autograph score that survive. From these drafts Beethoven was able to salvage much of a projected trio into the impassioned and exuberant duet "O namenlose Freude" ("Oh Nameless Joy") that celebrates the reunion of Florestan and Leonore after two years of torment.

In the summer after the first public performance of the *Eroica* in April 1805, Beethoven completed *Leonore*. The first of its three performances took place on November 20, only a few days after Napoleon's Vienna invasion. After the final performance, without Sonnleithner's knowledge Beethoven turned to his childhood friend, now a civil servant, Stephan von Breuning, to revise the libretto, which resulted in the deletion of three numbers from the domestic component of the plot. At the center of these domestic scenes is Marzelline, the daughter of the jailor Rocco, who has abandoned her beau, the doorkeeper Jaquino, in favor of a newfound love for Rocco's capable new assistant Fidelio (Leonore in disguise). Aside from the removal of Rocco's so-called gold aria, "Hat man nicht auch gold beineben" ("If You Haven't Gold as Well"), the reordering of several numbers, and the new *Leonore* Overture no. 3 (an expanded version of *Leonore* no. 2), the 1806 revisions were relatively inconsequential. In an important structural change, the first two acts were reduced to one, a reduction made possible by the elimination of several hundred measures. Despite two successful performances on March 29 and April 10 with most of the original cast intact, Beethoven, who felt cheated by the theater office, demanded the score and withdrew the opera.

The Congress of Vienna met from September 1814 to June 1815 for the purpose of restoring as much as possible of the former social order in Europe in the wake of Napoleon's fall. The congress provided an opportunity to celebrate Vienna's favorite musical son whose star had already noticeably risen at the end of 1813 when his overwhelmingly popular *Wellington's Victory* and Seventh Symphony were premiered and repeated to great success. The early months of 1814 from January to April included more performances of *Wellington's Victory*, Beethoven's most popular symphonic work during his lifetime, the Seventh and Eighth Symphonies, the *Ruins of Athens* and *Egmont* Overtures, and the *Archduke* Piano Trio, op. 97, the latter marking Beethoven's final documented performance as a pianist. Riding the coattails of the pending congress, the directors of the court theater asked Beethoven whether he was agreeable to staging a revival of *Fidelio*. According to Friedrich Treitschke, a producer, stage manager, and prolific dramatist at the court opera, Beethoven agreed "on the unequivocal condition that many changes be made" (Forbes 1964, 572) and asked Treitschke for his help in crafting these changes.

The 1814 version, first performed on May 23, although like the 1806 version divided into just two acts, contained revisions far more substantial than those of the 1806 revision. Some scholars and musical directors prefer aspects of the earlier versions, and several even prefer the early versions overall, especially their treatment of the dramatic climax in the final act. Those interested in hearing a reconstructed 1805 version can turn to a recording conducted by John Eliot Gardiner released in 1997. Along with the music the reconstruction contains Gardiner's impassioned defense of this version in his introductory essay "The Case for Beethoven's *Leonore*." Beethoven preferred this title, but the Theater an der Wien insisted he title the work *Fidelio* for the 1805 performances in order to avoid confusion with Gaveux's *Léonore*.

Despite these dissenting views, the 1814 *Fidelio* has emerged as the version of choice in the vast majority of performances and recordings, and it is this version that will serve as the focus of this chapter. Nevertheless, before discussing the final *Fidelio*, it might be helpful to provide an encapsulation of the principal changes Beethoven made between February and May 1814, largely at the instigation of Treitschke.

- The opera began with the fourth overture Beethoven had composed for the opera, the overture now known as the *Fidelio* Overture. Since this overture wasn't ready until a performance three days later, audiences at the first performance of the 1814 version probably heard the overture to *The Ruins of Athens*.
- The opening aria for Marzelline and the duet between Marzelline and Jaquino were reversed in order.
- The trio for Rocco, Jaquino, Marzelline, "Ein Mann is bald genommen" ("A Husband Is Soon Acquired"), no. 3 in 1805 and no. 10 in 1806, was removed.
- Rocco's "gold" aria no. 5 in 1805, and removed in 1806, was reinstated as no. 4.
- The duet between Marzelline and Leonore, "Um in der Ehe froh zu leben" ("To Live Happily in Marriage") no. 10 in 1805 and no. 9 in 1806, was removed.
- "Ach, brich noch nicht" ("Ah, Break Not Yet"), the recitative that precedes Leonore's "Komm, Hoffnung," was replaced by a new recitative, "Abscheulicher!" ("Monster!"), but this did not take place until the performance for Beethoven's benefit on July 18.
- A second prisoner's chorus, "Leb wohl, du warmes Sonnenlicht" ("Farewell, Warm Sunlight"), was added to complete act 1.
- A new third section in F major of Florestan's aria was added, "Und spürich nicht linde, sanftsäuseinde Luft?" ("Do I Not Feel a Gentle, Soft-Stirring Breeze?").
- The final scene was moved from the dungeon to the prison courtyard.
- A new chorus in C major opened the finale.

These changes by no means exhaust the alterations in the dialogue and music Treitschke and Beethoven brought to the score, which was immensely successful, running seven performances between May 23 and July 18. The opera soon made its way to houses outside of Vienna, beginning with a successful performance conducted by Weber in Prague on November 27. In October 1815 the opera was heard for the first time in Berlin.

The 1814 *Fidelio* gained classical status even during Beethoven's lifetime. When the opera returned to Vienna on November 3, 1822, for the first of six performances (November 3–4, December 2 and 17, and March 3 and 18, 1823), "Beethoven's masterwork in the area of opera" was "performed with the greatest success, and received with lively pleasure" (Senner 2001, 236). The new production launched the long association between Wilhelmine Schröder (after 1823 Schröder-Devrient) who performed the role of Leonore, according to the *Wiener allgemeine Theaterzeitung*, "with such diligence, such exertion, such fire, that although we are accustomed to only the most vital and brilliant performance from her, she nevertheless surprised us." Schröder, often considered to be opera's first great singing actress, would soon experience a comparable triumph as Leonore in Dresden and Berlin in 1823, and she sang the role to great acclaim at the first performances of the opera in Leipzig (1829), Paris (1830), and London (1832).

OUR *FIDELIO*: A GUIDE TO THE 1814 *FIDELIO*

Overture

The *Fidelio* Overture composed in 1814 was the shortest of the four overtures for this much-revised opera. Unlike *Leonore* Overture no. 2, which introduced the opera in 1805, its reworked replacement *Leonore* no. 3 in 1806, and *Leonore* no. 1, composed for a Prague performance that failed to materialize in 1807, the fourth *Fidelio* Overture does not contain specific musical references to the opera. In contrast, the three earlier *Leonore* overtures all place the central section of Florestan's act 2 aria at their centers, and no. 2 and no. 3 also bring in the trumpet call that heralds the arrival of Don Fernando, the officer who arrives fortuitously to the rescue at the opera's end, bringing Florestan's corrupt and vicious captor to justice. The *Fidelio* Overture is also the only member of the overture quartet in the key of E rather than C major. Although C major will play a significant role throughout the opera and the opera will end in this triumphant key, the key of E major, the key of Leonore's solo aria in act 1 brings the music closer to a specific crucial character in lieu of a more generic heroic backdrop. The overture begins with a fanfare that anticipates the main theme. After an *Adagio*, a return of the fanfare, and another *Adagio*, the central portion of the overture consists of a clear and concise sonata form (exposition, development, and recapitulation). The overture concludes with the fanfare and *Adagio* followed by a vigorous *Presto* that prominently features the opening rhythmic gesture of the fanfare and introduces the previous silent trombones. The choice of E major also conveniently serves as dominant of the first sung number of the opera in A major.

Act 1: The Courtyard of the Prison

No. 1, Duet: "Jetzt, Schätzchen, jetzt sind wir allein" ("Now, Sweetheart, Now We Are Alone"; Jaquino, Marzelline)

Before the 1814 revisions the opening number was Marzelline's C minor aria (see no. 2), which began where the *Leonore* overtures ended, in C major. The 1814 version opens with the previous no. 2, the duet between Jaquino and Marzelline. As with the other music of these two domestic characters (and also Marzelline's father Rocco), this duet evokes an eighteenth-century classical style, in one duet in particular: the opening number between Figaro and Susanna in Mozart's *The Marriage of Figaro*, "Cinque, dieci" ("Five, ten"). In this famous predecessor Figaro and Susanna are in love, but instead of focusing on his future bride, at the beginning of the scene Figaro is preoccupied with measuring the room while Susanna tries to transfer Figaro's attention to her bridal hat. Eventually Figaro notices Susanna's hat and starts singing her tune, but up to this point they sang different musical lines—each character in their own private world. In "Jetzt, Schätzchen" the characters are not quite ready for marital bliss. Instead Jaquino presses Marzelline for a wedding date and Marzelline puts him off. Beethoven expresses this conflict by giving each character a separate and conflicting key even as they sing the same basic tune, an unmistakable sign of their fundamental (but eventual) compatibility. The orchestral introduction sets up the conflict by moving from A major to B minor and back to A major after which Jaquino sings his first phrase in A major and Marzelline answers in B minor. When Jaquino moves to Marzelline's key, Marzelline shifts back to A major. Although unreconciled, for the sake of musical convention the warring couple manages to conclude together in Jaquino's A major.

No. 2, Aria: "O wär' ich schon mit dir vereint!" ("O Were I Now United with You"; Marzelline)

In a spoken confession prior to her aria, Marzelline acknowledges that Jaquino was perfectly acceptable as a marriage partner before Fidelio came into her life. Her aria displays two contrasting modes (minor and major), tempos (*Andante con moto* and *Poco più allegro*), and moods (A–B–A–B), a livelier version of the same juxtaposition in the *Marcia funebre* of the *Eroica*. The slower A sections in C minor reflect Marzelline's disappointment that she has not made inroads into Fidelio's affections, while the more lively B sections express the hope beating in her breast that Fidelio will eventually want to marry her. The aria closes with Marzelline's deluded vision of a love that will never come to pass. Indeed, although the opera eventually concludes in a hopeful C major, Marzelline's hopes of marrying Fidelio are dashed when his/her identity is revealed.

No. 3, Quartet: "Mir ist so wunderbar" ("A Wondrous Feeling Fills Me"; Marzelline, Leonore, Rocco, Jaquino)

Fidelio (Leonore) enters carrying chains. This leads to the quartet "Mir ist so wunderbar," which opens with a distinctive sound world of divided violas and cellos playing softly and with *legato* above a soft *pizzicato* bass line before the entrance of the winds momentarily leaves the simpler, domestic world and the traditional *Singspiel* far behind. The key is G major, later the key of Leonore and Florestan's passionate reunion in act 2, "O namenlose Freude!" ("O Nameless Joy!"). The serene music of the quartet is a canon, which means that each successive vocal entrance presents the identical melody. The serenity and compatibility of the music masks the strongly contrasting emotions and texts, each expressed as an aside. Marzelline continues to dream of a future with Fidelio while Leonore feels the pain and danger of Marzelline's feelings toward her. Rocco, who is greatly impressed by his new assistant, contemplates a pending marriage between his daughter and Fidelio, while Jaquino expresses his sense of hopelessness and loss of Marzelline's love. This magical quartet, during which time seems to stop, may be the point at which *Fidelio* stops being a simple domestic comedy and begins to explore deeper musico-dramatic territory.

No. 4, Aria: "Hat man nicht auch Gold beineben" ("If You Don't Have Money Too"; Rocco)

After considerable vacillation Beethoven decided to restore this three-minute aria, removed in 1806. Like Marzelline's aria, Rocco's "gold" aria is in two parts, each repeated: the A section in a moderately fast two-fourths time, and the B section in a more rapid six-eighths time with a concluding coda in the same tempo and style of A. The jailor's key fits symbolically in Bb major, the key of the Prisoner's chorus to follow later in the act. The simple melody, mostly supported by steady eighth-note rhythmic values, presents a simple man with simple values. In the A sections the pragmatic Rocco philosophizes that gold is as crucial as love in a marriage, while the B sections revel in the prospect of a prosperous marriage.

No. 5, Trio: "Gut, Söhnchen, gut" ("Good, My Son, Good"; Rocco, Leonore, Marzelline)

This substantial trio marked the end of act 1 in the three-act version of 1805. In the preceding dialogue Leonore learns about a prisoner who has been incarcerated for the past two years now placed on starvation rations by Pizarro, the prison governor. As the trio begins Leonore asks to join Rocco the next time he visits the special prisoner. Packed with small, repeated orchestral motives, not unlike an orchestral movement, the trio moves briefly to a seemingly triumphant C major as the characters express their mutual desire for a happy ending. To music clearly reminiscent of the duet between Papageno and Papagena in *The Magic Flute*, "Pa-Pa-Pa-Pa-Pa-Pa-Papagena," Rocco agrees to ask the governor to allow Fidelio to help him with his work in the deeper regions of the prison while Marzelline asks her father to obtain the governor's permission to marry the jailor's helper.

No. 6, March

Pizarro's entrance is accompanied by a short instrumental march about two minutes in length. The march is in two parts; the first and shorter part (A) contains only eight measures and is stated only once. The second part is thirty measures long, in three parts, and repeated. The first portion of the second part is the same as A (eight measures). After A, Beethoven presents a new tune, B, also eight measures long, another eight-measure theme (C), and a six-measure cadential phrase (D) to round out the second part. The key is Bb, the same as Rocco's "gold" aria and the Prisoner's Chorus. The material of B, C, and D is rhythmically regular and square.

Not so the A section. It opens with what sounds like an upbeat (the fourth beat in 4/4 time). This works fine for the first three measures. Beethoven then plays a trick on Pizarro (and us) by short-changing him a beat in the fourth measure. Beethoven accomplishes this by removing the fourth beat (which actually has been the *first* beat all the time as we can see in the score if not hear in the music). This is how we *hear* the first four measures: 4–1–2–3 (measure 1), 4–1–2–3 (measure 2), 4–1–2–3 (measure 3), 1–2–3–4 (measure 4). The fourth measure is the only measure to begin on the downbeat for a true 1–2–3–4 measure, but ironically because of the way Beethoven set up the irregularity in the first three measures, this metrically correct measure sounds wrong. Although Pizarro begins his march on the wrong foot, might makes right. Pizarro manages to figure things out after three measures of the A section, but he will be thrown off each time he returns to the beginning of the section. Mozart inserted a similar metrical trick when he has Donna Elvira enter on the wrong beat in her aria "Ah, chi mi dice mai" ("O, Who Can Tell Me Now") in *Don Giovanni*, and Beethoven's teacher Haydn was full of similar metrical trickery in his instrumental work, a trait that may have rubbed off on his student.

No. 7, Aria with Chorus: "Ha, welch'ein Augenblick!" ("Ha! What a Moment!"; Pizarro)

In the same key and angry mood as the Queen of the Night's aria "Der Hölle Rache" ("My Heart is Seething") from *The Magic Flute*, Pizarro's vengeance aria rants and raves. After five measures of a *crescendo* from *pianissimo* to *fortissimo* on the dominant, including first two "Ha's!" the third "Ha!" arrives on the tonic D minor on a powerful high D. For the rest of the aria Pizarro will only reach as high as a half step above this high D, six Eb's, including three in a row on the phrase "to plunge in his heart," but he will return to his D obsessively for nearly *fifty* repetitions, usually on the longest-held notes. When he reaches the words "Now it is my turn to murder the murderer," the music shifts menacingly to D *major*, but Ds remain frequent and prominent on strong beats even as Pizarro sings above the chorus of guards. Perhaps more than any other aria in the operatic canon, Pizarro's aria vividly characterizes, even embodies, the power, rage, and obsession of a vengeful and ruthless man.

No. 8, Duet: "Jetzt, Alter, hart es Eile!" ("Now, Old Man, It Is Urgent!"; Pizarro, Rocco)

In this duet Pizarro tries through flattery and financial reward to persuade Rocco to kill a prisoner. To capture this intention musically, Beethoven gives Pizarro an ominous and subversive descending major seventh on the word "Morden" (murder). When Rocco responds that murder is not in his job description, Pizarro shows his dagger and offers to kill the prisoner himself. The orchestra softly joins *der Gouverneur* as he describes how he will creep up on the prisoner and kill him with a single blow ("ein Stoss"), depicted by two unaccompanied pitches after a ferociously dissonant *fortissimo* chord in the orchestra. It only lasts a few seconds, but it is nonetheless significant that when Pizarro refers to "that man down below," he sings a descending C major scale to which Rocco confirms, also in C major, *pianissimo*, that Pizarro is referring to the man in the dungeon who will soon perish from starvation. Eventually C major will triumph, but in the meantime Beethoven is beginning to make insinuating and meaningful connections between C major and Florestan.

No. 9, Recitative and Aria: "Abscheulicher! Wo Eilst Du Hin?" ("Monster! Where Are You Hurrying?"; Leonore)

Leonore has overheard the sung conversation between Pizarro and Rocco and responds in her opening recitative, which Beethoven had completely rewritten for the 1814 performances. Before she arrives at the lyrical *Adagio* aria portion in E major, the recitative responds harmonically with Leonore's turbulent emotional state. When she sees the promise of a rainbow after the present dark clouds finally lift, a return to her calm and peaceful life with Florestan, the harmony tellingly shifts to a prolonged C major tonality. This brings Leonore to the first part of her two-part (slow-fast) aria in E major, "Komm, Hoffnung" ("Come, Hope") in the key of the Fidelio Overture. The *Adagio*, supported by three horns (as in the trio of the *Eroica scherzo*) three times, features vocal pyrotechnics on the word "erriechen" (reach) in a musical phrase that graphically depicts the promise that love will help her reach her goal of saving her beloved husband. On the third statement Beethoven emphasizes the word "Lieber" (love) for more than a full measure on a high E. In the *Allegro con brio* that follows, Leonore responds to the horn fanfares with a vigorous and wide-ranging aria, the music of which matches her determined resolve to *reach* her Florestan. Her music viscerally demonstrates that Pizarro has more than made his match.

No. 10, Finale (Prisoner's Chorus)

In response to Leonore's request to allow the prisoners (but not Florestan) to come up for air, the finale of act 1 focuses on their two choruses along with some plot developments. Strings and then horns and winds softly introduce an ascending sixteenth-note figure with syncopated accents on alternate measures. As they get their bearings the prisoners gradually move from a single-note melody to more melodically varied but declamatory and collective musical lines with a high note on "Luft" (air). The key is Bb, the key of Rocco's "gold" aria and Pizarro's march. An individual prisoner (a tenor) sings of his trust in God in G major (the key of "O namenlose Freude"). The opening chorus quickly introduces the word "free" as an adjective "in freier Luft" (in freer air) but with the musical emphasis on "Luft." The tenor then emphasizes the word "frei" (free) as the culmination of the phrase "wir werden frei" by giving it the highest and longest pitch (E). Tellingly, when the chorus returns to express the concept of "Freiheit" (freedom), Beethoven gives it a dark C minor mode since both freedom and C major remain in the distant future. Another prisoner, a bass, notices a guard. Over a series of chromatic and tense chords the prisoner admonishes his compatriots to be wary and speak softly and to keep quiet about expressing their desire for "Freiheit." The prisoners then reprise their original chorus.

Through a series of shifting tempos, keys, and melodic developments, much happens musically and in the plot development in the section between the two prisoner choruses. First we learn from Rocco that Pizarro has granted permission for the marriage between Jaquino and Fidelio and also that Fidelio can join Rocco later that day when he goes back into the prison. Leonore learns she will be helping Rocco to dig a grave that might be intended for her husband. The music accelerates and shifts to C minor on the word "Pflicht" (duty) as Marzelline and Jaquino rush in to inform Rocco that letting the prisoners come up for air has incurred Pizarro's wrath. The resourceful Rocco persuades Pizarro that this breach will actually be interpreted as a magnanimous gesture on the king's name day to show this public display of compassion. The prisoner's return to Bb and sing a second chorus, "Leb wohl, du warmes Sonnenlicht," ("Farewell, Warm Sunlight"), which Beethoven newly wrote for the 1814 performances. Marzelline, Leonore, and Jaquino take the prisoners back to their cells, Pizarro instructs Rocco to get on with the grave digging, and the unhappy jailor gets ready to fulfill his grim duty ("Pflicht"). The act ends with a sparsely orchestrated *pianissimo*.

Act 2: A Dark, Subterranean Dungeon

No. 11, Introduction and Aria: "Gott! Welch Dunkel Hier!" ("God! What Darkness Here!"; Florestan)

During an extended orchestral introduction we see Florestan sitting alone on a stone, exhausted from starvation, and chained to the wall. The first four measures in F minor unmistakably resemble the first four measures (in C minor) of the *Joseph Cantata* composed fifteen years before the 1805 *Fidelio*, although in the *Joseph Cantata*, the first two measures are *piano* and the second two *mezzo forte*, whereas in *Fidelio piano* alternates with *forte*. In both dark introductions the first and third measures sound an octave in the strings and the second and fourth measures strike a chord in the winds (flutes, oboes, clarinets, and bassoons) and horns. The chord on the fourth measure has been softened from a biting diminished triad in the cantata to a major chord in the opera. Also in the cantata Beethoven returned to the opening four bars after two intervening measures of winds and horn and three measures of a unison melody in the strings. The introduction to act 2 in *Fidelio* prepares us to confront Florestan's solitary existence and, despite its *Grave* tempo marking, moves quickly from soft to loud and major to minor. After three statements of an ominous melodic figure in the violas and cellos, Beethoven settles on a diminished-seventh chord in sixteenth-note triplets in the strings above the timpani, unusually tuned a tritone apart (i.e., three whole steps, another name for the interval, the augmented fourth or diminished fifth) to emphasize the dissonant interval imbedded in this mysterious chord.

Both the somber melodic figure and the tritones in the timpani return in the first part of Florestan's recitative, which opens with the famous (and sometimes ridiculed) seeming surprise at the darkness of his cell. Considering its brevity, Florestan's recitative contains four tempo shifts and even more numerous key shifts. On the word "Wille!" (will) the music presents a glorious moment in Leonore's key (E major), from which key Florestan soon moves to a dominant seventh of Ab major (the relative major of the opening F minor) for the first portion of the aria, *Adagio cantabile*.

The final section of Florestan's aria, *Poco allegro*, was added in 1814. In 1805 and 1806, Florestan simply collapses in exhaustion. In 1814, the directions in the score describe "an exaltation akin to madness" in which Florestan sees a vision of Leonore as a rescuing angel ("ein Engel, Leonoren") represented by the oboe in the highest sounding orchestral part. F minor has metamorphosed into F major, despair into hope. The second time Florestan describes the angel as "so like my wife Leonore," the voice joins the oboe in a musical phrase we will soon learn possesses additional meaning. Earlier in the aria Florestan sang three times about his duty ("Pflicht"). In the delusionary vision of the *Poco allegro*, he does not speak of a literal freedom ("Freiheit") from prison, but the freedom of death led by his wife, the angel Leonore. To mark his resignation, even his desire for a release from his suffering, Florestan sings the word "Freiheit," the word we heard so often in the Prisoner's Chorus, no less than nine times in the space of the next twenty-seven measures. In the end, his angel will lead him "zur Freiheit ins himmlische Reich!" (to freedom in the heavenly kingdom!). After a final commentary by the oboe, Florestan "sinks exhausted on the stone, hiding his face in his hand."

No. 12, Melodrama and Duet: "Nur Hurtig Fort, Nur Frisch Gegraben" ("Make Haste, Dig On"; Rocco, Leonore)

Melodrama was a novel style of musical and dramatic presentation developed in France in the late eighteenth century in which a spoken monologue or dialogue alternates or occurs simultaneously with instrumental passages. Mozart contemplated using this technique in portions of his unfinished *Singspiel*, *Zaïde*, but *Fidelio* is the first work in the mainstream operatic repertoire to use the technique. The *Fidelio* melodrama consists of a conversation between Rocco and Leonore juxtaposed between instrumental passages as short as a single measure and no longer than six. When they reach the prisoner in the cold darkness, he is so motionless that until he stirs they do not realize he is asleep and not dead. In a resourceful touch, Florestan's movements in sleep and Rocco's conclusion that he is sleeping (two measures of *Poco adagio*) are accompanied by the oboe playing the phrase associated with the words, "An angel, Leonore, so much like my wife." Clearly, the implication is that the sleeping Florestan sees his beloved wife in his dreams on the threshold of heavenly freedom from life's burdens.

It is time to dig—to a constant triplet accompaniment and a persistent six-note motive in the bass line fittingly heard, considering the location, in the lowest possible register by the double basses and the contrabassoon. Engrossed in his work, Rocco sings primarily mechanical repeated notes alongside Leonore's tuneful melody. The jailor urges Leonore to hurry their work in anticipation of Pizarro's arrival while Leonore tries unsuccessfully to determine the prisoner's identity. The central plot may be Leonore's rescue of her husband, but when she fails to recognize the identity of a suffering prisoner, she nonetheless asserts that "whoever you are, I will save you, by God!" From now on we know that the opera is about securing justice and Freiheit for *all* humanity. Significantly, Beethoven has Leonore celebrate this moment by turning to C major and by emphasizing her active promise to free ("befrei'n") this unknown man: "Ich will, du Armer, dich befrei'n!" (I will free you, poor man!). The sentiment is so important she repeats it, the second time with a virtuosic coloratura (i.e., an agilely ornamented) passage lasting nearly three measures on the word "befrei'n," still in C major, before Rocco brings the music back to the central key of the duet, A minor, the relative minor.

No. 13, Trio: "Euch werde Lohn in bessern Welten" ("May You Be Rewarded in Better Worlds"; Florestan, Rocco, Leonore)

In the dialogue that follows Leonore recognizes Florestan by his voice but does not let on. Florestan learns that it was Pizarro, the man whose criminality he had exposed, who had him incarcerated. No water is available but Leonore can give her husband some wine and, in the course of the ensuing trio, which begins and ends in A major, a piece of bread to complete a symbolic reenactment of the Eucharist. Once again, the musical symbolism embodied in the sanctity of C major returns when Rocco agrees to let Leonore give the dying man a taste of bread: "Da nimm das Brot, du armer Mann!" (Here, take the bread, you poor man!). Florestan thanks this angel to the words and A major music in which the trio began: "May you be rewarded in better worlds."

No. 14, Quartet: "Es sterbe!" ("Let Him Die!"; Pizarro, Florestan, Leonore, Rocco)

Rocco signals Pizarro, and the governor enters for the kill, dagger drawn. Since Pizarro is firmly in control at the beginning of this fast and frenetic quartet, the music is in the key of his act 1 aria, "Ha, welch' ein Augenblick!" this time in D *major.* As with most of the ensemble numbers, the quartet contains considerable action. When Pizarro goes to stab Florestan, Leonore places her body in front of her husband and challenges Pizarro to "first kill his wife!" on four unaccompanied notes, the last rising a fifth to a long and high Bb, a dissonance in the quartet's key of D major but a hopeful pitch that anticipates the key of the offstage trumpet fanfare soon to follow. Leonore pulls out her pistol and on the dominant of D exclaims, "One more sound and you are dead!" Ironically, instead of the expected D major, the music swerves to Bb (the note heard on "wife" and the music of the Prisoner's Chorus). The fanfare freezes the action, all but Pizarro praise God, and the fanfare returns closer and louder as the minister and soldiers arrive in the nick of time to expose Pizarro's treachery. In the 1805 and 1806 versions Rocco takes Leonore's pistol with him as he leaves with Pizarro, leaving the future of the conjugal partners in doubt. A number of Beethoven scholars find the earlier version more satisfactory than the revised conclusion of the quartet in which Pizarro and Rocco, the latter making a sign to heaven, leave the couple fully armed and able to celebrate their imminent freedom in the secure knowledge they are now out of danger.

No. 15, Duet: "O namenlose Freude" ("O Nameless Joy!"; Leonore, Florestan)

In G major, the key of the serene canon, "Mir ist so wunderbar" from act 1, Leonore and Florestan express the jubilation of their reunion and escape from tyranny. The main melody of "O namenlose Freude" is nearly identical to the duet from the otherwise rudimentary *Vestas Feuer* drafted in 1803, and aside from an added note on *O,* the 1805 version is indeed identical. In *Vestas Feuer* and the 1805 *Fidelio,* the duet partners sing in parallel thirds as Volivia/Leonore ascends to a high B. In 1814, Leonore first sings a line and Florestan answers with the same music, but both phrases stop at G rather than ascend to a B. Thus in 1814 the highest note of the phrase is an A, which descends to a G on the word "Freude" (joy). After repeating their first exchange and a new one, Leonore and Florestan sing four measures together in parallel thirds before resting underneath a fermata on a C major triad on the word *lust* (delight). Beethoven then interrupts their jubilation the second time they sing the words "unnenbaren Leiden" (unspeakable suffering), still in parallel thirds but now *Adagio*. After this almost prayerful moment of reflection on their past suffering, the main duet material returns bringing their declaration of joy, delight, and love to an exuberant conclusion.

Change of Scene

Once Beethoven had settled on his fourth and final *Fidelio* Overture by the third 1814 performance, *Leonore* no. 3 was cast out of the opera. Despite its presumed destiny as a concert overture, *Leonore* no. 3, however, would not be so easily disassociated with the opera. As early as the 1840s the composer and conductor Otto Nicolai inserted no. 3 between the two acts, a practice followed by Hans Richter in the 1870s. Also beginning in the 1840s some conductors adopted the practice of playing *Leonore* no. 3 *between the two scenes* of act 2. Conductors who favored this use of no. 3 included Carl Anschützt (Amsterdam and London, 1849), Michael William Balfe (London, 1851), Anton Seidl (New York, 1890), and Walter Damrosch (New York, 1896). By far, the most influential exponent of this practice was Gustav Mahler, who informed the Vienna orchestra in 1904 that "from now on, gentlemen, we shall play the third *Leonore* Overture after the dungeon scene, because this work compresses the drama's whole gamut of emotions into a great climax" (La Grange 1999, 6). From Otto Klemperer (Cologne, 1919) and Richard Strauss (Vienna, 1920) to Arturo Toscanini (Milan, 1927), numerous high-profile conductors followed suit.

The sets of Mahler's stage designer Alfred Roller were so heavy and cumbersome for the 1904 production in Vienna that it took the entire thirteen to fourteen minutes of the overture to move everything in order to be ready for the next scene. Although the idea of placing *Leonore* no. 3 between these scenes did not stem from Beethoven, and the practice has drawn criticism for its lack of authenticity as well as on dramatic grounds, many directors and conductors have retained the decision even when it was no longer necessary to fill the time needed for a set change. The practice remains controversial, but also popular, and continues to generate strong feelings pro and con.

Mahler also revived the practice of retaining the dialogue that immediately precedes the final scene in which Rocco informs the conjugal partners that Florestan's name was not officially on the minister's prisoner list. This dialogue clarifies the significant point that Florestan's imprisonment was brought about entirely by Pizarro's personal desire to avenge Florestan's exposure of the governor's crimes.

No. 16, Finale

Whether or not accompanied by *Leonore* no. 3, the scene has shifted to the bright exterior of the parade ground. For the 1814 performances Beethoven wrote a new and exuberant chorus in C major, with women's voices added to what was previously an all-male prisoner's chorus. The mixed ensemble creates a powerful audible fulfillment of the smaller moments of C major interspersed throughout the opera. Readers might recall the triumphant moment in the coda of the *Eroica* Symphony's first movement when Beethoven finally allows the main theme to be answered by its dominant and then repeats the culminating resolution four times. In the *Fidelio* finale, before the chorus begins with its "Heil sei dem Tag" (Hail the day), the orchestra states *thirty-three* measures of nothing but tonics and dominants, including six repetitions of alternating two-bar phrases, as in the *Eroica* coda—two measures of tonic followed by two measures of dominant. The speech that follows, in which the minister Don Fernando denounces tyranny, was also added in 1814. Rocco explains how "Fidelio" came to rescue her beloved Florestan, whom Fernando presumed to be dead. Pizarro is led away and Fernando gives Leonore the key to free her husband from his chains.

The music Beethoven has chosen for this magical "moment," sung to the words, "O Gott! Welch' ein Augenblick" (O God, what a moment), is the same music Beethoven used to express the coming of the "light" (as in the Enlightenment) in the *Joseph Cantata*, the second significant borrowing from this important work from Beethoven's youth in Bonn (the first being the orchestral introduction to Florestan's aria earlier in the act). In English, the cantata's words translate as, "Then mankind climbed into the light." Strikingly, the melody in the oboe part is precisely the same and in the same key as the music that begins the moment of Freiheit in the opera. In the cantata the oboe states the entire melody and the soprano repeats it with a simple accompaniment. In the opera, the oboe, the instrument that embodied Leonore in Florestan's vision at the end of his aria and his dreams during the melodrama, begins its melody, above which Leonore sings her first "O Gott!" as a counter line and the second "O Gott!" and "Welch' ein Augenblick!" on the same pitches at the continuation of the oboe melody. The oboe then begins the second phrase of the tune, soon joined by Florestan, after which both the oboe and vocal lines depart from the melody of the cantata. After Fernando, Marzelline, and Rocco sing their own counter lines above the oboe, the oboe returns to the original cantata theme as an accompaniment to all the principals (minus Jaquino) and the mixed chorus. The passage expresses a true hymn to freedom.

The music ends poised on the dominant (G major), which is resolved after two measures of *Allegro* to the most exuberant of all *Fidelio* choruses in a resounding C major. The opening text of this chorus is taken from Friedrich Schiller's "Ode to Joy": "He who has won a true and loving wife may join in our rejoicing," a phrase that would be reused in the second choral variation of the Ninth Symphony finale. The opera ends with a tribute to the courageous and loving Leonore and an unbridled celebration of Freiheit.

BEETHOVEN'S ODE TO FREEDOM

Although scholars rightly question Beethoven's alleged (and undocumented) remark that of all his musical offspring *Fidelio* endured the most painful labor and was therefore treasured as especially dear, that Beethoven labored over this composition is amply supported by an extraordinary number of extant sketches. Beethoven revised works extensively prior to their publication (and in some cases after), but only with *Fidelio* do we observe a work that exists in two complete versions composed eight years apart, 1806 and 1814. The 1805 *Leonore* was never published, and it is not always certain how to make a precise reconstruction, although we do know that Beethoven removed about five hundred measures from this version and what these measures were. The only musical number from 1806 that was lengthened was the overture, *Leonore* no. 2, which had 530 measures, and *Leonore* no. 3, now with 638 measures. The *Fidelio* Overture occupies less than half the length of no. 3 (307 measures).

Although most directors and audience members have concluded that the 1814 version constitutes a considerable improvement over the earlier versions, the revised opera continues to inspire division about the extent to which it improved a flawed work. The central criticism remains that the opera in all its versions demonstrates an irreconcilable opposition of classical and heroic styles. In particular, even though Beethoven removed an entire trio and duet, critics continue to find the domestic ("eighteenth-century") scenes overlong and uninspired, especially when compared with the psychological interpersonal nuances explored by Mozart in works such as *The Marriage of Figaro*. Conversely, commentators sometimes find it difficult to fathom the incongruous profundity of the quartet, "Mir ist so wunderbar," the first number in which Leonore, a seeming musical interloper, sings—even though this ensemble foreshadows the depth of Leonore's aria, the two prisoner choruses to follow in act 1, and virtually all of act 2. Some find the powerful thematic content, the liberation of humanity, while lofty, inherently undramatic. Further, while the intervention of a benevolent minister is certainly a welcome development, it also might be seen as reinforcing aristocratic values of the past rather than those of a new and more egalitarian era.

Beyond political interpretation, some biographical interpretations speculate that Beethoven may have identified with Florestan's suffering and isolation in prison since the composer similarly suffered and felt imprisoned by his deafness. Others have noted that the heroic and courageous love of Leonore for Florestan might be viewed as an idealization of Beethoven's lack of fulfillment in this arena, most recently emphasized in his failed romance with Josephine Brunswick that ended about the time the composer was working on the 1805 version of *Fidelio*. In any event, listeners continue to empathize with the suffering and political oppression, and many stagings are set in fascist and totalitarian regimes. Whatever the setting, audiences continue to be inspired by Leonore's heroism and love and the optimistic and idealistic celebration of a potential new world, a world that celebrates the word and powerful concept of Freiheit that brings to a stirring close Beethoven's one and only opera and one of his greatest works.

5

SYMPHONIC ALTERNATIVES TO THE HEROIC STYLE (1808–1814)

So also does the instrumental music of Beethoven open the realm of the colossal and the immeasurable for us (Forbes 1971, 152).
—E. T. A. Hoffmann's review of the Fifth Symphony in the *Allgemeine musikalische Zeitung*, July 4 and 11, 1810

THE ACADEMY CONCERT OF DECEMBER 22, 1808

After the Academies of April 2, 1800, and April 5, 1803, the next Academy, again at the Theater an der Wien, was delayed until December 22, 1808. This concert, a major focus of the present chapter, was without doubt one of the major public events in Beethoven's career. In the extraordinarily productive years between 1803 and 1808, other major orchestral and choral works of Beethoven were performed publically at only slightly less grandiose occasions. One year after several private and helpful performances, including the famous run-through in 1804 at Prince Lobkowitz's residence, the *Eroica* received its first public performance at the Theater an der Wien in April 1805. The performance of the first two versions of *Fidelio* occurred in November and the following spring. In December 1806 Vienna first heard the Violin concerto at the Theater an der Wien. At the home of Prince Lobkowitz in the spring of 1807 private audiences heard Beethoven's first four symphonies, the Fourth Piano Concerto, the *Coriolan* Overture, and arias from

Fidelio. The Mass in C followed in Eisenstadt September 1807. In April 1808 the first public performance of the Fourth Symphony took place at a charity concert; the Triple Concerto, at the Augarten in May.

Despite these important milestones, nothing can compare with the sustained barrage of magnificent sounds that Beethoven audiences heard on a cold day in December 1808. Here is how this concert was announced in the *Wiener Zeitung* a few days before the event:

On Thursday, December 22, Ludwig van Beethoven will have the honor to give a musical *Akademie* in the R. I. Priv. Theater-an-der-Wien. All the pieces are of his composition, entirely new, and not yet heard in public. . . . First Part: 1, A Symphony entitled: "A Recollection of Country Life," in F major (No. 5) [*Pastoral* Symphony published as no. 6, op. 68]. 2, Aria. [*Ah! Perfido*, op. 65]. 3, Hymn, with Latin text, composed in the church style with chorus and solos [*Gloria* from the Mass in C Major, op. 86, designated as a hymn to circumvent the restrictions on liturgical music in a theater]. 4, Pianoforte Concerto played by himself [Fourth Piano Concerto, op. 58].

Second Part. 1, Grand Symphony in C minor (No. 6) [Fifth Symphony, op. 67]. 2, "Sanctus," with Latin text composed in the church style with chorus and solos ["Sanctus" from the Mass in C]. 3, Fantasia for Pianoforte alone. 4, Fantasia for the Pianoforte which ends with the gradual entrance of the entire orchestra and the introduction of choruses as a finale. [Fantasia for Piano, Chorus, and Orchestra in C Minor/C Major (*Choral Fantasy*), op. 80].

Boxes and reserved seats are to be had in the Krugerstrasse No. 1074, first story. Beginning at half past six o'clock. (Forbes 1964, 446)

The composer and writer Johann Friedrich Reichardt described his view from Prince Lobkowitz's box: "There we continued, in the bitterest cold, too, from half past six to half past ten, and experienced the truth that one can easily have too much of a good thing—and still more of a loud" (Forbes 1964, 446). The inadequate heating system was not the only snafu. As a result of a quarrel with Beethoven, Anna Milder refused to sing the scene and aria "Ah! Perfido," a work first performed when Beethoven was touring in Leipzig in 1796 and published in 1805. Unfortunately, Milder's replacement, the inexperienced Josephine Killitschgy, the sister-in-law of Ignaz Schuppanzigh, was not up to the task. Although sources do not entirely agree on the nature and precise location of the problem, a counting error in the *Choral Fantasy* made it necessary to start over. We also learn from the seventeen-year-old Carl Czerny, who turned pages during Beethoven's performance of the Fourth Piano Concerto, that the composer inserted a number of alternative passages to those in the edition published in August. The original autograph has disappeared, but the copyist's score confirms that Beethoven entered numerous decorative alternatives in over a hundred measures of the piano part. After the December performance Beethoven's jottings do not resurface in future scholarly or commercial editions and remained unpublished until an article by Barry Cooper in 1994.

Before discussing the two symphonies, concerto, and choral fantasy heard at this remarkable concert, I would like to set the record straight on Reichardt's recollection concerning the length of the concert, a memory repeated in nearly every subsequent description of this alleged marathon. If we do the math, we discover that while the length of this concert would be longer than most concerts today, the total length of the concert—assuming for the sake of argument that Beethoven's improvisation in part 2 corresponds roughly in length to the written-out improvisation at the beginning of the published Fantasy—clocks in just under two hours and forty minutes. This adds up to about ten minutes longer than Hector Berlioz's *Damnation of Faust*, more than an hour short of the four hours Reichardt thought he suffered through and generations of scholars have readily accepted:

Part 1 (97 min.)

1. *Pastoral* Symphony (43 min.)

2. *Ah! Perfido* (12½ min.)

3. *Gloria* from the Mass in C (9 min.)
4. Fourth Piano Concerto (33 min.)

Part 2 (61 min.)

1. Fifth Symphony (31 min.)

2. "Sanctus" from the Mass in C (11 min.)

3–4. Improvisation and Fantasy (19 min.)

PART I: (1) SYMPHONY NO. 6 IN F MAJOR (*PASTORAL*), OP. 68 (LABELED SYMPHONY NO. 5)

Programmatic Elements

In contrast to works with added-on nicknames such as the *Moonlight*, *Tempest*, and *Appassionata* sonatas, the title *Pastoral* was clearly Beethoven's choice and appears on the original title page of the Sixth Symphony. The subtitle reads in English, "Memories of Country Life" and "more the expression of feelings than tone painting." By tone painting Beethoven meant the construction of musical counterparts to pictorial or programmatic images and story lines. In various notes in the sketches he reminds himself, and retrospectively us, that he wanted to deemphasize pictorial or programmatic musical representations, as evident in such remarks as, "All tone painting loses its value if pushed too far in instrumental music" (Cooper 1999, "Symphony No. 6," iii). Still, in his vast instrumental output, with the exception of the *Les Adieux* Piano Sonata op. 81a, the *Pastoral* Symphony is the only work in the standard genres in which Beethoven added titles for each movement. Here are the titles found in Beethoven's final autograph and copyist's score before they were altered by the publisher when the score appeared in 1809.

1. Pleasant, cheerful sensations awakened on arrival in the country-side
2. Scene by the brook
3. Merry gathering of the country people
4. Thunder storm
5. Shepherds song: Beneficent feelings bound with thanks to the Godhead after the storm

Beethoven clearly thought these titles, along with some obvious examples of tone "painting" such as bird calls and thunder, would be sufficient to evoke "memories of country life." Less literally, in the beginning of the symphony he also depicts this life with bare fifths in the violas that create a drone not unlike a shepherd's bagpipe, along with a jaunty shepherd-like tune in the violins. When the "shepherd's" tune returns moments later, Beethoven entrusts it to the oboe, an instrument commonly associated with a shepherd's pipe. Soon one can easily imagine the twittering in the flutes as an evocation of bird sounds.

First Movement: *Allegro ma non Troppo*

Although the first movement is clearly in sonata form, the first movement of the Sixth differs considerably from Beethoven's earlier symphonies, especially the Fifth Symphony, the work that would open the second part of the Academy program. Listeners are often struck by the amount of repetition along with the absence of goal-oriented musical development, again such as found in the Fifth. As an example of repetition without a clear sense of development we might listen to what Beethoven does with the second measure, the descending five-note motive,   dum-da-da-dum-dum   (eighth-sixteenth-sixteenth-eighth-eighth). As the opening melody comes to a close after fifteen measures (sometimes with different pitches but still maintaining the five-note rhythm), he continues to state this rhythm. But instead of using the five-note rhythm as a source of melodic and harmonic development, Beethoven prefers to maintain musical stasis.

The section that corresponds to a sonata development is still more extraordinary. Of its ninety-four measures, no less than seventy-two are based on a melodically altered variation of the descending five-note melody and rhythm of the second measure (dum-da-da-dum-dum). After hearing the five-note motive four times in the first twelve measures of the development in Bb major (the subdominant of F major), Beethoven states the motive alone twelve times in the next twelve measures. After that he shifts without preparation or warning to D major with the same motive for another twenty-four repetitions over the next twenty-four measures. For contemporary music lovers who also appreciate music using loops, from dance riffs to the repeated rhythmic figures of Steve Reich, Beethoven may acquire new prestige as a precursor.

Next comes a ten-measure break during which time Beethoven states the first four measures of the opening theme. He follows this with a return to the rhythmic and melodic motive based on measure 2 twelve times in the next twelve measures in G major (the subdominant of D major) and twenty-four measures on the unexpected and thoroughly unprepared key of E major, a key that does not strictly belong in F major at all. But E major is the dominant of A major, and that's where Beethoven goes next with another statement of the opening theme.

Finally, Beethoven is ready to use another idea from the first theme, the four-measure melody that initially followed the opening theme, the last measure of which uses the rhythm of the second measure but with new pitches. All together we hear these four measures from the opening, each of which ends with the rhythm of measure 2 seven times, three times in A major, twice in D major answered by G minor (the *only* touch of minor in the entire movement), and twice in C major. From there Beethoven returns to Bb major, which is where the development began. Instead of moving from subdominant to the dominant in order to make a persuasive harmonic return to the tonic F major, Beethoven subverts the dominant and precedes directly from the subdominant to the tonic, a plagal or Amen cadence (a harmonic cadence from IV to I rather than an authentic V–I cadence; see functional harmony in the glossary) that sounds more like the resolution of a hymn than the expected strong tonic resolution (i.e., authentic cadence) that links the returns to the recapitulation in most works by Haydn, Mozart, and earlier Beethoven.

Second Movement: Andante Molto Moto

In the second movement, Beethoven's "unreliable narrator," Anton Schindler, is plausibly but without firm evidence identified as the yellow-hammer bird (usually identified in the Beethoven literature as a goldfinch). This occurs in the passage the composer labeled "Solo" in the repetitive rising *arpeggio* flute part of the development section from "scene by the brook" (1966, 144–45). Near the end of the brook scene, Beethoven left no doubt of his intentions when he designated three wind instruments as particular birds and twice lets them chirp contrapuntally as they might be heard in nature, albeit unanswered by other members of the orchestra: the nightingale (flute), quail (oboe), and cuckoo (clarinet). Beethoven does not assign a label to the continuous rolling accompaniment underpinning to be played with mutes for most of the movement as "the brook," but it would take some imagination to refrain from this assumption. What is less obvious is that the nightingale shares much of the brook's motive, even its exact pitches. This is the kind of musical connection that links the programmatic *Pastoral* with the vast majority of Beethoven's abstract instrumental works.

Third Movement: Allegro

The oboe as shepherd's pipe will reappear prominently in the third movement, especially its humorous duet with the laconic, even primitive, rustic bassoon confined to three basic notes in the second part (the trio part of the minuet-trio form). In fact, virtually all the tunes in the third movement are clearly suggestive of folk music, including a rustic dance in two-fourths time inserted between the trio and the return of the minuet. In the Fourth Symphony Beethoven expanded the *scherzo-trio-scherzo* format by repeating the trio *scherzo* to create a five-part form. After strongly considering but ultimately rejecting a similar expansion in the Fifth Symphony, he offers the following expanded structure for the minuet and trio in the *Pastoral*, albeit unlabeled: minuet in three-quarter time, trio in three-quarter time, rustic dance in two-fourths, minuet-trio-rustic dance, and minuet. Perhaps in another nod to rustic simplicity and in contrast to his practice in earlier symphonies, Beethoven keeps all of these dance-like sections in the same key, F major.

Fourth Movement: Allegro

In the third statement of the minuet, Beethoven cut the music short, first by speeding up the music from *Allegro* to *Presto*, that is, from fast to very fast. What happens next is the most pictorial movement in the symphony, the movement titled "Thunder Storm." As it might occur in nature, rain interrupts the "merry gathering of the country folk" before they have a chance to finish their dancing. The storm begins unobtrusively with a soft ominous repeated note in the cellos and basses (a few raindrops). Next arrives a repeated eighth-note figure in the second violins with a melody in the first violins that opens with tritones, still soft, hesitant, and full of expectancy. Before the arrival of the storm the minor mode darkened a total of four measures in the first four movements. Now all is minor. After a crescendo the timpani enter, for the first time in the symphony, with a ferocious *fortissimo* drum roll, while the cellos (five sixteenth notes) and basses (a four-note figure) play their respective repetitive short scalar figures. The harmony offers a heavy dose of tense and dissonant diminished sevenths, a chord Beethoven studiously avoided in the early movements. Unmistakably, even without Beethoven's identifying title, the music *sounds* like a thunderstorm.

Beethoven reinforces the storm's ferociousness by introducing the trombone, an instrument new to symphonic audiences. The trombone will return in the finale of the Fifth Symphony, which Beethoven had composed prior to the Sixth.

Fifth Movement: Allegretto

The storm dissipated in less than four minutes, and just as the storm arrived with relative suddenness so does the final movement, beginning with a shepherd's song on the clarinet followed by an Alpine horn call on the horns. The final movement brings us back to a peaceful country scene with a simple tune in six-eighths time, a meter often associated with pastoral themes.

PART 1: (4) PIANO CONCERTO NO. 4 IN G MAJOR, OP. 58

After an approximately twenty-minute segment devoted to solo and choral vocal music, the first part of the program concluded with what was perhaps Beethoven's final public appearance as a soloist. Beethoven had completed his Fourth Piano Concerto by the middle of 1806, and many scholars contend, even in the absence of definitive documentary evidence, that it was this concerto that Beethoven performed at a private concert at the house of "Prince L." (presumably Prince Lobkowitz). The fact that Beethoven performed the concerto in such a high-profile venue as an Academy demonstrates that Beethoven's deafness had not yet progressed to the point where such a feat would have been impossible. When the Fifth and final piano concerto, the *Emperor*, received its first Viennese performance in February 1812, the pianist would be Carl Czerny, not Beethoven.

First Movement: *Allegro Moderato*

Those familiar with classical concertos of Haydn, Mozart, and Beethoven relish the drama of waiting for the soloist to make his or her grand entrance after an orchestral introduction that might last several minutes. Listeners familiar with Mozart's Concerto in Eb Major, K. 271, may recall that after the briefest of orchestral fanfares, five beats, the soloist replies with an answer lasting a grand total of seven beats, after which both the orchestra and the soloist repeated the pattern. As in other well-behaved opening ritornellos, the pianist then disappears until it is time to introduce the exposition. Most listeners in 1808 were probably unfamiliar with this Mozart concerto. But even if they recalled it, they might still be surprised to hear a five-measure piano solo at the beginning of a concerto. In fact, the audience might be excused if it thought the program had inadvertently substituted the word *concerto* for *sonata* or perhaps that the improvisation had begun. Indeed, many in the audience might be confused, although perhaps delighted by the beauty of the phrase.

But after five measures, a somewhat unusual length for a classical phrase, a few seconds later the orchestra makes its entrance, an entrance that also offers at least two surprises. The first surprise is that after repeating the first measure recently introduced by the soloist, the orchestral rhythm is the same, at least for the next two measures. After that the orchestra continues with its own related but distinctly different tune, as if in disagreement with the soloist about how the tune should go. The second surprise is that, while the soloist's phrase is in the key of the concerto, G major, the orchestra (actually only the strings, and *pianissimo* at that) enters in B major, a distant major mediant (the chord on the third degree of the scale), which does not readily belong to G major. The link between these two melodies and distant harmonies occurs in the opening orchestral measure, which uses the same note as the main melodic note in the piano introduction, the note B, the third of the piano introduction in G major and the root of the orchestral B major answer in B major. The answering tune in the strings lasts eight measures and takes the harmony back to the tonic. This time the piano will disappear until the music arrives at the piano exposition, where it will begin with a musical line based on the opening rhythm. Many readers will hear something familiar in the opening rhythm of the concerto, since it is the same as the ubiquitous motive that pervades the Fifth Symphony, the work that opens the second half of the Academy concert. Since in the concerto the motive consists of a short eighth-note rest (a notational symbol to indicate a particular duration of silence) followed by a short-short-short-SHORT rhythm and in the symphony the motive consists of an eighth-note rest followed by short-short-short-LONG, it is possible we might be listening too much into this, although most commentators are persuaded by the connection.

While still in the opening ritornello, the rest of the orchestra joins the strings when G major returns. A few measures later Beethoven presents a new theme in A minor, the theme that will eventually return in D minor as an answer to the second exposition theme, which is in the expected dominant, D major. In most classical concertos the second theme of the ritornello will also be the second theme of the exposition, and in most concertos this second ritornello theme will be in the same key as the first theme. Contrary to expectations, in this concerto we instead hear two separate but equal first themes, each in its own key in the opening ritornello and two separate second themes, one in the ritornello and one in the exposition.

The first movement, indeed the entire concerto, contains an abundance of harmonic and textural surprises, including a far-flung development that dwells for a long time in the remote key area of C# minor with a theme that does not seem on the surface to be derived from any of the many themes presented in the ritornello and exposition. Nevertheless, at the end of the development, the soloist and the orchestra together dutifully take us back to the main theme.

But which one? The answer to this question reveals yet another surprise, since not only do we hear the piano theme, now played *fortissimo*, in the home key, but also it is actually played by the pianist. The idea of beginning a recapitulation with the soloist is so unusual that it may be unprecedented in any previous concerto by Haydn, Mozart, or Beethoven. As in the opening ritornello, but not at the beginning of the exposition, the orchestra enters with *its* theme, still in B major and still in the strings only and *pianissimo*, but this time accompanied by triplet figuration in the upper register of the piano.

Second Movement: *Andante con Moto*

The second movement is probably the shortest and perhaps the swiftest of any middle movement in a Beethoven concerto, and probably those of Mozart as well. As in the first movement, the second movement opens with a dialogue between strings and the piano, this time starting with the strings (in E minor) and the piano answering, as it did in the first movement, in B major (now the dominant), before returning to the home tonic. In the first movement the soloist and the orchestra play different versions of a tune that is nonetheless readily perceived as similar. In the second movement the piano and the orchestra, although in constant dialogue, speak in markedly contrasting musical languages, the strings, the sole orchestral players, *sempre* (always) *staccato*, the piano *legato* and *molto cantabile* or *molto espressivo*. The result is analogous to a dialogue between two people who see the world from different perspectives and express themselves in an opposite way. The orchestra plays for five measures (the same length of phrase as the piano in the first movement) and ends in silence, the piano sounds for eight measures also ending in silence, the orchestra plays another five measures ending in silence, and the piano concludes the first long musical unit with eight measures.

The dialogue continues. This time the eighth measure overlaps with the orchestral answer and the phrases become shorter: three measures of orchestra, two measures of piano, two of orchestra, then two piano, and then a series of one-measure units separated by the shortest of orchestral responses. After several longer alternating phrases, the piano is allowed its longest passage, still legato but with short, sporadic, single *pizzicato* eighth notes in the strings. The piano alone then plays a written-out cadenza that features tritones, both ascending in the right hand and descending in a sextuplet figure in the left. The cellos and bass return to the opening string material, now sustained rather than *staccato*. The piano has the last word, ending on the melodic note that will begin the third movement, a rondo.

The music of this intensely dramatic middle movement is unmistakably conversational and dramatic, and over the years numerous writers have tried to explain what this suggestive music might mean. Although often attributed to Franz Liszt, it was the theorist and influential Beethoven champion Adolph Bernhard Marx who first shared the observation that the music was about the great mythological musician Orpheus confronting the shades of hell. Other well-known commentators on Beethoven, perhaps most noticeably Donald Francis Tovey, imagined he was hearing a musical scenario not unlike Orpheus's confrontation with the furies in Christoph Willibald Gluck's opera that stages this story. More recently, Owen Jander has offered a wide range of sources to support a hyperbolic argument that this movement is arguably the most programmatic of any in the classical literature (2009).

Jander's theories have received some support, but they have also endured considerable criticism for their lack of supporting evidence.

No one denies the dramatic nature of the movement, but since Beethoven was conspicuously and uncharacteristically reticent about the presence of a program, even in his private sketches, it is not possible or prudent to offer such specific programmatic elements as fact. The *Pastoral* Symphony had meaningful titles provided by the composer; the *Eroica* was unmistakably about a hero. Beethoven made these extra-musical ideas clear, even public. As with other so-called abstract works, listeners are free to create their own stories, whether or not these stories were intended by the composer. But in the end, in contrast to the *Pastoral* and *Eroica*, a programmatic connection with the Orpheus legend in the second movement of the Fourth Piano Concerto, while plausible, is unsupported.

Third Movement: *Rondo: Vivace*

The rondo too begins with a dialogue. For the first ten measures, which are double the opening phrase lengths of the first two movements, Beethoven gives the opening tune to the orchestra before the piano answers with its own ten-measure phrase. Not only is such an opening unusual, but also it is the only final movement in all the Beethoven concertos to begin with the orchestra rather than the soloist. In contrast to the first movement, the orchestra and the piano for the most part plays the same tune, although the piano plays a somewhat varied version. In the first movement the orchestra answered the piano in a strikingly different key, and in the second movement the piano answers the orchestra in a different key. In the rondo the two entities are finally united by key.

They may be in the same key, but Beethoven quickly introduces another jolt to the musical order when we discover that *both* the orchestra and the piano are in the same *wrong* key. The key signature and the putative key is G major, the tonic key of the concerto. The rondo tune, however, is clearly in C major, the subdominant. After the piano finishes its statement, the music does indeed move to the tonic, but within a few measures the movement returns to the main theme and key, now *fortissimo*, thus emphasizing even more emphatically the wrongness of the key. By now listeners have heard the rondo theme twice, but they have not yet heard the main theme in the tonic. How is this going to end?

Setting aside the correct key for now, the piano takes the lead on a lyrical second theme in the dominant, D major. A short new tuneful section follows, after which the main theme returns once again in C major. A long preparation on the dominant, twenty-seven measures, brings us to the second theme in the tonic G major (the dominant of C). After several harmonic digressions the music returns to the main theme, yet again in C major rather than the tonic G major.

This is the coda, one nearly one-third the length of the movement, in which we will eventually hear a recognizable variant of the main theme in the tonic in a playful and ingenious dialogue between soloist and orchestra, including a counterpoint between the piano, its own internal dialogue between the hands, and the clarinets and bassoons against a long-held note in the horns. But Beethoven manages to delay this long-awaited tonic arrival until measure 520 out of 600. The music soon changes to *Presto* and after ten measures on the dominant of G, we hear the main theme in the wrong key of C major, one final time, *fortissimo*. With eighteen measures to go, Beethoven has finally and firmly arrived with the main theme in the tonic G major. The music closes with the opening rhythmic gesture of the main theme, four times in direct succession, all in G, a rousing conclusion to a most unusual and wonderful concerto, perhaps Beethoven's most popular.

PART 2: (1) SYMPHONY NO. 5 IN C MINOR, OP. 67 (LABELED SYMPHONY NO. 6)

The symphony that opened the second half quickly became one of the most famous and iconic works in the entire orchestral literature. An early turning point in the work's reception arrived a year and a half after the December concert when the symphony received a review by the critic and composer E. T. A. Hoffmann in the leading Leipzig music journal *Allgemeine musikalische Zeitung*. Hoffmann's review was the first rigorous discussion of a Beethoven composition. It was also effusively positive. From the first sentences Hoffmann was not shy about expressing his high opinion of Beethoven's C Minor Symphony and the powerful impression it made:

The reviewer has before him one of the most important works of the master whose stature as a first-rate instrumental composer probably no one will now dispute. He is profoundly moved by the object he is to discuss; no one can reproach him for stepping beyond the usual bounds of criticism and striving to capture in words the feelings this composition aroused deep within his heart. (Forbes 1971, 150–51)

After taking his readers through the first movement, Hoffmann makes an observation about the extraordinary unity exhibited in the work that has proven a lasting one:

There is no simpler motive than that on which the master based the entire Allegro [Hoffmann is of course referring to the famous short-short-short-LONG motive that opens and pervades the symphony]. With great admiration, one becomes aware that Beethoven knew how to relate all secondary ideas and all transition passages through the rhythm of that simple motive so as gradually to unfold the character of the whole work. (156)

First Movement: *Allegro con Brio*

However, Tovey made the point that "no great music has ever been built from an initial figure of four notes" and that "the first movement of the C minor symphony is really remarkable for the length of its sentences" (1944, vol. 1, 38). Still, the opening of the Fifth with its four-note unison motive in the strings doubled by the clarinet, ending below a fermata and repeated a step lower, concluding with another fermata, prompted Marx to make an analogy between the motive and fate and Schindler's memorable but unverified recollection that Beethoven referred to the motive as "fate knocking at the door." In part due to the fitting coincidence that the rhythm of Beethoven's four notes are the same as the Morse code for the letter V, Beethoven's motive became the Allies' rallying cry for victory as early as 1941.

It is indeed remarkable how Beethoven was able to use the V-motive as the foundation for a seemingly infinite variety of thematic content, as the symphony makes its progressive and triumphant journey from C minor in the first movement to the roaring C major of the finale, a trajectory already noticed by Hoffmann in his 1810 review. We have observed a similar gradual anticipation of C major in *Fidelio*, but that work lacked the strong C minor presence in the first and third movements of the Fifth Symphony. The *Marcia funebre* in the *Eroica* contrasts the central march in C minor with a section in C major. Marzelline's aria in act I of *Fidelio* also juxtaposes a first section in C minor with a hopeful section in C major. The Fifth Symphony takes this idea to a culminating level, so much so that the overcoming of C minor and the triumph of C major in the finale make this symphony one of the central works of Beethoven's "heroic" style. The striking organicism of the work—the way the V-motive pervades the work from beginning to end—has also made the symphony a central example of thematic unity, a central value in the nineteenth century and beyond in which music is directly analogous to a living organism.

The V-motive is seldom absent for long. In fact, the short-short-short-LONG rhythm or its variant short-short-short-SHORT appears in virtually every measure of the first theme and transition to the second theme. When the horn introduces the second theme in the relative major (Eb), it also does so with the motive. Although the strings answer the horn with a new theme in even quarter notes, even here Beethoven immediately inserts the primary motive in the bass, or cello and bass, in response to this second theme. Beethoven also makes a melodic as well as a rhythmic connection between the opening theme and the second theme. The organic connection merits the trouble it takes to explain it. Here goes.

If one were to strip the V-motive of its rhythmic component to reveal its melodic content, we can easily discern that the opening motive consists of four distinct pitches (G, Eb, F, and D), dispersed over the eight notes of the first two four-note descending statements of the motive: G–G–G–Eb (short-short-short-LONG) and F–F–F–D (short-short-short-LONG). The distance between the first pair of notes, G and Eb, is a major third; the distance from F to D is a minor third. When the horn introduces the second theme, the motive is enlarged into a descending fifth, Bb–Eb, followed by a second descending fifth F–Bb, the first pair with the three shorts, the second pair without. Not only does the new theme contain four distinct pitches, but also two of these notes, the second and third, are the same as that of the original motive, even though we have moved to a new key. This is the kind of motivic unity between themes that would become a hallmark of musical style for the next two centuries. This is organicism at work.

The closing theme offers yet another variant of the V-motive, this time a LONG followed by fifteen measures of "shorts." After still more short-short-short-LONGs to conclude the exposition, the development returns to the opening short-short-short-LONG with a fermata underneath the LONG, followed by a continuous presence of the motive in various states of clarity, including *forte* and *più* (more) *forte* statements in the full orchestra. In the second half of the development, Beethoven turns to the second theme in several keys, subjecting it to fragmentation and eventually reducing it to two notes, the second and third notes shared between the first and second theme.

The recapitulation returns to the V-motive in the tonic C minor with a roar in the entire orchestra. Soon, however, when the music arrives at its third fermata, the pause is prolonged still further and the music given over to the oboe for what amounts to a one-measure cadenza marked *adagio*. Interestingly, the melody of the cadenza is derived from two elements from the first theme, a four-note descending scale from G down to D and a scalar filling in of the opening pitches G–Eb and F–D.

After the oboe cadenza the recapitulation follows the exposition closely, that is, until near its end, when for the first time in the movement, and of course the symphony, the recapitulation ends and the coda begins with the full orchestra playing the V-motive *fortissimo* in the *major* mode (introduced in the second theme). The expanded first-movement coda, one of Beethoven's central modifications of sonata form (in fact the four formal sections are nearly identical in length, ranging from 122 to 127 measures), offers Beethoven another opportunity to develop his motives further and tie loose ends. At the end of this second "development," Beethoven returns to the V-motive and its sequential repetition one final time, with the minor mode regaining its initial supremacy.

Second Movement: *Andante con Moto*

The second movement presents two contrasting sections, A and B, the A section beginning and ending in Ab major and the B section beginning in Ab major and modulating to *C major*. The return of the A section contains an ornamental variation of the first A, while the return of B contains additional rhythmic movement but less variation. The pattern repeats for another Ab variation and a varied B section, again in Ab and C major. The final variation starts in Ab *minor* before returning to Ab major. Instead of a final return of the B section, a coda brings the music back to Ab minor with an incomplete variation and a partial return of the B section in the tonic major.

To conclude the A theme, Beethoven offers three statements of the short-short-short-LONG rhythm. As if to call attention to the V-motive, albeit with a brand new set of pitches, Beethoven reserves its most prominent version for a grand *fortissimo* in the horns, trumpets, and timpani, supported by the oboes, in C major, thus anticipating the heroic presence of C major in the finale. Beethoven will repeat this emphasis on C major *fortissimo* and with brass and timpani at the end of the second and third A–B pairings. The rhythm for each of the three blaring C major passages is an elongated yet unmistakable version of short-short-short-LONG.

Third Movement: *Allegro*

The third movement *scherzo* begins with a mysterious introductory melody in C minor, a melody noticeably similar to the C minor "Sinfonia" sketch that dated from Beethoven's Bonn years. In the Fifth Symphony *scherzo*, Beethoven adds the V-rhythm to this theme, now introduced by the horns, and stated no less than nine times of the next few measures. For the rest of the *scherzo* portion of the movement, the primary motive occasionally disappears, but never for long. The trio, in C major throughout, starts with the cellos and basses, a challenging passage for the latter instrument destined for many bass auditions, and answered in counterpoint, first by the violas and bassoons and then by the second and first violins. After the *scherzo* returns in a somewhat streamlined version, the timpani taps the primary rhythm on a C, but the basses and cellos move to a prolonged Ab instead. Although the cellos and basses return to G to produce a pedal point on the dominant of C minor, the timpani repeats and the inner strings dramatically sustain a prolonged C in anticipation of the tonic. In response to the overwhelming tension, the music erupts into an ascending fanfare-like melody in C major reinforced by three trombones, a contrabassoon (first heard in *Fidelio*), and a piccolo, the first time any of these instruments had appeared in a symphony.

Fourth Movement: *Allegro*

The imaginary hero has triumphed over C minor as the four-note V-motive persists in new triumphant guises. Its first return arrives in the continuation of the main finale theme after four measures. This is the short-short-short-SHORT version of the theme heard with a variety of melodic material in the first movement. After a distinctive second "first" theme in C major, introduced by two horns in harmony with two trumpets, the music modulates to the dominant for a second theme based entirely on the V-rhythmic motive, short-short-short-LONG and stated no less than twenty-four times in succession. Again, as with the first movement, even the closing theme, which begins with the clarinets and bassoons, clearly imbeds the short-short-short-LONG into its simple scaler theme.

Until the end of the development the primary rhythm rarely disappears from the background and eventually assumes the foreground. Surprisingly, a lengthy *fortissimo* passage on the dominant fails to return to the expected recapitulation. Instead Beethoven returns to C *minor* and the main short-short-short-SHORT melody from the *scherzo* for one final delay of heroic gratification before the recapitulation returns in a blaze of C major glory. From now to the end of the symphony C major is here to stay.

In the first movement Beethoven presented a coda equal in length to the other central parts of the sonata form. In the finale the exposition and recapitulation both contain eighty-six measures, but the development is completed in sixty-six measures and the abbreviated return of the *scherzo* lasts only fifty-three. Considering these proportions, the coda occupies an astonishing 150 measures, in four sections. The first section emphasizes the material of the second theme; the second focuses on the last part of the 1. "second" first theme. For the third section Beethoven completes the acceleration of the previous measures until he achieves a *presto* based on the closing theme. This time Beethoven reinforces the short-short-short-LONG component of the theme by giving the central rhythm to the cellos, basses, and contrabassoon eight times. Still *presto*, the fourth part returns to the main theme, *fortissimo*, beginning with a canon between the cellos and basses and then joined with the rest of the orchestra. Remarkably, these final forty-one measures consist of only two chords, the major tonic and the dominant, culminating in twenty-nine measures of tonic only. In the final measures Beethoven states a final round of three shorts (pause), a final short (pause), and one final LONG underneath a fermata.

PART 2: (3) "FANTASY FOR PIANO ALONE" AND (4) "FANTASY FOR THE PIANO WHICH ENDS WITH THE GRADUAL ENTRANCE OF THE ENTIRE ORCHESTRA AND THE INTRODUCTION OF CHORUSES AS A FINALE"

The *Wiener Zeitung* announcement listed two sections of the program devoted to improvisation, a talent for which Beethoven was invariably praised throughout his lifetime. While it is possible that the "fantasy for piano alone" was distinct from the three-minute improvisatory introduction to the *Choral Fantasy*, op. 80, it seems at least reasonable to inquire whether they were and remain one and the same. In any event, we simply do not have a reliable record of what Beethoven played at the concert but did not write down. The published score for the *Fantasy* does contain a substantial notated, but improvisational in character, "fantasy for piano alone," which introduces the work before the orchestra enters in a section labeled "Finale." The Fifth Symphony that began the second half of program started with C minor in the first movement and then, after some conspicuous returns of C major in the second and third movements, explodes into C major for the finale. The *Choral Fantasy* follows this basic tonal trajectory from C minor to major, also identified in *Eroica*'s *Marcia funebre* and Marzelline's aria from *Fidelio*.

The piano introduction to the *Choral Fantasy* begins with a distinctive musical idea, stated twice in C minor, once on the minor subdominant (F minor) and then as a prolonged dominant seventh of Eb major that is only momentarily resolved in that key (Eb is the relative major of C minor). The harmony next veers in several directions, as improvisations do, before one final statement of the original motive in E major, a move that duplicates the harmonic trajectory of the C minor piano concerto, in which the first movement is in C minor; the second movement, in E major. The virtuosic and presumably unnotated introduction to the work Beethoven composed hastily to serve as a rousing finale concludes, and the orchestra enters *pianissimo* in C minor in the basses. This initiates a dialogue between orchestra and piano, a dialogue analogous to the conversation between orchestra and soloist in the second movement of the Fourth Piano Concerto that ended the Academy concert's first half. After five measures of horns and oboes answering each other in fifths, like hunting horns, the main theme begins.

Most listeners readily detect strong musical family resemblances and even a number of identical phrases in common between this theme and the vastly more famous "Ode to Joy." The *Choral Fantasy* tune also has a prehistory, which can be traced more than a decade earlier to the main (and major mode) portion of Beethoven's song from 1794–1795, "Seufzer eines ungeliebten / Gegenliebe" (Sigh of one who is unloved / Love returned), which similarly starts in C minor and moves to C major for the "Gegenliebe" portion. The melody of "Gegenliebe," much of which was retained in *Ode*, offers persuasive musical evidence that the gestation of Beethoven's final symphony took place over a span of thirty years, probably long before Beethoven seriously considered incorporating this melodic material into a symphonic composition.

As with the Ninth's "Ode to Joy," much of the *Choral Fantasy* consists of a theme and variations, beginning with a self-contained theme in the piano supported by a simple accompaniment in the horns. After a short cadenza shortly before the theme comes to a close, Beethoven offers four complete variations, all with recognizably audible melodic connections with the main theme. In the first variation Beethoven has the flute present a varied version of the theme accompanied by the simplest of chordal accompaniments in the piano. In the second variation the oboes play another variation of the tune in parallel thirds, again with the simplest of piano accompaniments.

Along with the coldness of the hall and the alleged four-hour length of the concert, the most frequently recorded moment was a breakdown in communication in the orchestra, a miscommunication that created enough cacophony to force Beethoven to stop and start over. This is how the incident was reported in the *Allgemeine musikalische Zeitung* review the following month:

> Most striking, however, was the slip that took place during the final fantasy [variation 2, mm. 90ff.]. The wind instruments [starting with the flute in variation 1] were playing variations on the theme that Beethoven had previously stated on the pianoforte. Now it was the oboes' turn. The clarinets [featured along with the solo bassoon, without piano, in the third variation]—if I am not mistaken!—mis-

count, and enter at the same time. A curious mixture of tone arises; Beethoven leaps up, tries to silence the clarinets; but he no sooner succeeds in this than he very loudly and somewhat angrily calls out to the entire orchestra: "Quiet, quiet, this is not working! Once again— once again!" And the orchestra so praised must be satisfied with starting the bungled fantasy over again. (Senner 2001, 49)

After this embarrassing communication breakdown, Variation 3 gave the theme to the solo clarinets and bassoon; Variation 4, to solo strings—both variations with the piano playing along. And Variation 5 consisted of a restatement of the theme in full orchestra. After a coda in which the piano and orchestra participated in a playful dialogue and another short cadenza, the piano brought the music back to C minor with a vigorous, *Allegro molto* and *fortissimo* outburst answered by the full orchestra. The music returns to C major to conclude this section, one marked by freer references to the central theme rather than a strictly formal variation. The clarinets and bassoons supported by the viola and a piano trill introduced a new slow section in the remote key of A major, after which Beethoven launched another new section, this time in F major, which consisted of a march-like variation in the winds, brass, and timpani punctuated by short chords in the strings, a section that Beethoven designated *Marcia, assai vivace*.

Instead of a firm affirmation of C major, Beethoven presents a harmonically ambiguous transition leading to a return of the material that introduced the orchestra (before we heard the theme), this time with one short piano cadenza in lieu of a dialogue between the piano and the orchestra. As in the beginning of the theme and variations, we hear the open fifths of the horns, now answered by the clarinets, while the piano plays a continuous accompaniment that contains nothing but *arpeggios* punctuated by periodic short notes in the strings. Finally the chorus makes its long-awaited entrance with a full statement of the main theme, first in the sopranos and altos, along with a continuous piano accompaniment and sparse *pizzicato* notes in the strings.

No author's name appeared in the published score, and no one seems to know for sure who wrote the new text that substituted for "Gegenliebe." The most likely suspect seems to be Christoph Kuffner. If this is correct, it would be his most famous poetic text and, like the concert itself, serves as a tribute to the spiritual power of art and music perhaps guiding humans to Enlightenment ideals: "When magical sound is in command and words convey devotion, wonders must take shape; night and tempest turn to light."

The second choral statement features solo tenor and bass parts with a similar accompaniment, and in the third statement the entire chorus joins the full orchestra (but without the piano) in yet another complete statement of the theme, this time *forte*. A long and elaborate coda presents new melodic material as well as contrapuntal passages in which parts of the main theme appear in staggered entrances. The chorus drops out shortly before the end, but the piano maintains its presence to the end of the work, concluding with a brilliant series of C major *arpeggios* reinforced by the orchestra's triumphant dominant to C major tonic harmonies.

THE ACADEMY CONCERT OF FEBRUARY 27, 1814

In the years following the monumental Academy concert of 1808, a number of new Beethoven works with orchestra received their premiere performances. Highlights of this performance activity start with a repeat public performance of the oratorio *Christ on the Mount of Olives* for chorus, orchestra, and three soloists at the Theater an der Wien in 1809. This is the work that premiered at the Academy concerto of 1803. While *Christ* is seldom heard today, it had its Viennese followers in the early nineteenth century and was probably the most popular Beethoven work in the United States in the composer's lifetime. The first performance of the incidental music to Goethe's *Egmont* was heard in 1810; the first performances of Beethoven's fifth and final piano concerto were heard in Leipzig late in 1811 and Vienna early in 1812. Also in 1812 the incidental music to *King Stephen* and *The Ruins of Athens* received three performances at the opening of a new theater in Pest (now Budapest).

There were private run-throughs of the still-new Seventh and Eighth Symphonies at the Archduke Rudolph's palace in April 1813 and a return engagement of the Fifth Symphony at the Augarten. After that, the Seventh Symphony, op. 92 (composed in 1811–1812), and *Wellington's Victory*, op. 91 (composed in 1813), received their first public performances on December 8 and 12, 1813, at University Hall and repeat performances at the Grand Redoutensaal one month later on January 2 along with music from *The Ruins of Athens*, all to immense acclaim. During these peak years of Beethoven's popularity, audiences demanded that the second movement *Allegretto* of the Seventh Symphony be encored at both December performances. At the third concert, a profitable venture, according to the *Wiener Zeitung*, "many things had to be repeated, and there was a unanimous expression of a desire on the part of all the hearers to hear the compositions again and often and to have occasion more frequently to laud and admire our native composer for works of his brilliant invention" (Forbes 1964, 571).

On February 27, 1814, also at the Grand Redoutensaal, audiences heard the Seventh Symphony once again as the first work on the program. *Wellington's Victory* appeared last. The two works in the middle were the trio for soprano, tenor, and bass, *Tremate, empi, Tremati!* ("Tremble, Guilty Ones, Tremble"), op. 116, composed in 1802 and perhaps revised in 1814, and the first public performance of the Eighth Symphony, composed in 1812. As in past performances, the Seventh Symphony and *Wellington's Victory* were received with enormous applause and audiences demanded that the second movement of the former and the battle portion of the latter be repeated. According to the report in the *Allgemeine Musikalische Zeitung*, Beethoven's latest symphony, the Eighth, fared less well, "and the applause which it received was not accompanied by that enthusiasm which distinguishes a work which gives universal delight" (Forbes 1964, 575). The reviewer did not attribute this lesser reception to the quality of the work but more to the fact that it had to follow the overwhelmingly popular Seventh on the same concert. The review concludes with the confident assertion that, "if this symphony should be performed *alone* hereafter, we have no doubt of its success" (Forbes 1964, 575). This prediction did not morph into fact. On the contrary, the Eighth Symphony, even when performed without competition from the Seventh Symphony or other Beethoven works, has continued to suffer in comparison with its more extrovert, readily accessible, and popular twin. The remarks that follow will attempt to shed light on why the Eighth lives in the shadow of the Seventh and to make a case for its extraordinary craft and comic genius.

SYMPHONY NO. 7 IN A MAJOR, OP. 92

We can thank Richard Wagner for what has become the most-quoted encapsulation of Beethoven's Seventh. Wagner's epiphany first appeared in *The Artwork of the Future* (1849): "The Symphony is the Apotheosis of the Dance itself: it is Dance in its highest aspect, the loftiest deed of bodily motion, incorporated into an ideal mold of tone." In these and other statements it is clear that for Wagner, who absorbed much of Beethoven's Seventh in his own youthful Symphony in C (composed only five years after Beethoven's death), the symphony as a genre was derived from dance, and Beethoven's symphony was its apotheosis. Indeed, from Wagner's time to ours, the dance-like (or rhythmic) aspects of the Seventh have served as the gateway to understanding what Beethoven accomplished in this well-loved work.

After two symphonies that began with introductory phrases but without formal slow introductions as in the First, Second, and Fourth symphonies, Beethoven opens the Seventh with the longest introduction he would ever compose, sixty-two measures of pomp and circumstance that begin and end in A major with important harmonic digressions to the remote key areas of C major and F major. By now deeply concerned with harmonic unity over the span of a large work, we probably should not be surprised to learn that the composer will return to these remote areas in the movements that follow.

First Movement: *Poco Sostenuto-Vivace*

Each of the four movements in the Seventh focus on a particular distinctive rhythm, usually for the duration of the movement. At the beginning of the *Vivace* sonata-form movement that follows the first-movement introduction, Beethoven introduces a three-note jig-like rhythm pattern (dotted sixteenth-sixteenth-eighth) that will rarely disappear. Even in the development, after the first two measures, only two other measures manage to avoid this catchy, repetitive rhythm. The simultaneous presence of octave drones in the horns and sometimes in the winds evokes the bagpipes of the Sixth Symphony and contributes to a folk-like flavor. As in the Fifth Symphony, recognizable melodic elements of the first theme also continue in the second theme and form the starting point of the closing theme. Another characteristic of the exposition is its boisterous nature with more than half of the total measures sounding *forte* or louder.

As the primary rhythmic cell begins to assert the primary rhythm in the development, where it will continue uninterrupted, Beethoven also inserts near its beginning a four-part canon based on a melodic variation of the main theme. It appears in the following sequence: cellos and basses, first violins, second violins and violas, oboes, flutes, and bassoons. Near the end of the development we hear a D minor *fortissimo* outburst of the primary rhythm that eventually moves up one pitch (E) to the dominant that will take us back to the tonic A major along with the first theme to begin the recapitulation.

The primary rhythm also seldom abandons the coda, which begins with a surprising *pianissimo* digression in Ab major. Although Beethoven soon moves to the tonic, including another *fortissimo* statement in the full orchestra, even this statement avoids placing the tonic solidly in root position. Such a tonal affirmation will have to wait until the exciting final tonic *fortissimo* (a wait richly rewarded) in the final seconds of the movement.

Second Movement: *Allegretto*

The second movement in A minor features another pervasive rhythmic motive: LONG-short-short-LONG-LONG. This rhythm pervades a remarkable tune—simple, sturdy, and memorable. It begins in the lower strings (violas, divided cellos, and basses) immediately following the opening chord in the winds (minus the flutes) and horns. The opening LONG-short-short part of the pattern corresponds to the poetic dactyl, a rhythm, perhaps following Beethoven, even more favored by Schubert in numerous works. As with the primary rhythm of the first movement, the two-measure pattern in the second movement, an *Allegretto* rather than a slow movement, is nearly continuous throughout the opening A section. The presentation suggests a series of variations with added layers building on a fundamentally simple tune.

The B section presents a new tune in A major that features triplets in the first violin. The tune remains supported by ubiquitous dactyls (LONG-short-short) but now without the following LONG-LONG's of the A section. The return of the A section and A minor is less reliant on the original rhythmic pattern, although the pattern continues to manifest its insistent presence in the cellos and basses. Later in this second A section the original tune serves as the starting place for an extended fugato, an imitative passage leading to a *fortissimo* rhythmic unison statement of the primary rhythm in the strings, brass, and timpani, accompanied by continuous sixteenth notes in the winds. A much-abbreviated B section in A major, again supported by unwavering dactyls in the bass, leads to a short coda, still based on the dactyls and sometimes ending with two longs and other times with one. The movement concludes with a restatement of the opening A minor chord, scored as before, but now voiced with an additional low A in the bass, a note absent from the opening chord.

Third Movement: *Presto*

The third movement is a *scherzo*-trio form in F major with a second trio, a third *scherzo*, a third snippet of a trio, *piano*, and an abrupt five-note *Presto, fortissimo*. Although Beethoven does not present a single pervasive rhythmic figure as he did in the earlier movements, he does emphasize one rhythmic idea over all others in both the *scherzo* and the trio portions. The prominent *scherzo* rhythm (LONG-short) with the long half note and the short quarter note, first heard in the strings and then the flute twelve measures into the movement, appears only four times in the first half of the *scherzo*, including three times in succession within a four-measure span. In the second half of the *scherzo* section, the LONG-short pattern becomes pervasive, including twelve measures in a row near its beginning, all *pianissimo*, five times in the flute and clarinets, four times in the violins and violas, and three times in the cellos and basses. After a brief, full orchestra *fortissimo* outburst, Beethoven then repeats the entire sequence. The second part of the *scherzo* also includes a false return of the *scherzo* theme, that is, an early return of the *scherzo* tune in the "wrong" key of Bb major before the tune enters in the correct key of F major.

According to Abbé Stadler, a composer, music historian, and friendly acquaintance of Beethoven, the main theme of the trio section is based on a pilgrim's hymn, an assertion still waiting to be authenticated and the hymn yet to be discovered. In any event, the new or perhaps borrowed tune features a new rhythm that will be heard in nearly every measure. It consists of a half note tied to an eighth followed by a quarter note on the downbeat of the second beat in triple time. Above the trio tune, which begins in the clarinets, bassoons, and horns, the violins sound a high drone, an inverted pedal tone.

Fourth Movement: *Allegro con Brio*

At the outset of the finale Beethoven introduces a four-note rhythm (eighth note, two sixteenth notes, and eighth note, or LONG-short-short-LONG), a powerful motive that he will repeat numerous times throughout the movement, much as other distinctive rhythmic motives saturated earlier movements. As with the first and second movements, the Seventh finale focuses on a *primary* rhythm, in this case a seven-note motive lasting a single measure of two-fourths time and an eighth note followed by six sixteenth notes (LONG-short-short-SHORT-short-short-short) with a *sforzando* on the third sixteenth note (i.e., the "Big Short"), which places the accent on the weak second beat.

Sandwiched between three statements of the seven-note motive on one side and three on the other is a single measure that contains a dotted eighth-, sixteenth-, and quarter-note pattern (LONG-short-LONG) with a *sforzando* on the quarter note. Underneath the entire theme is a dominant pedal point drone with a *sforzando* accent on the second beats in synchronization with the principal melody. Throughout the movement Beethoven also offers repeated statements of a two-note dotted eighth-sixteenth note cell and its variant (dotted eighth-sixteenth note followed by a quarter note). Aside from a recurring scalar idea that closes many phrases, virtually all the material in the movement is based on these distinctive rhythms.

It has been noted since George Grove's pioneering study of the symphonies originally published in 1896 that this finale tune bears a strong musical resemblance to an Irish tune, *Save Me from the Grave and Wise* (also known as *Nora Creina*), Beethoven set as part of a group of songs in George Thomson's collection composed in February 1813 and published in Edinburgh. Indeed, the recurring phrase of Beethoven's tune constitutes a rhythmically altered but recognizable paraphrase of the Irish tune and the odd measure in the middle contains the same upward major sixth as the borrowed tune. Altogether Beethoven set 169 different (and 179 total) Scottish, Irish, Welsh, British, and Continental folk songs between 1809 and 1820, of which 126 were published. The finale of the Seventh Symphony strongly suggests that he might have found a way to incorporate at least one of these songs into one of his most ambitious symphonic works.

The relentlessly exciting and constantly moving finale framed by the opening music turns the lilting Irish tune into a vigorous stomping dance. Although Beethoven doesn't travel too far harmonically, at least for long, he does offer a large dose of C major and smaller amounts of F major (the two unusual keys he introduced in the first-movement introduction) and even a short digression to the even more remote key of C# minor. In the coda Beethoven takes the opening rhythm, alters the pitches slightly, and treats the altered version as a source of counterpoint for more than fifty measures. Accompanying this passage is a recurring E–D# pattern in the bass that lasts for nearly twenty-six measures. Shortly before Beethoven breaks this E–D# pattern, and for another ten measures after that, Beethoven omits the D# and states only the dominant E. This leads to a rare *fortississimo* (*fff*, very, very loud) climax in the tonic key.

SYMPHONY NO. 8 IN F MAJOR, OP. 93

After the vocal interlude that featured the trio "Tremate, empi, tremate!" audiences heard the first performance of Beethoven's shortest, least understood, and most underrated symphony, a work that at first glance seems to look backward rather than forward. Beethoven's only symphony to be published without a dedicatee is also decidedly nonheroic in nature, perhaps even antiheroic. Czerny is responsible for reporting that when Beethoven discovered the Eighth was received less favorably than the Seventh, he replied it was "because it is much better." Without taking sides on whether the Eighth is "much better" than the Seventh or any of his other popular symphonies, the present chapter will espouse the view that Beethoven's most classical symphony from his middle years is a work of great sophistication, humor, and joie de vivre, and listeners can reap tremendous rewards from the work if they give it a chance.

First Movement: *Allegro Vivace e con Brio*

> In my beginning is my end.
> — T. S. Eliot, "East Coker" (1940)

The first movement suggests a fast minuet or Viennese *Ländler*. Jean Jacques Rousseau opened his *Confessions* with the announcement that his birth was the first of his misfortunes. In Beethoven's Eighth its first "joke" or trick arrives in the opening two seconds: a six-note phrase in the violins. As in Haydn's G Major Quartet, op. 33, no. 5, in which the first movement begins (and ends) with the same decisive closing phrase, so Beethoven's first six notes could just as easily serve as the end of the movement as its beginning. When in the final seconds of the movement we hear the last six notes of the movement, unison and *pianissimo* in all the strings, we realize that we had already heard the end of the movement at its beginning. After the first six notes the movement continues with a twelve-measure theme divided into three four-measure phrases. The first and third phrases are played by the full orchestra. The middle, and functionally unnecessary, phrase features the winds.

The next trick is difficult to hear (and grasp) since it challenges a sacred harmonic convention of sonata form. The convention in question, which Beethoven had adhered to in the Seventh Symphony, is to prepare harmonically for a move to the dominant as the second key and then go there (in some works, for example, the *Waldstein*, Beethoven prepared for a key area other than the dominant and then arrived to this alternative goal). In the Eighth, Beethoven prepares the second key as if it *would* be the dominant (C major), that is, he *pretends* to follow the convention, but instead of arriving at the dominant, Beethoven offers the dominant (Bb) of the seventh degree of the scale (Eb major). Even Beethoven understood that this would be a strange and unprecedented goal for a second key area and indeed does not *actually* go there. Instead he goes to the dominant of D major, another unusual but not unprecedented second key, since D is the sixth degree of the F major scale, the submediant. Adding to this harmonic trickery, the second theme plays a rhythmic trick in which the first beat of its first three measures is anticipated with a syncopation on the upbeat of the previous measure, thus making it nearly impossible to discern a downbeat until the new theme is well underway several measures later. After one full statement of this new theme Beethoven finally decides to offer the long-delayed dominant seventh of C major and then repeats the second theme in C major, the dominant of F major we expected all along. Once arrived, Beethoven remains in the dominant, C major, until the end of the exposition, which will contain a closing theme stated twice with the orchestra playing *fortissimo*. The exposition closes with an octave figure that sounds like a caricature of the famous four-note Fifth Symphony motive. Who knows if Beethoven meant it as such?

In any event, throughout much of the development Beethoven will stick with this octave motive, possibly borrowed from the Fifth Symphony's central motive. When not presented in isolation, the octave motive also accompanies numerous statements of the opening six-note motive played successively by the bassoon, clarinet, oboe, and flute three times over the space of a minute or so. He next subjects the six-note subject to a canon, first in various isolated voices and then in overlapping entrances. Altogether we can hear the opening six-note motive at least once per measure for an astonishing twenty-eight measures in succession. Surely Beethoven cannot be *serious*. After this mock-obsessive development, the composer allows the octave motive that usurped the rhythm of the Fifth Symphony motive to take the listener back to the recapitulation.

The recapitulation opens with a statement of the main theme in the cellos, basses, and bassoon, with the entire orchestra playing *fortississimo* (*fff*), that is, very, very loud, a dynamic marking we have heard only once before near the end of the Seventh. We expect this is the climactic moment. Beethoven subverts the expected climax, however, with his decision not to provide the entire twelve-measure main theme. What he does instead is to state the first four measures and the last four measures and deletes the middle four, which as noted at the outset were unnecessary anyway. After that, he returns to the first four-measure phrase, now in the winds and *piano*, supported by timpani *pianissimo*, and follows the first phrase with the second, still in the winds, before he allows the cellos and basses to lead to the cadence that marked the original twelve measures, now extended to twenty.

It may not seem too amusing at the time, but the coda introduces an odd note and an odd harmony that will bear tremendous consequences in the finale. The note is Db, known in classical parlance as the flat submediant (or flat sixth) of the tonic F. It does not really fit in too well in F major, however, especially in the coda, the place where we have a right to expect matters to wrap up and attain closure. We then hear the leaping octave Fifth Symphony motive in the bassoons on an isolated F after which violas enter on the same motive on Db while the clarinets play the first four measures of the main tune, also in Db major. Soon Beethoven will extricate himself from this harmonic predicament brought about by beginning the coda in such a far-fetched key and bring in the entire orchestra with the first four measures of the main theme, on the tonic, *fortissimo*. Instead of offering a firm resolution in the welcome tonic, however, Beethoven interrupts by allowing the full orchestra to enter *fortississimo* for two measures with a Db harmony before finally settling permanently, still *fortississimo*, on the tonic.

Despite landing in the home key, Beethoven creates the sense of an anticlimax during his final measures by suddenly shifting to a *piano* dynamic and offering a dialogue between *pizzicato* strings and the winds and brass. First we hear two pairs with all three beats sounding, then two pairs with two beats sounding, and finally two measures with one beat each and *pianissimo*. P. D. Q. Bach's creator Professor Schickele said at the end of a live concert, "We have now reached the moment you have been waiting for . . . the end." And we have now reached the long-awaited conclusion of the first movement of Beethoven's Eighth, which paradoxically, and perhaps ironically, is where we started. Now, however, *pianissimo* replaces *forte*, as the movement closes with its opening six notes, again calling to mind, as with the first movement of the *Tempest* Sonata, the concluding words of T. S. Eliot's "The Hollow Men," "not with a bang but a whimper."

Second Movement: *Allegretto Scherzando*

As with the Seventh, the four movements of the Eighth do not include an "authentic" slow movement. The Seventh had the famous and often encored *Allegretto* in A minor. The Eighth offers a playful *Allegretto scherzando*. Until quite recently, and repeated as gospel in many commentaries on the symphonies to this day, the second movement of the Eighth was thought to be based on a canon in the same key (Bb major), *Ta ta ta, lieber Mälzel* (*Ta ta ta, dear Mälzel*). According to this theory, the little tune served as a comical tribute to the man who patented the metronome in 1815, Johann Nepomuk Mälzel (although historians now attribute its invention in 1814 to Dietrich Nikolaus Winkel). The rumor

of this connection, purported by Schindler, who forged entries in Beethoven's conversation books to support this claim, has now been established as false, along with the attribution of the canon published under
Beethoven's name in 1844. In the updated thematic catalog published
by G. Henle Verlag in 2014, the canon is banished to the appendix of
spurious compositions as WoO 162.

With its playful "tick-tock" sixteenth-note *staccato* pulse, a more
likely influence is the second movement of Haydn's Symphony no. 101,
aptly nicknamed *The Clock*. Although predominantly "metronomic," in
two places Beethoven plays with the meter by stating a series of identical five-note descending scales one sixteenth note *before* the downbeat.
As if this isn't confusing enough—that the scale is five notes rather than
four—every one of the five entrances falls on an irregular place in the
metrical scheme. The first time this happens occurs immediately prior
to the first return of the main theme, the second time shortly before the
end of the movement. On both occasions the sequence begins with a
crescendo followed by a *diminuendo* during the third statement, ending
in *pianissimo*. Shortly after the second five-note sequence is repeated
five times, Beethoven ends the movement with a *pianissimo* dialogue
between winds and the first violins *sempre pianissimo*, a *fortissimo* outburst in the full orchestra, a touch of *pianissimo* in the second violins
and violas, a repeat of this comical pattern, and finally a three-measure
crescendo from *pianissimo* to *fortissimo* that ends with comical abruptness.

Third Movement: *Tempo di Menuetto*

The third movement is a minuet trio that starts with a two-measure
introduction with heavy *sforzando* accents on each beat, the reverse of
what listeners might expect of an aristocratic dance movement. In the
second section of the minuet, Beethoven inserts a number of strong
sforzando accents on the *second* beat throughout much of the orchestra. These accents contribute further to the impression that we are
listening to a country dance rather than a classical minuet. The second
section introduces staggered imitative entries of the main subject. As
with the trio of horns in the trio of the *Eroica*, the Eighth Symphony
trio follows the strict constructionist meaning of a "trio" (and the origins
of the term) and features three instruments, each marked "solo." Bee-

thoven follows the trio with duet for two horns above an arpeggiated cello accompaniment, which continues as the solo clarinets answer the horns.

Fourth Movement: *Allegro Vivace*

The final movement of the Eighth, described as a contredanse, contains the basic elements of a sonata-form movement but one that is more than a little askew. In contrast to his first seven symphonies, Beethoven elects not to repeat the exposition (ninety measures), a decision that considerably alters the conventional balance. After a modest development (sixty-nine measures) and a recapitulation that modestly extends the length of the exposition (105 measures), Beethoven concludes with a coda (Italian for tail) that gives new meaning to the phrase "the tail wagging the dog," a whopping 236 measures. This is only thirty measures shorter than the first exposition, development, and recapitulation *put together*.

The finale transcends this grand formal joke with more musical surprises than can be described here. The present discussion will focus on one through-line joke, the foreshadowing of a particular "sore" note that has no business being so prominent in the key of F. Readers may recall that Beethoven had introduced a similar out-of-place note in the coda to the first movement. That note was a Db, the flat submediant. In the finale Beethoven calls attention to this same note, now disguised enharmonically as a C#. We hear it as a unison note *fortissimo* on the second (or offbeat) and the first beat of the following measure at the end of the first statement of the main theme, which has started *pianissimo* and concludes *pianississimo*. Perhaps it is not coincidental that, although the harmonic context has changed, C# happens to be the same sore note that stopped the opening theme of the *Eroica* in its tracks.

After the C# interruption, hopefully difficult to miss, Beethoven restates the first theme *fortissimo*. When he arrives at the second theme he performs the same trick as he did in the first movement by introducing the new theme in an unexpected key (this time Ab, the flat mediant) before restating it in the dominant C major to restore the sonata-form order. The development focuses exclusively on bits and pieces of the main theme, culminating in a *fortissimo* statement in A major, which means that the starting note of the theme is none other than the devil itself, C#.

After a full statement of the main theme that begins the recapitulation, Beethoven interrupts with the same *fortissimo* C# on the second beat of one measure and first of the next. Beethoven treats the interruption a little like an inappropriate guest at the dinner table, completely ignores the *faux pas*, and plays the main theme *fortissimo*. When he reaches the second theme, the incorrect key that he chooses is Db (i.e., the enharmonic to C#). Since he has thus far eschewed formal anarchy, Beethoven then restates the second theme in what was the expected tonic. After the short closing theme, the coda, more accurately a second development, commences.

After nearly a hundred measures of this coda, with some stops and starts and harmonic digressions along the way, Beethoven returns to the main theme in F major, the tonic of the movement and the symphony. This time he only offers the first four measures of the theme and then uses the opening three notes (two beats divided into two eighths and a quarter note, or short-short-LONG) as a point of departure, ending with three *pianississimo* repetitions, the first two followed by two beats of rest.

For the third repetition Beethoven swerves to a *fortissimo* Db in the full orchestra, as before on the offbeat and held over to the next measure. Again we see the three-note motive *pianissimo* (violins, violas, and cellos); again, the full orchestra *fortissimo* on Db (now spelled as C#); again, the three-note motive *pianissimo* (violins); and so forth. After the third Db/C# intrusion the strings no longer answer. Instead the full orchestra plays two more C#s in succession, each starting on the second beat. The C# can no longer be ignored.

Unlike the *Eroica* Beethoven never actually makes C# a point of harmonic arrival in the Eighth Symphony. Instead he turns C# into the dominant of F# (one half step above the tonic) and on this unorthodox harmony Beethoven states the main theme for the first time in the minor mode. After one last digression in D minor (matching the D major first statement of the second theme in the first movement), Beethoven reestablishes the tonic where the music will mostly remain for nearly another astonishing hundred measures.

WELLINGTON'S VICTORY, OR THE BATTLE OF VITTORIA (BATTLE SYMPHONY), OP. 91

Nearly ten years after the *Eroica*, "written on Napoleon," Beethoven wrote a shorter *Battle Symphony* that describes and celebrates the defeat of Napoleon's army led by the general's brother Joseph at the Battle of Vitoria (which Beethoven spelled Vittoria) in northeastern Spain on June 21, 1813, at the hands of Arthur Wellesley, Duke of Wellington. It was a decisive victory for the 121,000 English, Spanish, and Portuguese who outnumbered the 68,000 French troops and broke Napoleon's control of Spain. Two years later, also in June, Wellington and a contingent of British, Prussian, Austrian, and Russian troops defeated Napoleon and his army still more decisively, and famously, at Waterloo near Brussels, Belgium.

The symphony, conceived as an overture and lasting about fourteen minutes, contains two parts: the *Battle* and the *Victory Symphony*. The *Battle* is a programmatic reenactment of the Battle of Vitoria. First we hear the drums gradually escalating in volume followed by the trumpets on the English side and a full statement of Thomas Arne's march *Rule Britannia* in Eb major, first published in 1741. Next we hear a different drum roll and trumpet call in C major on the French side followed by a full rendition of the French march, *Marlborough*, in Beethoven's published score, designated *Malbrouk s'en va-t-en guerre*,[1] the tune known in English-speaking countries as *For He's a Jolly Good Fellow*. After a French trumpet challenge in C and a British trumpet counter-challenge in Eb, the *Battle* begins. Included in the detailed performance notes published in 1815 are Beethoven's instructions for two bass drums designed to produce the sounds of cannon shots and further instructions that the two cannons (bass drums) "must be located apart from the actual orchestra, on opposite sides, one side representing the English army, and the other the French army, as the hall permits, but neither one visible to the audience."

Beethoven even offers instructions in the published score indicating precisely where he wanted the cannons to go off, marking the English cannons with black ovals and the French with white ovals. Altogether listeners hear 188 cannon shots in the *Battle* and *Charge* sections within the space of about four minutes. To further depict escalating tensions, during the *Charge* the bass line ascends by half steps from Ab to A to

Bb to B, after which a *Presto* section adds a trumpet and rattles on the English side against a trumpet on the French. Soon we hear only English cannons. During the last French hurrah the music slows down to an *Andante* and we hear a minor version of *Malbrouk* underneath sporadic cannon shots from the English side.

In the second part, the *Victory Symphony*, Beethoven adopts a musical idea that corresponds to the new finale to *Fidelio* composed the next year, a victorious triumphant march that lasts nearly another four minutes. Since to the victors go the spoils, the music fittingly turns to *God Save the Queen*, a fourteen-measure tune divided unequally between a six-measure phrase and an eight-measure phrase. In the course of stating this anthem, in a *Tempo di Menuetto moderato*, in which Beethoven alternates between measures of *piano dolce* (sweet) and *fortissimo*, the music gets stuck on the twelfth measure. After seven repetitions of this measure, a three-note scalar figure each beginning with a ceremonial trill, we hear another three statements of the scale, each beginning on the second beat, *pianissimo*, and gradually coming to a halt.

Still beginning on the second beat and still in triple meter, the scale figure leads to an elaborate *Allegro* fugato variation on *God Save the Queen*, lingering in *pianissimo* before culminating in a *fortissimo* statement of the anthem in the full orchestra. The coda begins with (and eventually returns to) the central rhythmic motive of the Seventh Symphony first movement and concludes with other recognizable snippets of the anthem.

Wellington's Victory was undoubtedly the most popular orchestral composition of Beethoven's lifetime. While the septet of 1800 remained popular even in the 1820s, probably no Beethoven work, in any genre, generated more excitement and buzz than *Wellington's Victory*, not even the second movement of the Seventh Symphony. To some extent Beethoven's *Victory* was a Pyrrhic one, since the reviews were decidedly mixed. Although some early critics viewed the work positively, other early commentators expressed misgivings about Beethoven's desire to capture a historic event with such blatant musical realism, a realism that seemed to cross the line of good taste set by the *Pastoral* Symphony.

A decade later Beethoven's programmatic symphonic overture inspired what was perhaps the most negative critical response of a Beethoven composition to appear in the composer's lifetime. The review, published in 1825, appeared in the journal *Cäcilia* originating in Mainz. Its author was the theorist Gottfried Weber. The central topic of Weber's essay was tone painting, or Tonmalerei, which the critic objected to on principle. Naturally, he considered *Wellington's Victory* a particularly egregious example of the travesty: "These are not musical colors that Beethoven uses here, not the materials of a composer, but the trickeries of scenic acoustics" (Mathew 2013, 26). Beethoven was not pleased. When he received a copy of the article, he wrote some comments at the bottom of the page. The composer, who seems to have distinguished between the ambitious and timeless compositions such as his symphonies and lesser works designed for a particular occasion, took particular umbrage at the accusation that what he wrote was "nothing but an occasional piece" (27). Beethoven's defensive comment addressed to Weber may not be fit to print, but it is certainly worth quoting: "Oh you pitiful scoundrel, what I shit is better than anything you have ever thought" (27).

In the years since Weber's review Beethoven's potboiler has been regularly, if not invariably, maligned for its vulgarity and low artistic aspirations, especially among Beethoven scholars who consistently, but with some exceptions, tend to view the work as a degradation or a parody of the heroic style. For the past few decades scholars have been removing works in the canon of Renaissance icon Josquin Desprez because they fail to measure up to his highest compositional standards. It isn't so easy to pass off a Beethoven work to another composer or to deny the work's authenticity, but if they could get away with it, probably more than a few Beethoven scholars would enthusiastically reject *Wellington's Victory* as a work by the master. Gradually, however, some scholars are beginning to take a different tack. Since Beethoven himself never claimed he had written a symphonic masterpiece, perhaps we too could concede that a schlocky, lesser Beethoven work surpasses the schlocky, lesser works by other composers. Perhaps then we might better understand why Beethoven's warhorse has outrun so many others.

6

BEETHOVEN AND SONG

"Nimm sie hin denn, diese Lieder" (Accept them then, these songs).
—Title and opening line of song no. 6 from Beethoven's *An die ferne Geliebte*

Beethoven was the greatest melodist who ever lived.[1]
—Richard Wagner, 1879

BEETHOVEN AS A MELODIST

The epigraph that heads this chapter was taken from a diary entry diligently recorded by Wagner's doting wife Cosima Wagner (née Liszt) in response to Friedrich Nietzsche's "stupid" opinion that placed Beethoven beneath Franz Schubert as a composer of melody. While many commentators have eagerly embraced Wagner's famous characterization of the Seventh Symphony as "the apotheosis of the dance," they have taken an oath of silence when it comes to Wagner's striking assessment of Beethoven's melodic gifts. Indeed, some reading this chapter title might be wondering, What lyrical Beethoven? or Why does this book devote a chapter to the *lyrical* Beethoven?

As a first response to these questions we might note, with some surprise, that nearly half of Beethoven's six hundred known compositions are vocal. Although over a hundred of these compositions are songs, aside from *Fidelio*, the *Missa solemnis*, and the finale to the Ninth Symphony, Beethoven's vocal music is far less known than the instrumental compositions. Didn't Beethoven compose mainly symphonies, concertos, overtures, string quartets and other chamber music, and numerous piano, violin, and cello sonatas? Who knew he wrote songs?

Since the composer's time, singers have also been complaining vociferously about the vocal music they *do* know, especially the considerable demands Beethoven made on them. Even today tenors singing Florestan wonder how they will be able to negotiate a high G (G for *Gott*) to open act 2 of *Fidelio* after spending a silent act 1 on death row, which is troubling enough. More broadly, *Fidelio* has been faulted for its orchestral approach to opera. Since Beethoven's time, sopranos have complained about the high tessitura in the Ninth and how long they must sit waiting, like Florestan, before their first entrance, approximately forty-five minutes into the symphony. Instrumentalists are well aware that Beethoven makes considerable demands on them too, but somehow they seem to be getting used to it, although when he neared the end of his performing career, the virtuoso Alfred Brendel singled out Beethoven's *Hammerklavier* Sonata op. 106 as a work he would cease playing due to his arthritis.

Some of Beethoven's most famous instrumental works are known for their *lack* of lyricism and singability. Naturally, the first movement of the Fifth Symphony comes to mind. Surely this movement sounds more instrumental than vocal. On the other hand, its second movement, although it might pose a challenge for some to sing its principal melody, and even more so the variations that follow, by most criteria possesses a truly memorable melody. Unfortunately, the "motivic" Beethoven with all those melodic fragments ripe for development has led to the lack of appreciation of the "lyrical" Beethoven, despite many pervasively lyrical works such as the violin concerto, even during the heroic years (1803–1808). A significant exception is the "Ode to Joy," first heard in the lower strings before it is sung, which remains probably Beethoven's most famous tune. The second movement of the *Pathétique* is another certifiably singable melody. But certainly most of the instrumental works contain lyrical and "vocal" slow movements.

In the imaginary conversation "Why Beethoven?" in Leonard Bernstein's *Joy of Music* (1959), Bernstein (L.B.) challenges the claim voiced by his companion, Lyric Poet (L.P.), that "Beethoven is the greatest composer who ever lived!" (1959, 24) (note in the epigraph to this chapter that Wagner pronounced Beethoven as "the greatest *melo-dist*"). To sort this out, L.B. and L.P. take the musical elements one by one, starting with melody:

> L.P.: Let's see, melody. . . *Melody!* Lord, what melody! The slow movement of the *Seventh!* Singing its heart out——
>
> L.B.: Its monotone heart, you mean. The main argument of this "tune," if you will recall, is glued helplessly to E-natural.
>
> L.P.: Well, but that is intentional—meant to produce a certain static, somber, march-like——
>
> L.B.: Granted. Then it is not particularly distinguished for melody.
>
> L.P.: I was fated to pick a poor example. How about the first movement?
>
> L.P.: Just try whistling it.
>
> *L.P. makes a valiant attempt. Stops. Pause.*
>
> L.B. (*Brightly*): Shall we move on to harmony? (24)

Lyric Poet also strikes out with his next example, the slow movement of the A minor string quartet, op. 132, before salvaging the argument by offering "that glorious tune in the finale of the *Ninth*" (25).

On the other hand, starting in his lifetime and continuing throughout the nineteenth century, numerous Beethoven instrumental works were set to words and published as songs. A catalog from early in the nineteenth century lists more than thirty such settings. While melody is perhaps the most subjective of musical parameters to evaluate, the example of Beethoven demonstrates that it is possible to create extraordinarily memorable melodies, even lyrical melodies, that are perceived as less singable than, say, the melodies of dozens of tunes by his crosstown rival Schubert. Scholars have long argued that, although Beethoven's "heroic" works such as the *Eroica* and Fifth Symphonies, the *Egmont* Overture, and the *Appassionata* Sonata (and the less heroic *Ninth*) formed the dominant image of Beethoven that largely remains today, the works that influenced Schubert and the first generation of

Romantic composers tended to be nonheroic works. Interestingly, Beethoven composed a group of especially lyrical nonheroic works between 1809 and 1814, including the Eb Major String Quartet, op. 74, and the F# Major Piano Sonata, op. 78 (both composed in 1809), the Piano Trio (*Archduke*), op. 97 (1810–1811), and the final Violin Sonata in G Major, op. 96 (1812). Perhaps most conspicuously songlike from this group is the second movement in E major of the two-movement piano sonata in E minor, op. 90 (1814), whose main tune could easily be put to words and presented without suspicion as a song.

BEETHOVEN AS A WRITER OF SONGS

Beethoven wrote more songs than are extant, perhaps most famously an early setting of Friedrich Schiller's *An die Freude* for which two short sketches survive. From the first version of *An die Hoffnung*, op. 32, in 1805 to the revised version of *Der Kuss*, op. 128, in 1825, forty-three Beethoven songs were published with opus numbers during the composer's lifetime. Thirty-three songs were published without opus number (WoO), and another thirty-eight songs were published between 1836 and 1990. This adds up to 114 songs, coincidentally the same number of songs Charles Ives published at his own expense in 1922. Beethoven composed some of his songs considerably earlier than they were published. For example, most of the songs published as Eight Songs, op. 52, compiled between 1803 and 1805 and published the latter year, were composed during Beethoven's years in Bonn and the early years in Vienna. Based on publication dates, the trajectory of Beethoven's songs indicates fewer songs at the beginning and final phases of his career. Only ten songs survived from the Bonn years (1783–1792), the phase that also probably contains the most lost songs, and only seven songs Beethoven composed between 1817 and 1826 are extant, including the modestly revised *Der Kuss*.

Thirteen Beethoven songs were published during the early Vienna years (not counting the songs from op. 52) and twenty-five songs during the peak years of the "heroic" phase in the first decade of the nineteenth century. The high concentration of songs, thirty-five between 1809 and 1816, perhaps not surprisingly parallels the high concentration of lyrical instrumental pieces composed during these years. We noted in the previous chapter that Beethoven provided 179 arrangements of songs from the British Isles and the continent between 1809 and 1820 for the Edinburgh publisher George Thomson and that one of the Irish songs, *Save Me from the Grave and Wise* (known as *Nora Creina*), inspired the main theme of the Seventh Symphony finale.

It may be surprising to learn that songs necessitated proportionally more extensive sketching labor than instrumental movements. The manuscripts reveal numerous variants and alternatives to seemingly uncomplicated melodies. Those who think Beethoven could have conceived the relatively simple "Ode to Joy," if not in the shower (a later invention), perhaps on one of his daily walks, might be startled to see the extensive sketches for this tune, including numerous abandoned tangents. On occasion Beethoven set the same text more than once, a practice adopted to a far greater extent by Schubert. In the case of *An die Hoffnung*, Beethoven published both markedly dissimilar versions with opus numbers, op. 32 and op. 84, and no fewer than four versions of *Sehnsucht* with a text by Goethe without opus numbers together as WoO 134. A note on his autograph score for the latter set explains why: "I didn't have time to produce *one good one*, so here are several attempts" (Reid 2007, 250).

The two major approaches to setting a text during Beethoven's compositional years, and for years to come, were strophic and through-composed (the latter often referred by the German term *Durchkomponirt*). In a strophic song each stanza of text is set with the same melody, although the accompaniment can be greatly altered; in a pure through-composed song, each line of text receives its own music. Naturally, strophic songs are generally more straightforward and offer fewer opportunities for individual compositional nuances, especially when it comes to setting individual words. Strophic songs also tend to be more tuneful, folk-like, and more melodically memorable. Some through-composed songs, for example, the second setting of *An die Hoffnung*, also contain repetition, in this case a *da capo* of the main melody. Such hybrids may explain why one scholar contends that Beethoven composed an equal number of strophic and through-composed songs, while another scholar concludes that fully two-thirds of Beethoven's songs are strophic.

FIVE BEETHOVEN SONGS

Aus Goethe's "Faust" (From Goethe's "Faust"; known as the Mephisto's Flohlied, or Mephisto's Flea Song), Op. 75, No. 3 (1809; app. 2:00 min.)

The late publication date for this song is deceptive since we know from the manuscripts that Beethoven worked out much of it as early as 1790 while still in Bonn. More sketches appear among the earliest Vienna sketches in 1793. From these drafts we can determine that most of the tune is present as well as the recognizable roots of a piano part, the latter suggesting Beethoven's desire to musically capture the flitting nature of a particular flea (and his relatives). Sometime in 1809 Beethoven compiled a group of six songs, including three by Goethe, two by Christian Ludwig Reissig, and one by Gerhard Anton von Halem, and the songs were published together as a set in 1810 during the composer's most intense song phase. The song underwent melodic tweaking between 1793 and 1809, with the most conspicuous revisions focused on the rhythmic working out of the recurring flea music in the piano part. Interestingly, the song's punch line heard in the piano postlude cannot be detected in the earlier drafts.

The first three measures of the five-measure piano prelude introduce listeners to a flitting musical figure fit for a flea. In three stanzas with only minor melodic changes, altered to fit the varying syllabification of the text (i.e., the matching of musical notes to syllables), Mephisto, who has brought Faust to Auberch's tavern, responds to a student's song about a rat with a song about a flea. Mephisto's song tells the tale of a silly king who treats a pesky flea as a son, dresses it in princely garb, appoints it minister, and allows its relatives to run amuck and sting everyone in sight. Although the subjects were not allowed to "squash them and scratch them off their arms," in the end the chorus had enough and threatens to take the law (and the fleas) in their own hands—or in this case, thumbs—and smash the brutes.

One statement of the "flea motive" interrupts each stanza, and Beethoven follows each of the first two stanzas with an eight-measure piano interlude that features flea-like grace notes and trills, concluding with three statements of the flea motive. The music is set mostly in the minor mode (G minor) but with unpredictable and sudden moves to

major, for example, in the first stanza on the word wenig (a little) and
heran (duly), culminating in a dramatic and surprising (at the least the
first time) move to G *major* on the final note of each stanza. On each
occasion the piano thwarts this major mode conclusion by returning
hastily back to G minor.

At the end of the third stanza the "Chorus" enters with the music
formerly stated by the piano on the following words: "Wir knicken und
ersticken / Doch gleich, wenn einer sticht" (But we'll squash and suffo-
cate / Soon enough, if someone stings us). Instead of following the
interlude to its natural conclusion with the flea motives, the chorus
repeats its initial complaint with an angry and steady stream of sixteenth
notes, alternating between a measure that opens with the major melodic note B natural and major chord (G major) and one with a minor
mode statement (the note B-flat and a G minor chord). Major reigns
victorious as the voice concludes with five repetitions of the same note
that ended each stanza (a B natural) while the piano repeats a G major
triad topped by a B natural, four times in the penultimate vocal measure and eight times in the final vocal measure.

Also on this final sung measure the piano states another eight G
major triads against repetitive thirty-second-note melodic oscillations
between C and B natural. This figure becomes the basis for another six
thirty-second note figures, each with a short one-half or whole-step
descent. The score of the penultimate measure of the song includes
something not often seen in Beethoven's piano music, fingering markings in the right hand as it descends down the keys. Scholars believe
these marks to be genuine: C–B, A–G, E–D, C–B (the latter C–B one
octave lower). Above each of these notes Beethoven offers the same
fingering, a "1," which stands for the thumb. It may be bad form to spoil
a joke, but the following recollection of Frau Pessiak-Schmerling is
definitely worth retelling. Frau Pessiak was the niece of Beethoven's
friend Fanny Giannatasio del Rio, whose parents ran the private school
where Beethoven's nephew Karl boarded in 1816:

> On another day Beethoven brought with him a number of songs,
> including the one from *Faust* beginning: "Es war einmal ein König
> der hatt' einen grossen Floh" ("Once upon a time there was a king
> who had a large flea"). Laughing, Beethoven "took his seat at the
> pianoforte and played them the conclusion in which he pressed
> down two adjacent keys with his thumb at the same time and said:

'That's the way to kill him!' Mother and Aunt also had to have a try at this thing which had amused him so." (Forbes 1964, 666–67)

An die Hoffnung (To Hope), Op. 32 (1805; app. 5:20 min.)

Vocal music offers potential gateways to the autobiographical realm that instrumental works rarely reveal. For example, Beethoven's identification with and attraction to the ideas of freedom and conjugal love in *Fidelio* are rarely disputed. In the case of the first setting of *An die Hoffnung* (1805), *Dimmi, ben mio*, op. 82/1 (1809), and the cycle *An die ferne Geliebte*, op. 98 (1816), the time period in which they were composed, the choice of texts, and some direct evidence also point to autobiographical interpretations. We know, for example, that Beethoven had offered the 1805 setting of *An die Hoffnung* to Josephine Brunswick as a gift earlier that same year. Josephine, still sometimes presented as a candidate as Beethoven's Immortal Beloved, despite the absence of documentary evidence, was Beethoven's student and patron during her marriage to Count Joseph Deym. After Deym's death in 1804, Beethoven and Josephine became emotionally close and the fourteen extant letters between them clearly demonstrate the composer's love for Josephine along with Josephine's affection for Beethoven, albeit an affection that fell short of physical desire. In March 1805 Josephine wrote her mother about Beethoven's "present of a pretty song, *An die Hoffnung*" (Reid 2007, 62), but by the time the song was published later that year, the romance was over and the song contained no dedication.

The poem is part of a larger collection reprinted eleven times before 1837 by the now obscure Christoph August Tiedge whom Beethoven met in 1811. It is natural to conclude that Beethoven would gravitate to a song about hope, a state of mind also embodied in Leonore's aria "Komm, Hoffnung" (Come, hope), composed around the same time. The first stanza of this strophic setting highlights the word "Hoffnung" with a modulation from the tonic Eb major to C major, by leaping up a hopeful major sixth (the largest melodic leap of the song) on the word "hope," and by giving this word the longest and highest note of the song. But hope is quickly challenged, one measure after the hopeful leap, by the simultaneous presence of a dominant seventh of C in the voice and right-hand offbeat accompaniment against Cs on each beat in the left hand and then in the next measure where the return of C major is followed by C minor. Neither hope nor C major will return, and the next phrase sets up a return to Eb major that also will not recur. Instead, Beethoven concludes the first statement of these three lines with a diminished-seventh chord on C, a musical bridge to nowhere.

Since Beethoven chose to repeat the final lines of this stanza that begin with "hope," he needed to set the word again. This time he sets "hope" melodically with a tense tritone and harmonically with a dissonant diminished-seventh chord, an ambiguous chord carried over from an unfulfilled return to the tonic two measures earlier. The second time through these final lines, Beethoven offers virtually the same rhythms as the first statement before joining pitch and rhythm on the final words, "ein Engle seine Thränen zählt" (an Angel keeps record of his tears). Although Beethoven fulfills the tonal expectations of his era and ends the song firmly on the tonic, he nonetheless makes it clear that the lover's hopeful expectations were musically dashed, as Beethoven's hope with Josephine was dashed.

Beethoven's strophic setting offers a perfect match for the first stanza of the poem. The second and third stanzas are less precise. This is the perennial problem with strophic songs in which a single melody must fit all texts. Nevertheless, the words of these subsequent stanzas depict what might be interpreted as hopeful ideas, even if these too are ultimately thwarted touches due to diminished sevenths and delayed harmonic resolutions. Creating a musical setting that serves with comparable specificity is the inherent problem of strophic settings, a reality that perhaps inspired Beethoven ten years later to compose a through-composed setting of Tiedge's poem, op. 94. The advantage of a strophic setting is that it can sustain a mood, if not specific words, as in the case of op. 32, which convey the sentiment that emotional suffering and patience can be rewarded by hope. The piano sets all this up with an arpeggiated introduction that prepares for the tonic, an arpeggiated transition to the hopeful C major, the unfulfilled resolution to the ambiguous diminished-seventh chord before the second statement of "hope," and the return to the tonic. The memorable songlike melody is mainly stepwise with occasional leaps that fall on significant words. For some, including myself, the melody of Beethoven's first setting of *An die Hoffnung* possesses a directness and simplicity not found in its more complex successor, a lyrical melody worthy of Schubert.

Dimmi, Ben Mio, Che M'ami (Tell Me You Love Me), Op. 82, No. 1 (1809; app. 2:00 min.)

The poet of *Dimmi, ben mio* is unknown, although the well-known Pietro Metastasio wrote the texts for the other five songs of op. 82. In fact, the poem would probably be unknown were it not for Beethoven's setting. Several writers have suggested that, as with *Wonne der Wehmuth*, the five Italian songs published in this set were written with Beethoven's hoped-for beloved, Therese Malfatti, in mind, but it is also possible that the songs were completed before he met and fell in love with this young woman of Italian ancestry. In any event it is not difficult to imagine how the text might reflect Beethoven's strong feelings for Therese. Either way, within its two stanzas and eight lines, repeated all in less than three minutes, Beethoven clearly wrote an unabashed love song. Here is the poem as translated by Paul Reid in *The Beethoven Song Companion*.

Dimmi, ben mio, che m'ami,	Tell me, darling, that you love me,
Dimmi che mia tu sei,	Tell me you are mine,
E non invidio ai Dei	And I shall not envy the gods
La lor divinità.	Their divinity.
Con un tuo sguardo solo,	With a single glance,
Cara, con un sorriso	Sweetheart, with one smile
Tu m'apri il paradiso	You open for me the paradise
Di mia felicità.	Of my contentment.

The move from A major to C major without a proper modulation is the main surprise of the first statement of the text. One moment the music is stating a prolonged dominant seventh of A major; in the next the music fails to resolve to the expected tonic and swerves without warning directly to C major (beginning with "tu m'apri il paradiso" and concluding with the return of the opening word "Dimmi"). Including a false return of the main tune, Beethoven stays in C major nearly as long (eight measures) as he had remained in the tonic A major earlier in the song (the first eleven measures). During the second musical statement of the complete text, instead of returning to the remote region of C major, the music quickly (after five measures) turns to the subdominant or IV chord (D major) on the words "solo cara," with the word "cara" (sweetheart) repeated for emphasis. After two resolutions to the center of this key on the word "sorriso" (smile), the music returns without a clear modulation to A major on the "di" syllable of "paradiso" (paradise), reserving a brief confirmatory modulation for the final syllable of "felicità" (contentment).

In both stanzas Beethoven takes a liberty with the text by repeating the final line. Also, as with the "Trocknet nicht" exhortation we will observe in *Wonne der Wehmuth*, Beethoven selected first a word and then a phrase for special emphasis. In *Dimmi, ben mio, che m'ami*, the main singled-out word is "Dimmi" (tell me). We first hear the word repeated before the return of the second stanza when the voice utters this plea in a return statement of the main melody in the piano. At this point in the song the music is still dwelling in the remote key of C major. Immediately, the piano, still in C major, starts the main tune again but swerves to the dominant, where it is again answered by "Dimmi." Beethoven then prolongs the dominant another four measures on the words "Dimmi m'ami" (tell me you love me). Finally, the music returns to restate the beginning of the first stanza, only the first three measures of which are the same as the first statement. Beethoven also chose to repeat the final line, "Di mia felicità" (of my contentment) no less than three times in succession at the end of the first time through the text and twice at the end of the second, each time with different music.

When Beethoven repeats the final stanza one last time, he uses the same harmonic progression described earlier but with an almost completely new melody. This second time, instead of establishing D, Beethoven quickly shifts to the dominant of the original tonic, thus establishing a clear musical pathway to the original tonic (A major), along with a *crescendo*, to "paradiso." The climax of the song arrives one measure later when the music reinforces the singer's "felicità" on the highest repeated pitch of the song (an F#), the third of the subdominant, before resolving the immediately repeated word "felicità" solidly on the tonic. In the briefest of piano postludes, we hear the first musical line of text (without words) one last time before a scalar flourish and emphatic V–I cadence. Thus closes Beethoven's unfortunately barely known modest but masterful impersonation of the Italian *cantabile* style. It may not sound like the Beethoven we think we know, but it's a first-rate song nonetheless.

Wonne der Wehmuth (Bliss in Sorrow), Op. 83, No. 1 (1810; app. 2:50 min.)

Both Schubert and Beethoven set more songs to poems by Germany's famous poet, Johann Wolfgang von Goethe (1749–1832), than to any other poet, seventy-four by Schubert (out of more than six hundred songs) and twenty-two of the one hundred fourteen songs by Beethoven. In addition, Beethoven wrote the incidental music to Goethe's play *Egmont*, used the poet's text as the source of *Meeresstille und glückliche Fahrt* (*Calm Sea and Prosperous Voyage*) for chorus and orchestra, and contemplated composing music for *Faust* (beyond *Mephisto's Flea Song* discussed earlier). The great exponents of their respective domains were also well aware of one another, corresponded on a number of occasions, and met once or twice in 1812.

We have noted conjectures that *Wonne der Wehmuth*, like *Dimmi, ben mio*, was composed for Therese Malfatti, perhaps in response to an unrequited romance the same year. In any event, it is easy to imagine that the idea of Goethe's poem would fit a man shedding tears over an unhappy love. Within a few lines Goethe captures the poignant beauty and sadness of a loving memory and espouses the view that the inability to cry leads to a deadened emotional void. Here are Goethe's six lines as translated by Reid in *The Beethoven Song Companion*. The title has been variously translated. I prefer "Bliss in Sorrow" to Reid's "Joy of Melancholy."

Trocknet nicht, trocknet nicht,	Never dry, never dry,
Tränen der ewigen Liebe!	Tears of eternal love!
Ach! Nur dem halbgetrockneten Auge	Ah, how desolate, how dead the world appears
Wie öde, wie tot die Welt ihm erscheint!	To eyes that have even half-dried!
Trocknet nicht, trocknet nicht,	Never dry, never dry,
Tränen der ewigen Liebe!	Tears of eternal love!

Wonne der Wehmuth, the first of three Goethe song settings published as op. 83 in 1810, contains twenty-three measures and lasts less than three minutes. Only one measure, the first, is nearly identical to another, the first measure of the restated final pair of lines (measure 16). The repetition, a result of repeated lines and added statements of the phrase "trocknet nicht" ("never dry") prior to the third line of text and again at the end of the song, doubles the number of times the poet implores his subject not to dry his or her tears. In nearly every case (the exceptions are measures 1 and 16), the vocal line expresses these words with alternate pitches and several rhythmic possibilities and a repeated rapid descending scalar motive in the piano, a motive regularly interpreted as the flowing of tears. The song, for the most part through-composed, offers numerous interactions and dialogue between the singer and the piano.

The song's emotional center stems from its response to the plea, uttered eight times, not to dry one's tears. The second repetition on the second measure is the same as the first, intensified by its repetition one note higher. The third and fourth statements offer a single pitch in the voice on the second beat as the piano guides the singer with the music that began the song. The first statement is combined with the descending scale, the fourth without accompaniment, *pianissimo*, with a rhythm identical to the sound of the quail in the "Brook" movement of the *Pastoral* Symphony. The final statement is the same as the first four notes of the scale of tears, after which the piano answers with the same four notes before continuing the scale down an octave. The music moves from E major to minor on the word "Tot," and the voice repeats G, the minor third above E minor, six times. Toward the end of the song Beethoven returns to the note G, now up an octave, first in the voice on the word "Tränen" (tears) for the highest, loudest, fullest (a seven-note chord), most dissonant (a diminished seventh), and longest-held note of the song, and then repeated by the piano.

Der Kuss (The Kiss), Op. 128 (1822; app. 1:50 min.)

As with the *Flea Song*, *Der Kuss* demonstrates the humorous side of the composer even as he was deeply engaged with such grandiose compositions as the *Missa solemnis* and the Ninth Symphony. Also as with the

Flea Song, Der Kuss was begun years earlier. By 1798 he had completed a piano accompaniment of the song, an accompaniment not unlike that of the final version. In December 1822 he revised the song and finished a new autograph score, and the song was published in 1825 as an "Ariette." *Der Kuss* would be the last song published in Beethoven's lifetime.

Here is the complete text, written by Christian Felix Weisse, originally published in the collection *Scherzhafte Lieder* (*Light-hearted poems*) in 1758 and reprinted in Vienna in 1793, as translated in Reid's *Beethoven Song Companion*:

Ich war bei Chloen ganz allein,	I was all alone with Chloe
Und küssen wollt' ich sie;	And wanted to kiss her;
Jedoch sie sprach, sie würde schrein,	But she said she would scream,
Es sei vergebne Müh'.	And I was wasting my time.
Ich wagt' es doch, und küsste sie	I risked it nevertheless, and kissed her,
Trotz ihrer Gegenwehr.	Despite her resistance.
Und schrie sie nicht?	And didn't she scream?
Jawohl, sie schrie,	Oh yes, she screamed.
Doch lange hinterher.	But only long afterwards.

We have observed Beethoven's liberties with song texts, including his practice of repeating a stanza, especially key phrases and important individual words such as "Trocknet nicht" in *Wonne der Wehmuth* and "Dimmi" in *Dimmi, ben mio, che m'ami*. *Der Kuss* takes this practice to a new level and with many examples, only a sample of which can be included in the discussion that follows.

After a generous nine-measure piano prelude that introduces the main tune with its overall gradually ascending melodic line (first A–B–C#–D–E and then C#–D–E–F#–G#–A–B), the first line of text repeats the first measures of the prelude, emphasizing the first scale, after which the music states the C#–D–E on the second beats on the thrice-repeated word "küssen" (to kiss). The next line continues with another version of the opening ascending five-note scale from A up to E, this time with three repetitions of "sie würde schrein" (she would scream) with a long held note on the final "scream." Chloe "*would* scream" (in the German subjunctive, i.e., hypothetical sense) *four* times, but she never actually *does* scream, not even once.

In the second stanza Beethoven singles out the word "Gegenwehr" (resistance) for special treatment by creating five-note melismas on the first syllable (a melisma is a long melodic passage sung to a single syllable of text), the second melisma ascending the familiar scale from A up to E in the process but then immediately lowering the E an octave on the last two syllables as if to convey the idea that Chloe's resistance is a pretense. The piano returns to the opening phrase ending with C#–D–E, and the voice answers with the same notes on the words "Und schrie sie nicht?" (and didn't she scream?), now *Poco adagio*. In this slower tempo the piano repeats the question with an added trill. Back in tempo the vocal line ascends two notes further, F# and G# on the repeated words "sie schrie" (she screamed).

Above a new (and repeated) piano motive Beethoven now chooses to emphasize "doch" (but). After the second "doch," the score indicates a fermata followed by the verbal direction "lächelnd" (smiling) above the third "doch." This is a new starting point in the final line of text, "Doch lange hinterher" (but only long afterwards). The key word here is "lange" (long), a word Beethoven repeats no less than twelve times in the final seconds of this two-minute song, including *nine* times in a row. The implication is that the kiss lasted a long time and that Chloe was in no hurry to scream. The piano gets the last word in the briefest of postludes, just enough time to insert one more statement of the scale from A to E.

The recapitulation in the first movement of the Ninth symphony was famously described by Susan McClary in a 1987 issue of *Minnesota Composers Forum Newsletter* as a passage that expresses "the "throttling, murderous rage of a rapist incapable of attaining release." A modified and considerably toned-down version of this description, which appeared in *Feminine Endings: Music, Gender, and Sexuality* (1991), removes the rapist reference, but commentators perhaps more often prefer to cite the earlier and more incendiary description. Still, the day I first drafted my remarks about this song I came across a short article in my school newspaper called "Consent Basics: Pre-101," the gist of which is that the romantically inclined should get used to the idea they need to secure a person's consent before they kiss or touch. Since Chloe did not actually formally agree, if I were a Lieder singer I would hesitate before performing this song on a campus recital. Chloe's struggle might have been interpreted to be feigned in the 1820s, but in an age when no unequivocally must mean no, we might remain wary of the subtext of this seemingly innocent song.

AN DIE FERNE GELIEBTE (TO THE DISTANT BELOVED), OP. 98 (1816; APP. 13:40 MIN. TOTAL)

1. "Auf dem Hügel sitz' ich, spähend" ("I sit on the hill, peering"; Eb major; 2:40 min.)
2. "Wo die Berge so blau" ("Where the mountains so blue"; G major; 1:45 min.)
3. "Leichte Segler in den Höhen" ("Light clouds gliding aloft"; Ab major; 1:40 min.)
4. "Diese Wolken in den Höhen" ("These clouds high up above"; Ab major; 1:10 min.)
5. "Es kehret der Maien" ("May returns"; C major; 2:10 min.)
6. "Nimm sie hin den, diese Lieder" ("Accept them then, these songs"; Eb major; 4:15 min.)

One of the great Romantic musical inventions was the song cycle, a coherent and integral group of songs, usually but not invariably by a single poet. The most famous collections of this new and important genre were two groups of songs by Schubert, *Die schöne Müllerin* (*The Fair Maid of the Mill*), twenty songs set to the poetry of Wilhelm Müller in 1823, and the twenty-four-song collection *Winterreise* (*Winter Journey*) composed in 1827, also set to poems by Müller. The next major group of song cycles appeared a few years later during Robert Schumann's year of song, 1840, most famously *Liederkreis* (*Song Cycle*), op. 39 (twelve songs), *Frauenliebe und-leben* (*Woman's Love and Life*), op. 42 (eight songs), and *Dichterliebe* (*A Poet's Love*), op. 48 (sixteen songs).

The term "song cycle" used to label these sets by Schubert and Schumann (and later in the century Johannes Brahms and Hugo Wolf, among others) is rarely used with precision. In fact, only one of the "cycles" mentioned (*Frauenliebe*) is truly cyclic in the sense that earlier parts return in later parts of the cycle. The earliest significant song cycle in either its precise or more inclusive definition is Beethoven's *An die ferne Geliebte*. Beethoven set all six of these songs to the poetry of a single poet, Alois Jeitteles, who wrote the poems while a medical student and who later spent most of his career as a physician. Scholars conjecture that Jeitteles may have been introduced to Beethoven by a mutual acquaintance, the dramatist Ignaz Castelli, and that Jeitteles sent Beethoven a handwritten copy of the texts.

As with several of the songs discussed in this chapter, it is likely that Beethoven found personal meaning in Jeitteles poems about a love that is separated by time and distance and suggested that Beethoven expressly asked the poet for a group of poems on this subject. Assuming, as the majority of scholars still do, that the identity of his Immortal Beloved four years earlier was Antonie Brentano, by the time Beethoven wrote this cycle, she had since returned to distant Frankfurt with her husband and family.

The song begins with the poet sitting on a hill long separated from his beloved by physical distance and taking solace in his art. This is also not unlike the message of Beethoven's semi-suicidal message to his brothers in 1802, the document known as the Heiligenstadt Testament. The messengers of the poet's love are the composer's songs, "songs of lament that tell you of my anguish." In the final song the poet returns to the songs' message in a subtle reworking of the opening song. The poet asks his distant beloved to "accept them then, these songs which I sang for you, my love" and to "sing what I sang what sounded from my overflowing heart." As the music returns unmistakably to the first song, the poet optimistically affirms that "in the face of these songs, what kept us so far apart will evaporate." If ever a group of songs supported what we imagine Beethoven might have been feeling and thinking in 1816, it would be these six songs. In any event, Beethoven and Antonie maintained their musical communication, perhaps most notably seven years later when Antonie became the dedicatee of one of Beethoven's most important compositions, the *Diabelli* Variations discussed in the next chapter.

The songs themselves are almost folk-like in their simplicity, and all six exhibit some kind of a strophic structure. In some cases Beethoven alters a musical parameter, but he never departs from the essential melody of the opening stanza. In the first song he varies the accompaniment significantly in each of the five stanzas, while in the second song he offers what is perhaps the only internal modulation within a song (from G major to C major) and allows the piano, *pianissimo*, to repeat the initial melody with a repeated G in the voice, an ingenious touch that graphically reveals the singer's distance from the melody of his beloved. In the third song Beethoven varies the stanzas by largely retaining the original melody but switching from Ab major to minor for the third, fourth, and fifth stanzas.

Another striking feature of the cycle is Beethoven's desire to link the songs with transitions that make it difficult for any of the songs to be extracted from the cycle and performed separately. This is in sharp contrast to the independence (as well as interdependence) of most of the songs in Schubert's two cycles. Let's look further at these transitions.

At the end of the first song a brief piano postlude arrives at a prolonged octave G with Eb as the harmonic foundation. After two more Gs supported by Eb, the melody stays on G, but the harmony around it has changed from Eb to G. G major may be remote from Eb, but since they share a G (the tonic in G, the third in Eb), the change from Eb to G is natural and effortless, even though it does not constitute a true modulation. The transition to song number 3 is more sudden. One moment the music is in G major; the next moment it moves up a half step to Ab major (the subdominant of the original song). Since song numbers 3 and 4 share tonal centers, no transition is strictly necessary, but Beethoven provides one anyway as he takes a moment to move from the Ab minor where song 3 ended by sounding a prolonged (i.e., endless) Eb on the last word of song 3, on the words "ohne Zahl" (endless number) of tears. The transition from the Ab major of song 4 and the C major of song 5 is the most like a traditional harmonic progression, prolonged in an extended piano prelude (twelve measures) before we arrive at the main tune in C major.

At the end of song 5 Beethoven leaves the prevailing *Vivace* and adds several measures in an *Adagio* that take the music to C minor for the first time in a song that has reveled in C major. Without warning, Beethoven moves to the key of the first song, Eb, with a leisurely eight-measure piano prelude. Such an abrupt nonmodulation is possible because Beethoven moves to the tonic from Ab, which shares a common melodic note with C major/minor (C is the major third of Ab). The music shifts to the first stanza of this sixth song, the only through-composed stanza in the cycle.

But something far more unusual and ingenious is going on in this final song, which is more than twice the length of any of the previous four songs. As the poet asks the beloved to sing back the songs he sang to her, Beethoven's new song bears a noticeable family resemblance and melodic contour to the song that opened the cycle. Upon closer examination one discovers that the resemblance goes much further and deeper. In fact, the new song contains virtually all the notes of the earlier song. It is a magical variation, a true thematic transformation, a metamorphosis, and the more we hear the cycle the more we realize that we are hearing the original song, but with new insight. The second time through this new song the poet tells his beloved that "you sing what I sang," in other words that *her* song is *his* song. The music conveys the same message.

The piano then literally returns to the first song, and the poet joins in with words that inform the distant beloved that "in the face of these songs, what kept us so far apart will evaporate." The memory of their shared music will keep their love eternal. The tempo markings accelerate as the music moves from *Ziemlich langsam und mit Ausdruck* (rather slowly and with expression) to *Allegro molto e con brio* (very fast and with spirit). The first time Beethoven states the final line of text, "what a loving heart has blessed," he alters the ending slightly from the way it was in the first song and places a fermata above the final word. At the end of all five stanzas in the first song and the first two statements in the final song, Beethoven offers a low Eb. The final phrase of the cycle, the first and only *fortissimo* of the cycle, repeats the last line of text but with a new musical line in which all the emphasized notes are a high G, the highest note of the cycle with the strongest G accents on the *lie-* in "liebend" (loving) and "Herz" (heart). Beethoven emphasizes the word "liebend" further by repeating it and by giving each statement of this word a melisma that lasts an entire measure (a four-note melisma the first time, five notes the second). The piano gets the last "word" when it returns to the final phrase of the first song before it closes with a return to the opening notes of the cycle, the anticipation of yet another new beginning.

7

THE LATE PIANO MUSIC (1816–1824)

We had only needed, he said, to hear the piece to answer the question ourselves.

—Professor Wendell Kretschmar, a character in Thomas Mann's novel, on the question of why Beethoven did not write a second movement to the Piano Sonata op. 111. Thomas Mann, *Doctor Faustus* (1947)

Between 1795 and 1822 Beethoven composed thirty-two pianos sonatas, far more works than any other major instrumental genre. During the course of this survey we have looked at five sonatas from the early and middle years: no. 7 in D Major, op. 10, no. 3; no. 8 in C Minor, (*Pathétique*), op. 13; no. 14 in C# Minor (*Moonlight*), op. 27, no. 2; no. 17 in D Minor (*Tempest*), op. 31, no. 2; and no. 23 in F Minor (*Appassionata*), op. 57. In this chapter we will feature the last two sonatas from Beethoven's final quintet of piano sonatas composed between 1816 and 1822: no. 31 in Ab Major, op. 110 (December 1821) and no. 32 in C Minor, op. 111 (January 1822). Along with the three previous late sonatas, no. 28 in A Major, op. 101 (1816), no. 29 in Bb Major (*Hammerklavier*), op. 106 (1818), and no. 30 in E Major, op. 109 (1821), these bold and imaginative works demonstrate the central features of Beethoven's late style, including sharp contrasts between movements and within movements; movements and passages of extreme lyricism alongside moments that leave lyricism far behind; a sharply increased attention to counterpoint (including fugatos and fugues); and a predilection for theme-and-variation movements. It is also worth noting that at the same time that he began exploring new formal solutions, Beethoven retained the essential principles of classic sonata form in at least one movement of his late works, even as he challenged these principles in imaginative ways.

None of these sonatas, and for that matter none of the last five string quartets or other works of Beethoven's last years, with the exception of the Ninth Symphony, match the works of the middle years in popularity with performers and audiences. For the most part the later works were intended for connoisseurs and meant to be heard in private or in more intimate gatherings such as salons rather than concert halls. Public piano recitals were virtually unknown in Beethoven's lifetime. In fact, only one or perhaps two public performances of a piano sonata are known. The public string quartet concert arrived only in time for the late quartets. In the years since, Beethoven's final sonatas and quartets, staples of the public concert, have acquired enormous critical prestige, to the point where they are often regarded as among the wonders of musical civilization. With the ready availability of recordings in many formats, as well as frequent public performances, listeners have been amply rewarded for their willingness to give these works a chance to be heard and reheard to the point where it is probably fair to claim that Beethoven's challenging later works beyond the Ninth continue to gain increasing accessibility, appreciation, and audiences far larger than could have been foreseen in Beethoven's own time.

SONATA NO. 31 IN AB MAJOR, OP. 110 (1821)

After the adulation and attention during the Congress of Vienna in 1814 and the immense success of works such as the Seventh Symphony and *Wellington's Victory*, Beethoven's personal and musical fortunes began to take a downward turn. The death of his brother Carl in 1815 led to a five-year legal battle to obtain custody of his nephew Karl that ended with a Pyrrhic victory in 1820. Beethoven reached successful financial settlements with the heirs of Prince Kinsky and won financial claims against Prince Lobkowitz to restore the value of the original annuity of 1809, undermined by the post-Napoleonic currency devaluation. But with his legal and medical expenses, educational costs for Karl, and his own reduced productivity, Beethoven remained deeply concerned with money issues. In 1818 his hearing entered a steep decline, and although he never became fully deaf, for the rest of his life he would be dependent on conversation books, many of which have survived and have proven useful to Beethoven scholars and enthusiasts.

While his production never again matched the vigorous compositional output of 1800 to 1810, Beethoven managed to create a new style during the leaner years that followed, a style that by 1820 had taken root in a small but significant group of compositions that included the cello sonatas, op. 102 in 1815; the song cycles *An die ferne Geliebte* and the Piano Sonata op. 101 in 1816; the monumental Piano Sonata op. 106 in 1818; the first twenty-three of his *Diabelli* Variations in 1819; and the Piano Sonata op. 109 in 1820, the latter work begun shortly after the custody battle was settled in his favor and sent out for publication early in 1821.

The Ab Major Sonata op. 110 was the second of three sonatas commissioned by the Berlin publisher Maurice Schlesinger. Before he began concentrated work on the sonata, however, he returned to the *Missa solemnis* (begun in 1819) and the piano bagatelles that would one day comprise nos. 7–11 of op. 119. Shortly afterward he became sick, and the compositional record goes virtually silent for nearly nine months of 1821; some evidence warrants the conclusion that Beethoven was forced to remain in bed for six weeks. Due perhaps to a combination of factors, including the fact that some documents may have been lost in transport, no conversation books survive, and only four letters survive for the entire year of 1821. Still, by the end of the year Beethoven completed much of the final movements of his mass and was able to both start and finish op. 110. He then turned directly to his final sonata, completed it relatively quickly, and sent it to Schlesinger by February 1822.

With its considerable lyricism, humor, passion, and uplifting finale, op. 110 is probably the most popular and accessible of the late sonatas. It is also one of the most unified of any Beethoven sonata with its wide array of shared musical material from one movement to another. The work is nominally in three movements. However, the substantial final movement contains an introduction and two contrasting but connecting parts, each repeated with significant departures. The first movement *Moderato cantabile molto espressivo* is in a remarkably concentrated sonata form, and the middle movement, *Allegro molto*, is an A–B–A *scherzo*, although not labeled as such, in duple meter. The finale is a complex hybrid beginning with what has been described as an operatic scene with its "orchestral" introduction, recitative (so labeled), and an *arioso*, the latter labeled by Beethoven both in Italian as *Arioso dolente* or plaintive song and parenthetically in German as *Klagender Gesang* (an arioso is a heightened recitative, but falling short of a full-scaled aria). The finale's second part is a fugue (labeled FUGA), *Allegro ma non troppo*, after which the music returns to shortened versions of the both the *Arioso* and the *Fuga*. The entire sonata takes about nineteen minutes to play with the first movement about six and a half minutes, the *scherzo* about two minutes, and the finales a little over half of the grand total or about ten and a half minutes.

First Movement: *Moderato Cantabile Molto Espressivo*

The first movement is most definitely another candidate for the "lyrical Beethoven" designation discussed in the last chapter. It is also for the most part dynamically understated, beginning *piano* and only once escalating to *forte* for three measures when the second theme arrives at a clear resolution in the highest piano register to the dominant midway through the exposition. As with the Fifth Symphony much of the first movement (and the sonata as a whole) grows from the opening musical material, but this time Beethoven transforms his central motive into a song. In the reverse of the Fifth Symphony with its descending major third followed by a descending minor third starting one step lower, in the opening Ab major sonata melody, the melody I will call the "first" first theme begins in the first measure with a descending major third above a chordal texture followed in the second measure with a descending minor third starting one step *higher*. The interval of the third will also figure prominently in the "second" first theme that begins after four measures.

But before we get there it is important to mention a more significant melody imbedded in these opening measures. If for a moment the listener imagines that the opening chord (a tonic Ab major triad) is a one-note preamble to the main tune instead of two successive descending thirds, what this listener will hear is a melody consisting of two successive *ascending fourths*. The first serves as an upbeat to the second measure; the second, an upbeat to the third measure. In the fourth and final measure of this introductory "first" first theme, Beethoven provides the delayed third successive fourth and fills in the interval as a scale, first ascending then descending. Thus the melody that begins with two successive descending thirds in the first two measures evolves over the short course of the "first" first theme into a second melody consisting of three ascending fourths (the third delayed): Ab–Db, Bb–Eb, C–F (three ascending fourths). After a trilled fermata, a final fourth *descends* from F to C in the context of a scale. The arrival on C launches the "second" first theme.

At this early stage of the sonata the listener might ask, "How do we interpret the function of this 'first' first theme? Is it a theme that begins with two successive descending thirds or a theme with three ascending fourths?" It may take until we arrive at the FUGA to fully answer this question, but long before we get there we will learn that the main theme of the first movement, and significant parts of the second, consists of a theme based on fourths. Listeners will later discover that the subject of the FUGA consists of the *same* three fourths we heard in the first four measures of the movement, Ab–Db, Bb–Eb, C–F, and the descending scale down from F (F–Eb–Db–C). Thus the fugue subject, which we will in the end hear many times, because fugues state their subjects many times, serves as an audible return of the "first" first main theme. The fugue subject completes the "first" first theme more quickly but preserves both the melodic identity and the lyrical quality of the music that opened the sonata, although Beethoven will hide the identity of his central theme for another twenty minutes.

The "second" first theme is even more songlike, with a lyrical melody supported by a simple sixteenth-note accompaniment. The new theme, which consists of two four-measure phrases, also offers a number of thirds and fourths, but its central melodic identity is a series of broken triads, that is, *arpeggios*. On the eighth and final measure of this new theme, the thematic broken triads turn into rapid and *piano* thirty-second notes outlining arpeggiated triads that will serve as the transition section of the exposition that guides rather than pushes the music from the first key to the second, the latter in the dominant Eb. The arrival at Eb is far from a straight musical line, however, since Beethoven is slow to acknowledge this move to the dominant and slow to offer a clear-cut second theme at all. Instead, the music moves rapidly from melodic fragment to fragment until a series of trills in the left hand and a *cres-*

cendo proclaim the previously mentioned solitary *forte* and the first firm modulation to the second key. This part of the theme section states three ascending six-note scales (another unifying device throughout the sonata). The six-note scales are followed by a short, lyrical closing theme that comfortably but firmly rests on the dominant. Repetition may be the key to wisdom, but in this sonata, the exposition does not repeat.

In earlier chapters we have come across several substantial development sections, most notably the developments of the *Eroica* Symphony and the first *Razumovsky* quartet. Among the piano sonatas the development of the *Appassionata* Sonata was a few measures longer than the exposition. The late piano sonatas reveal a contrasting approach to classical sonata style. In fact, most of the first movements in the late sonatas are compact, concentrated, and pithy. The entire first movement of op. 101 lasts only about four minutes, of which the development occupies one of these minutes. The first movement of op. 109 is even shorter, roughly about three and one half minutes with the entire development lasting only thirty seconds. The development of the op. 111 barely outlasts its predecessor with a forty-second development. These are extraordinarily short developments. The development of op. 110 lasts about fifty seconds and occupies only sixteen measures. The only exception is op. 106, which boasts a first movement of nearly twelve minutes (with the exposition repeat), including a full-scale, two-minute development.

Classical composers enjoyed an abundance of options concerning what musical ideas from the exposition they chose to develop, and most composers take advantage of these opportunities. In op. 110 Beethoven decided to use only four notes from the exposition: the first four notes with the two thirds. The entire development consists of eight repetitions of these two third intervals, two measures each, to achieve its grand total of sixteen measures. After two longish chords to clear the formal palette, the first seven measures of the development start in the relative minor of Ab major (i.e., F minor) before moving to Db major (the subdominant), among other keys. Interestingly, although in a new key, the first F minor statement uses the identical four notes that opened the movement (C–Ab–Db–Bb). After its first appearance Beethoven varies the starting note four times during the course of the remaining fourteen measures. It is fair to say that Beethoven has reinvented the development once again, this time by shortening it instead of lengthening it, as he did in the *Eroica* and the first *Razumovsky* quartet.

At the ninth repetition of the four-note motive in the development, Beethoven returns yet again to the original opening notes (C–Ab–Db–Bb). We are now home in the tonic Ab major and ready for the recapitulation. The left hand, instead of duplicating the rhythm of the right as it did in the opening four measures of the movement, now accompanies the return of the "first" first theme with the thirty-second-note arpeggiated chords familiar from the transition of the exposition. Throughout his career Beethoven, unlike Mozart, rather than following the exposition closely, regularly offers significant departures in his recapitulations. The departures in the recapitulation of the op. 110 sonata not only surpass Beethoven's usual practice but also far surpass the level of harmonic and melodic *development* recently offered in the sonata's puzzlingly short development section. The first major departure occurs when Beethoven arrives at the "second" first theme. According to recapitulation protocol, he should still be in the tonic, where he would state the "first" first theme in the tonic accompanied by thirty-second-note *arpeggios*. Instead Beethoven states the "second" first theme in the subdominant, Db, a key area foreshadowed in the development. Since the note Db is the enharmonic C#, it is not difficult to move from Db major to C# minor, although this degree of harmonic "development" is rare in a recapitulation.

What happens next may not be easy to follow without precise references to measure numbers (for score readers the passage begins at measure 67), but it is well worth the attempt because of several fascinating subtle but significant connections between this piece, Beethoven's previous piano sonata, op. 109, and many later works by Beethoven and his successors. After one measure of C# minor, Beethoven moves one step lower on B to a dominant seventh of E major for two measures and in fact arrives at the promised land of E major. But E major is quite a remote key area in the key of Ab and far from where Beethoven should be at this late stage in the work. Some Beethoven scholars interpret this arrival in E major as a subtle harmonic link between op. 110 and op. 109, the main key of which is E major, but this conjecture is not easily proven. E is also the enharmonic of Fb, and Fb is a flatted sixth degree of the Ab scale (the flat submediant or bVI). At the risk of becoming impenetrably technical, E is also the sharped fifth degree of Ab sharped (#V). When theorists talk about this relationship, they usually label E the bVI, just as they would if we thought of this note as Fb. The move to the bVI, or flat submediant, was an important key relation that Beethoven started using regularly in his late period. We will observe it again in the Ninth Symphony. It is also a key relation favored in the music of Beethoven's contemporary Schubert and later romantics.

Transitions in expositions modulate, usually to the dominant as in op. 110, but there are other possibilities. Transitions in recapitulations usually do not need to modulate because the music has already reestablished the tonic. But when you're in E major in the key of Ab, a composer needs to think about modulating in order to get *back* to the tonic. Since Beethoven wishes to refrain from tonal anarchy, he will return to the tonic abruptly in time for the second theme, after which the remaining material of the recapitulation closely parallels that of the expositions. A coda merges smoothly from the closing theme, after which the thirty-second note *arpeggios* return for several measures, in Ab major. In the closing moments we hear the first measure of the "first" first theme one more time in the left hand.

Second Movement: *Allegro Molto*

The second movement, a lightning-fast *scherzo* in duple meter and F minor, begins in the relative minor of Ab, a key foreshadowed at the beginning of the development. In the interest of continuity the last note in the first movement was a C (the third of Ab), and the first note in the second movement is the identical C, now the fifth of F minor. The link is subtle but nonetheless presents an audible seamless connection between these contrasting movements. In the interest of full disclosure, I am not the first to notice this subtle and effective transition from one movement to the other. The main theme of the *scherzo* begins with a descending six-note scale, starting on the C and ending on E-natural. Some scholars have suggested that this theme is based on the once-popular song *Unsa Kätz häd Katzln ghabt* (Our Cat Has Had Kittens), but the musical resemblances are superficial.

More credible is another alleged musical allusion in the second part of the *scherzo* section that outlines a fourth. This tune, *Ich bin lüderlich, du bist lüderlich* (I Am Slovenly, You Are Slovenly), was proposed as a borrowing as early as A. B. Marx's life and works of Beethoven published in 1859. Some evidence points to the possibility that Beethoven knew the tune: the rhythm between the tune and the sonata is identical for the first three measures, and with the exception of one note (at least in Marx's transcription), the pitches are identical for the first two measures. If we give one note for each of the first five syllables in the song's title, Marx's transcription states Ab–Ab–G –G–Eb, which Beethoven altered to Ab–Ab–G–F–Eb, thus filling in the descending scale. Unfortunately, modern scholars who consider Beethoven's theme as a borrowing of *Ich bin lüderlich* also invariably alter Marx's transcription so that it matches Beethoven perfectly, but the two tunes nevertheless are quite close melodically.

The middle (trio) section presents a distinctly non-tune-like, rapid-fire melody in which every phrase begins on the offbeat and in which the first two notes of each phrase begins with a descending fourth. After a return of the *scherzo*, the last four measures of the coda feature an *arpeggio*, strongly reminiscent of the frequently heard *arpeggios* in the first movement.

Third Movement: Recitative/Adagio, ma Non Troppo—Fuga: Allegro ma Non Troppo

The third movement begins with an extensive vocally inspired improvisatory instrumental recitative, which interestingly duplicates the striking move to E major we witnessed in the first-movement recapitulation thus marking another significant link between movements. Although we have dismissed the presumed connection with *Unsa Kätz*, the borrowing *not* suggested by Adolph Bernhard Marx, the descending six notes that began the *scherzo* nonetheless bear a concrete connection with the opening of the *arioso* theme in Ab minor, the parallel minor of the sonata's tonic. In fact, the opening of the *scherzo* and the opening of the *arioso* are melodically identical.

We have already explained where the fugue subject comes from. As with textbook (i.e., J. S. Bach) fugues, the first fugue, marking a return to Ab major, begins with the fugue subject in isolation followed by further statements of the subject in other parts, or voices, in this case three (see Musical Forms: Fugue in the glossary). This is the fugue exposition. In contrast to most Bach fugues, however, in which the fugue subject drops out in alternating sections called episodes, Beethoven's fugue in this sonata never lets go of the subject for long. It is easy to miss, but at the end of the first fugue Beethoven unobtrusively but unmistakably inserts the first phrase of the *arioso*, yet another of the many connecting links among movements in this tightly intertwined sonata.

After the first presentation of the fugue in the tonic Beethoven moves down a half step to the leading tone, G, and returns to an abbreviated but still substantial modified statement of the *arioso* in G minor, now described as *Perdendo le forze, dolento* (Italian), *Ermattet klagen* (German), and in English "exhausted, lamenting." After a solid cadence on G minor Beethoven states ten G major triads in a row, each only a sixteenth-note long, separated by rests and all on the third note of three-note groupings. Another *arpeggio*, this time rising three octaves in G major, takes the music to an abbreviated and reworked return of the fugue.

Beethoven begins this second fugue with a restatement of the subject (still in G major) and offers a description in the score of what is happening in case listeners do not perceive that all the notes of the original subject are now going in the opposite direction. The technical term for this is inversion, a technique found in the second fugato of the *Eroica* finale. In op. 110 Beethoven actually labels the technique "the inversion of the Fuga," both in Italian, *L'inversione della Fuga*, and in German, *Die Umkehrung der Fuge*. A few measures later he places the subject in its original right-side-up position and in G minor. To call attention to this turn of events he doubles the note values of each note. This technique is called augmentation and is used in several Bach fugues. A few measures later he combines the augmented version of the theme with a version in which the notes are halved. This is called diminution. Thus in the space of less than a minute Beethoven offers three tricks of the fugue trade: inversion, augmentation, and diminution.

Meanwhile we should note that from the end of the G minor *arioso* until the diminution, Beethoven instructs the pianist to place his or her foot on the *una corda* pedal. This is the pedal on the left on modern pianos that shifts the keyboard so that only one string (*una corda*) is struck. Just before the end of the second fugue Beethoven writes *poi a poi tutte le corde* ("little by little all the strings"). Soon after that he asks for the music to get progressively faster, presumably for the rest of the movement, the final two pages of the score. For these final moments Beethoven abandons the counterpoint of the fugue in favor of a homophonic statement with its rising fourths, first with a statement in the left hand and then in the right hand for the rest of the movement, accompanied by a sixteenth-note figuration. (The word "homophonic" is the adjective form of homophony, a texture in which a single melody is supported by chords, in contrast to polyphony with its simultaneous combination of two or more melodies.) The fugue subject continues to rise as it accelerates and increases in volume to proclaim the first *fortissimo* of the entire sonata before erupting into a four-measure flurry of sixteenth-note *arpeggios* on Ab to bring the work to a triumphant close, the only sonata of the final trilogy to end with such affirmation.

Beethoven was reticent about inserting autobiographical clues or programs that might shed light on the meaning of his music. Scholars have reached a consensus, however, that Beethoven's declarations in the published score of thanks to God ("Heiliger Dankgesang") for giving him renewed strength in the pairing of the hymnlike *Molto adagio* and *Andante* in the third movement of the A minor string quartet, op. 132, was in response to getting over a recent illness. Even in the absence of any printed description, the basic meaning of what is happening *musically* in the *arioso*-fugue pairings of op. 110 would be clear. The words "exhausted" and "lamenting" at the return of the *arioso* is followed by a description of what is about to take place. The Italian is *poi a poi di nuovo vivente* (little by little with new life).

And little by little there is clearly new life in the music as Beethoven first asks the performer to let go of the *una corda* pedal, the striking rising half-step movement from the dying G major that returns the music to life on the tonic Ab major, and finally the unwavering increase in the tempo until the end of the work. With its vocal melodies in the first movement, the fragments of a popular tune in the second, and the recitative, two *ariosos*, and lyrical fugue in the finale, op. 110 is perhaps the most consistently lyrical of all Beethoven's late works and, despite the display of learned fugal techniques, remarkably non-academic sounding. And perhaps only the finales of the Ninth Symphony and the C# Minor String Quartet op. 131 match the sonata in its affirmation of Beethoven's "nuovo vivente."

SONATA NO. 32 IN C MINOR, OP. 111 (1822)

Beethoven had a predilection, if not an obsession, for the key C minor and what has been called "the C minor mood" (Kerman 1967, 70; 1994, 217–37). The first extant instrumental work, composed and published in 1782 at the age of eleven, was the Piano Variations on a March by [Ernst Christoph] Dressler. Twenty-four years later he published his only other variations in a minor key, the thirty-two variations on an original theme, WoO 80, like the nine *Dressler* Variations also in C minor. During his early years in Vienna between 1793 and 1800, Beethoven composed six major C minor instrumental works in five central genres: the Piano Trio op. 1, no. 3; the String Trio op. 9, no. 3; the Piano Sonatas op. 10, no. 1, and the *Pathétique*, op. 13; the String Quartet op. 18, no. 4; and the Third Piano Concerto op. 37. A Violin Sonata in C Minor, op. 30, no. 2, the Funeral March movement of the *Eroica* Symphony, the *Coriolan* Overture, and the Fifth Symphony followed in the years 1802–1808. The sonata in C minor, op. 111, Beethoven's third piano sonata in this key, would be the last instrumental work in this key.

In several works, as we have also seen in *Fidelio* (especially the first two versions) and still more prominently in the Fifth Symphony, and to a lesser extent the Mass in C Major, a work we have not explored here, Beethoven presents a musical struggle in which C major eventually triumphs over C minor. Readers may recall, for example, how Beethoven subtly prepared for the coming of C major in *Fidelio* and how significant moments of C major in the second and third movements of the Fifth Symphony paved the way for the triumphant C major finale marked by the trombones.

The final C minor piano sonata conveys a similar struggle, albeit in two movements rather than the usual three or four. Although it is by far the largest of its kind, op. 111 is not the first two-movement piano sonata. Between the large sonatas known as the *Waldstein* op. 53 and *Appassionata*, op. 57 (1803–1805), Beethoven sandwiched a more modest two-movement sonata in 1804, op. 54, with both movements in F major about thirteen minutes in length. Five years later he wrote a second two-movement sonata, op. 78, with both movements in F# major that takes a little longer than ten minutes to play. A third two-movement sonata about fourteen minutes long followed in 1814, the

Sonata in E Minor, op. 90, with a dynamic first movement in the minor mode and the songlike second movement rondo in E major, a sonata singled out in "Beethoven and Song" (chapter 6). Op. 111 revisited this idea on a larger scale with a fast sonata-form movement in C minor, about nine minutes in length, this time prefaced by the third substantial piano introduction of the thirty-two (the others are the *Pathétique*, op. 13, and *Les Adieux*, op. 81a). The second movement is long and slow, twice the length of the first, a theme-and-variations movement in C major.

First Movement: *Maestoso/Allegro con Brio ed Appassionata*

The introduction, *Maestoso*, rather than slow is both dramatic and tense and lasts for just under two minutes. It begins in the left hand, with the tense melodic interval, the diminished seventh, Eb descending to F#, immediately followed by the tense diminished-seventh chord on F# that fills in the notes of the diminished-seventh interval (F#–A–C–Eb). The diminished-seventh chord, which consists of a stack of three minor thirds (in this case F#–A, A–C, and C–Eb), was not only the tensest but also the most ambiguous chord in Beethoven's time, tension and ambiguity working together as natural allies. A century later it still served as the quintessential chord in horror films and suspense dramas. The chord lacks both a center and a direction, traits that also serve ambiguity. The chord can and often does, however, resolve by contracting into a goal-oriented triad such as the dominant. The diminished seventh on F#, the only chord in measure 1, resolves G, the dominant of C minor, in the second measure. The third measure repeats the process, first the diminished-seventh interval and then the diminished-seventh chord, this time on the diminished seventh on B-natural (B–D–F–Ab), contracting to the tonic in the next measure.

Beethoven is not yet ready to establish the home key. Instead he repeats the process a third time, this time on the only diminished seventh left unused (in the twelve-note chromatic scale, only three diminished sevenths are possible, each with its own collection of four notes). This is the diminished seventh based on E-natural (E–G–Bb–Db). In contrast to the first two diminished-seventh chords, this one does not contract or resolve, at least not right away. Instead, the dotted, almost march-like rhythms attached to this last diminished seventh continue with a reduction in dynamics from *piano* to *sempre* (always) *pianissimo* before the music swerves back to the dominant of C, where it remains for the remaining six measures of the introduction. At the same time, the beginning of a future theme emerges, a simple scale of four notes starting at G and ending on C, first in the middle range and then an octave lower.

The music *crescendos* and accelerates and we hear the four-note scale once more, now fast, then with two notes added, and finally one more time to become the first full statement of the main theme of the *Allegro con brio ed appassionato.* Everything we have heard in the fast part and will hear for the next few measures of the fast section is played by both hands one octave apart and *fortissimo.* When the theme returns with a more conventional homophonic texture Beethoven reverts to a *piano* dynamic. The first theme, twice interrupted by instructions to suddenly hold back the tempo (*poco ritenente*) before reaccelerating, lasts only a few seconds. After a brief contrapuntal rapid transition based on the main theme in sixteenth notes along with a new counter-theme in eighth notes, two pairs of half notes, each leaping several octaves, take the music to a new key, Ab major (VI), the central key of op. 110. For two decades Beethoven has been challenging sonata-form conventions by moving to keys other than the dominant, when the work is in major, or the relative major, when the work is in minor. But of the nine previous major multimovement works in C minor, only one does not establish the relative major for its second key. The exception is the *Pathétique*, which first travels to Eb *minor* instead of Eb major before concluding the exposition on Eb major. By moving to the key on the sixth or submediant degree of the scale rather than the third degree (the relative major), op. 111 breaks a pattern more than thirty years in the making.

The second theme is the sole respite in the first movement, a moment of lyricism and momentary leisure amid the otherwise constant, even relentless, movement. Although it returns to the dotted rhythms of the introduction, its altered melody is in marked contrast to the first and transition themes. The new theme quickly shifts to a *piano* dynamic and in quick succession slows down from *meno* (less) *allegro* to *ritardando* and *adagio.* Then with dramatic abruptness and a *fortissimo* dynamic and return to the original swift tempo, Beethoven brings back the diminished-seventh chord, the two hands playing an octave apart. A closing section also derived from the main theme concludes the exposition, which unlike op. 110 is repeated, albeit without the introduction.

Within the twenty measures and approximately forty seconds of the development, Beethoven focuses on the main theme, first in octave unison between the hands and then in counterpoint with one hand playing an augmented statement of the first four notes of the theme and the other hand playing the entire theme. In the retransition that prepares for the return of the recapitulation and C minor, Beethoven takes the first three notes of the main theme and harmonizes each statement with the three diminished chords heard in the introduction and in the same order.

The diminished sevenths of the introduction have thus linked every conceivable part of this movement. At the outset of the coda Beethoven returns one final time to the same three diminished chords once again in the same order, this time on off beats. In the final measures of the movement Beethoven introduces a new idea that presages the second movement, a series of C major triads, each introduced not by the dominant of C but by the minor form of the subdominant (F minor), an amen (or minor plagal) cadence with a twist. The introduction of C major in the final seconds is powerful but also subdued since everything is *piano* until the final two measures which *diminuendos* still further to a barely audible *pianissimo*.

Second Movement: *Arietta, Adagio Molto Semplice e Cantabile*

After the mostly fast and furious first movement with its unexpected soft landing on the C major tonic at its close, the theme that follows sounds like a slow song and is in fact labeled *Arietta* (a small aria) with the tempo designation *Adagio molto semplice e cantabile*. Where the theme of the first movement was angular and frenetic, the *Arietta* theme fits Beethoven's tempo description. Melodically and harmonically it couldn't be more *semplice* (simple), either in melody, rhythm, harmony, or in its accompaniment that matches the melody rhythmically almost note for note, and it could hardly be more *cantabile* (singing). When we next turn to the *Diabelli* Variations, we will learn that by the time he started to work on op. 111 he had composed twenty-three variations on Diabelli's theme, also in C major, in 1819, and it has been noticed that the opening theme in the second movement of op. 111 and

Diabelli's theme are related, and that Beethoven will incorporate audible elements of the op. 111 theme in the final variation 33 of the
Diabelli.

The two parts of the *Arietta* are eight measures each, each repeated
and with separate first and second endings in each part indicated in the
score, whereas Diabelli's theme consists of two repeated sixteen-measure parts with identical endings. The main melodic similarity between
the *Arietta* theme and its predecessor occurs in the openings where a
descent of a fourth from C to G is followed by a descent of a fifth from
D to G. The central difference is that in Diabelli the first half of the first
part, eight measures, prolong this simple melodic movement by repeating the Gs ten times each after the C and the D, whereas in the *Arietta*
theme Beethoven states the Gs only twice, thus compressing eight
measures of Diabelli's theme into two measures of his own.

The rest of the *Arietta* theme maintains the simplicity, singing line,
and serenity established at the outset. The harmony also matches the
melody in its simplicity and directness. The first half of the theme
modulates smoothly to the dominant. The second half begins with four
measures on A minor (the submediant) before moving down one step to
the dominant (G major), from which the music returns smoothly and
easily to the tonic C major. As with the first part, the left hand in the
second matches the melody nearly note for note and only one chord is
not conveyed in its simplest form, root position, that is, with the lowest
note of the chord in the bass.

The trajectory of the variations is one of increasing movement.
Interestingly, while the tempo remains *Adagio molto*, the reduction of
note values makes the music sound as though it is traveling at increasingly greater speed in each of the five variations, none of which is
numbered in the score. To prepare for the rhythmic subdivisions to
come, Beethoven in variation 1 adopts the unusual time signature of
nine-sixteenths, nine beats per measure and sixteen subdivisions. In the
theme, three beats sound like one, which means that Beethoven could
have just as easily notated the theme in a slow waltz time (three-quarter). In this variation Beethoven's choice of nine-sixteenths makes sense
since each of the nine beats gets its own sixteenth note. The arrangement thus consists of three groups of three sixteenths (3 + 3 + 3) for a
total of nine, and since the tempo is glacially slow, the music can be
counted and felt as nine beats per measure. This is quite an unusual

phenomenon. Those curious can locate viewable and downloadable copies of Beethoven's autograph manuscript and first published edition online at IMSLP.

Beethoven changes the meter in the second variation to six-sixteenths. This change allows him to increase the rhythmic motion from nine subdivisions per measure to twelve subdivisions, arranged in three groups of four (4 + 4 + 4). Again the tempo does not change (*L'istesso tempo*), but the increased motion most definitely has the feeling of a faster tempo. The syncopations and irregular *sforzandi* within the subdivisions in variation 3, the first variation with a *forte* dynamic, has frequently been described as proto-swing. Indeed the music does sound jazzy. And while the tempo still does not change, the subdivisions have increased the sense of motion still further. This is new metrical territory in the classical tradition, and Beethoven had to invent a new meter, 12/32, to notate what he wanted. Since what is heard doesn't exactly match this metrical sign, I will focus on what is heard rather than to try to make sense of Beethoven's time signature. The motion in variation 1 consisted of three groups of three sixteenth notes each (3 + 3 + 3); and variation 2, three groups of four sixteenth notes each (4 + 4 + 4). Variation 3 ups the ante with three groups of eight thirty-second notes each (8 + 8 + 8).

Variation 4 returns to nine-sixteenths time yet offers still more rhythmic motion, this time three groups of nine thirty-second notes each (9 + 9 + 9). Remarkably, within the space of four variations Beethoven has moved from nine to twelve, twenty-four, and twenty-seven units per measure. In the fourth variation, which begins and remains *pianissimo* throughout, Beethoven presents what is known as a "double" variation, which means that each part of the variation is written out to produce a variation of a variation. This is a common practice in variations beginning with the big slow penultimate variation (variation 23) and occurs as early as the *Righini* Variations (1790–1791). In the first half of the first part of variation 4, Beethoven places both hands deep in the bass range with the left hand muttering repeated rumbles. In the second half of the first part Beethoven moves skyward to the upper range with three groups of three notes each (3 + 3 + 3) in the left hand, each supported above by three thirty-second notes (9 + 9 + 9). The pattern of low sounds in the first half and high in the second is maintained in the second part of the variation.

After the fourth variation Beethoven departs from the standard two-part form of the theme and variations and instead offers a freer variation of the theme marked by twelve measures of continuous trilling, first in a middle voice for six measures and then two measures of double trilling in the two upper voices against a portion of the main theme in the bass. For most of the next three measures Beethoven sounds only one voice, still trilled. For the next two measures Beethoven places a part of the tune in the highest register of the keyboard available to him while the left hand plays the lowest notes available, a wide expanse of sound that would have been new to both performers and audiences in the 1820s and remains unusual, if less radical, today.

The developmental interlude moved away from C major for the first time, to Eb major and Ab major, the latter the key of op. 110. Beethoven then returns to the *Arietta* and C major, one statement of each of the two parts of the theme, with the melody sounding above and two rhythmic layers in the lower voices, nine sixteenth-notes in the middle voice (3 + 3 + 3) and twenty-seven thirty-second notes in the lowest voice (9 + 9 + 9). After completing the theme Beethoven extends the variation material freely for an additional twelve measures.

The coda returns to the first part of the theme one more time, *pianissimo*, now in the middle voice with a high continuous trill in the upper range and the three groups of nine thirty-second notes below (but still relatively high). To close the work Beethoven replaces the opening C to G with three statements of D to G. This is followed by a harmonious musical line in thirty-second notes in parallel thirds between hands then descending scales in sixths between the hands, two statements of the opening C to G, and finally the first two notes inverted (G up to C) for a quiet *pianissimo* landing on a C major triad.

Op. 111 was published in two cities in 1823, first by Maurice Schlesinger in Paris and shortly thereafter in the Berlin wing of the firm run by Maurice's father Adolph. After receiving the sonata both father and son wrote to Beethoven inquiring whether he had accidentally neglected to send the final movement. In his biography first published in 1841 Beethoven's unpaid secretary Anton Schindler addresses this issue and the master's response when he asked "why he had not written a third movement appropriate to the character of the first" (Schindler 1966, 232). Beethoven's response was similar to the note he wrote on his autograph after drafting no less than four settings of the song *Sehn-*

sucht (WoO 134), in which he explained he provided four attempts because he did not have time to compose a good one. According to Schindler, in the case of op. 111 "he replied casually that he had not had time to write a third movement, and had therefore simply expanded the second" (232). Obviously missing the likely possibility that Beethoven was pulling his leg, Schindler continued to "deplore" the decision not to add the missing third movement: "I could not then and still cannot understand how two movements of such sharply differing character could possibly produce an integrated and satisfying whole" (232).

At the end of the nineteenth century the great but fictitious German composer Adrian Leverkühn in his youth hears his organ and composition teacher Wendell Kretschmar deliver a lecture in which he revisits the question posed by the Schlesingers and Schindler: "Why did Beethoven not write a third movement to the Piano Sonata Opus 111?" The scene appears in Thomas Mann's fictional biography of Leverkühn, *Doctor Faustus* (1947), in which the hero makes a pact with the devil, giving up love and long life in exchange for twenty-four years of creativity. At the end of the lecture Kretschmar offers an answer that remains a sensible response: "We had only needed, he said, to hear the piece to answer the question ourselves." Speaking metaphorically, Kretschmar announced further "that the sonata had come, in the second enormous movement, to an end, an end without any return." Kretschmar meant not simply the end of op. 111 but "the farewell of the sonata form" more generally. In the light of Schubert's final piano sonatas and the chamber music of Schumann and Brahms, Kretschmar's historical verdict seems premature. But op. 111 was most definitely the last of Beethoven's thirty-five piano sonatas, going back to the three *Elector* Sonatas of 1783 forty years earlier.

THIRTY-THREE VARIATIONS ON A WALTZ BY A. DIABELLI, OP. 120 (1819–1823)

When it came to describing his monumental set of variations on the title page of his new work published as op. 120 in 1823, Beethoven chose the word *Veränderungen* (transformations) rather than the customary *Variationen* (variations) of his other major variation sets, including the *Eroica* Variations, op. 35, and the variations op. 34 and WoO 80 on original themes. To encapsulate the well-known origins of this work, the starting point was a publicity "gimmick" generated by the publisher and composer Anton Diabelli who in 1819 invited fifty composers to each contribute a variation on Diabelli's ingenuous waltz in two parts, sixteen bars in each. The composers who accepted Diabelli's invitation represented a Who's Who of the day and, in the case of the eleven-year old Franz Liszt, the future. Schubert's contribution, a waltz in C minor, a small gem, has been included in various collections of the composer's smaller piano works.

According to Schindler, Beethoven "did not care for the theme with its 'cobbler's patches'" (Schindler 1966, 252) and declined the invitation. Although Schindler's recollection enjoys no other biographical or documentary support, the idea that Beethoven disdained Diabelli's theme has until recently been repeated unchallenged. Even after the discovery of Schindler's forged entries in Beethoven's sketchbooks, mainly those prior to 1822, and considering the likelihood that Schindler did not know the composer until late that year, the story is apparently too good not to be true. One fascinating exception to the cavalier acceptance of Schindler is found in Moisés Kaufman's well-researched play 33 Variations that appeared on Broadway in 2009 starring Jane Fonda in which a musicologist, Dr. Katherine Brandt (Fonda), is working on the sketches and compositional process of the work. In the course of her research Brandt perceptively observes that "it was Schindler who started the legend that Beethoven hated Diabelli's waltz" and that "he is the only source that tells us that Beethoven found the theme commonplace" (Kaufman 2011, 67).

The manuscript record reveals that instead of contributing a solitary variation, Beethoven composed no less than twenty-three variations in 1819 (one would eventually remain unused), returned to the work in 1822 after completing his final sonata trilogy and the Missa solemnis, and then wrote eleven more variations. The musicologist in Kaufman's play says that "we truly have no idea what Beethoven thought of Diabelli's waltz" (67), but in fact we do. The evidence can be found directly in the work itself. Clearly Beethoven thought enough of the waltz, at least its musical potential, to compose what Charles Rosen concluded was a work "that can lay claim to being his greatest work for piano—at least it is the work that allows us best to grasp almost all the facets of his genius" (2002, 247).

The two fundamental approaches to theme and variations are variations that preserve the harmony of the central theme and those that largely retain the melody of the theme. Prime examples of the harmonic approach include Bach's *Goldberg* Variations, which Beethoven would have heard about and probably knew, and Beethoven's thirty-two variations on an original theme, WoO 80. The *Eroica* Variations used the *Basso del Tema* as a starting point but also offered variations in which the contredanse theme is clearly present. Examples of the melodic approach include the *Righini* Variations, WoO 65, and the six variations on an original theme, op. 34.

Beethoven's variation sets often combine the two approaches. In the *Diabelli* Variations he often preserves the original harmony of the theme (with a few interesting departures here and there), and in nearly every variation Beethoven uses one of a number of the distinctive musical elements found in the original melody. A variation such as variation 4 presents a paraphrase of nearly the entire theme in which all the main notes are present, usually on important beats but separated by so many other new notes that the effect is one of a brand-new melody. It is not always a simple matter to detect what element is being used, and how, but the more one hears *Diabelli*, the more one will hear something of the original theme as well as its harmonic underpinning.

The present chapter can only offer only an introductory survey of this complex work. For more expansive and authoritative writing on the *Diabelli*, the reader is advised to turn to the essay and the book by William Kinderman cited in the bibliography. I will limit the discussion to an overview of the work and a range of selective details, starting with the way Beethoven builds all or a part of a variation around a distinctive feature of the original theme.

Take, for example, the opening upbeat grace note on a D and the turn that follows from C to B, still on the upbeat, and rests on C, the downbeat of the first measure. Numerous variations preserve this upbeat, but some actually start with a clear reference to the turn figure in the original theme. Examples include the trill that begins and subsequently pervades variation 6 and the turn itself that pervades every measure in variation 9, the first of only four variations in the minor mode (C minor). A gentler triplet version sounds in every measure of variation 11. The *Largo, molto espressivo* variation 31, by far the longest variation, the variation that parallels the slow and aria-like twenty-fifth variation in Bach's *Goldberg*, begins with a seven-note turn, with the original turn figure occupying the third through sixth notes, all before the downbeat of the theme's first measure.

What follows is a selective profile of the variations as a whole:

1. Chronology: The eleven variations Beethoven added in 1823 are variations 1–2, 15, 23–26, 28–29, 31, and 33. The majority of these added variations occur in the last eleven variations, eight of which were newly written four years after the original twenty-two composed in 1819.

2. Meter: The theme and twenty-one variations are in triple meter as is Diabelli's original waltz, eleven variations are in duple meter, and one variation (var. 21) alternates between duple and triple.

3. C Minor: Four of the thirty-three variations are in the minor mode. These include the violently comical C minor variation based on the opening turn (var. 9) and a trio of successive C minor variations near the end of the work (var. 29–31), including the longest and slowest variation 31.

4. Counterpoint: Two variations are fugal in nature, var. 24 is a little fugue, labeled *Fughetta* by Beethoven, and var. 32 is a full-scale fugue, labeled *Fuga* by Beethoven. The fugue is widely described as in Handelian style, in part because it adopts Handel's practice of presenting its subject and countersubject together as a pair and perhaps in imitation of a famous Handel fugue consisting of many repeated notes.

5. Rhythm: While the rhythm of the theme is recognizable in most of the variations, it recedes in eleven of them, including the final five variations (var. 29–33).

6. Timings: The work as a whole takes a little over fifty minutes to play if one observes all of Beethoven's indicated repeats. One variation, var. 31, is over five minutes in length; no others last more than four minutes. Four variations last between three and four minutes (var. 14, 20, 24, and 33), three variations last between two and three minutes (var. 9, 30, 32), and eleven variations last between one and two minutes (including the first four variations). The largest single group, comprising no fewer than fourteen variations, clock in at less than a minute each, including

three variations that last between thirty and forty seconds (var. 10, 14, and 22).

ORGANIZING THE *DIABELLI* VARIATIONS: SEVEN GROUPS

In contrast to the meticulous three-variation groupings and larger architectural structures in Bach's *Goldberg*, Beethoven's *Diabelli* does not offer a clear-cut formal plan, despite considerable parallels and contrasts of tempo, mood, and virtuosity between groups of two or three variations and a persuasive musical and psychological trajectory. The outline that follows proposes a meaningful, if irregular, collection of variation groups—providing a framework to make listening to the set more of a satisfying whole.

Group 1: Theme and Variations 1–5

The first five variations each contain unmistakable melodic connections with the waltz, ranging from parody to paraphrase. Scholars have suggested that the first two of the 1823 variations were added to support Beethoven's evolving idea to open the work with variations that clearly reveal the theme. The first two variations also share the keyboard register of Diabelli's original waltz.

Group 2: Variations 6–14

This large group includes at least four variations based on the opening turn figure (var. 6, 9, 11, and 12) including the first variation in C minor (var. 9). Looking at the first two groups together, it is striking that five of the first fourteen variations last under a minute in duration; the longest variation in the first thirteen is just under two minutes. Only one variation, the first slow variation 14, *Grave e maestoso*, among the longest in the set, lasts almost as long as four minutes, a stately finale to this exceptionally varied group of variations. Variation 9, with its overexaggerated insistence on the opening turn, and variation 13, with its comic responses to the silence, are among the wittiest variations of the entire set. But other variations exhibit an engaging comic spirit, in particular the swift variation 10, a variation that exhibits relentless staccato trills and trilled *pianissimo* bass rumblings in the second half of each part. Maintaining its *presto* tempo marking, the growing *crescendo* in the second part escalates to a *fortissimo*, and the variation is over in thirty seconds flat.

Group 3: Variations 15–19

With its clear return to both the original theme and the original register, variation 15 clearly marks a new beginning not quite halfway through the set. Not surprisingly, this variation was added in 1823. In fact, along with variations 1–2, variation 15, with its galloping staccatos, is the *only* other variation before variation 23 that Beethoven had conceived prior to 1823. Each of these new variations exhibits a considerable closeness to Diabelli's theme. A detail: If the third variation of op. 111 suggests jazz, the bass of variation 16 suggests boogie-woogie, a connection made vivid in the imaginative realization recorded by Uri Caine from 2002. Variation 19 begins with a veritable cascade of lively, inventive arpeggios—something of a Beethoven signature as listeners like yourself, who have voyaged thus far in this listener's guide, well know.

Group 4: Variations 20–24

Variation 20 marks another beginning, low and slow, grave and meditative, soft (the loudest dynamic marking is *piano*, and the majority of the variation is *pianissimo*), and full of rich, chromatic, harmonic ambiguities that take the music far afield from the theme and most of the variations. This group also includes the much-discussed variation 22, the shortest in the set, which, even in the absence of Beethoven's verbal clue, *Alla "Notte e giorno faticar" di Mozart* would be recognizable as a borrowing from Leporello's opening aria at the beginning of Mozart's *Don Giovanni*. The group concludes with a lyrical *fughetta*, variation 24, added in 1823.

Group 5: Variations 25–28

With variation 25, for the first time since variation 15 Beethoven unmistakably returns to Diabelli's theme and its original register. As with variations 1–2 and 15, which also closely resemble the waltz, variation 25, was newly composed in 1823. The final variation of this group is harsh and dissonant with dissonant *sforzandi* on each beat.

Group 6: Variations 29–31

These final three minor mode variations form their own group. The first and third variations are slow; and the second, a moderate *Andante* tempo. Variations 29 and 30 also conspicuously alter the previously invariable repetition of each section in the earlier variations. Variation 29 adds several new measures that do not correspond to the theme and do not divide the variation into two repeatable sections in contrast with most of the variations. Variation 30 repeats only the last four measures of the second part. In Variation 31, seemingly inspired by variation 25 in Bach's *Goldberg*, the original theme is ingeniously disguised but can be nonetheless perceived with help from a pianist who can bring out the musical line. Even on its terms variation 31 is arguably one of Beethoven's most ingenious as well as profound and moving slow movements.

Group 7: Variations 32–33

Following Beethoven's tribute to Bach in variation 31, the set closes with tributes to Handel (variation 32) and Mozart (variation 33), the two composers Beethoven admired most. The Handelian fugue emphasizes the repeated notes of Diabelli's waltz while the Mozartian minuet (*Tempo di Menuetto*) thoroughly transforms the lowbrow waltz into an elegant variation that begins with an imaginative reworking of the opening turn figure and ends with a substantial coda.

In the lecture that concludes Kaufman's play, *33 Variations*, Brandt conveys her findings: "Beethoven chooses to end the set of variations with a minuet. A graceful dance. And I find such beautiful symmetry in his design. We start with a beer-hall waltz and end with a delicate, spiritual dance. Variations on a dance should end with a dance. What an elegant idea—and so eloquently articulated by the master. This from a man who could not dance" (Kaufman 2011, 102).

POSTSCRIPT: *FÜR ELISE* OR BAGATELLE IN A MINOR, WOO 59

Each of the *Diabelli* Variations is intended to serve as a part of a whole, but if taken individually they resemble another genre that Beethoven would visit from time to time. This is the bagatelle, the French word for trifle or in German *Kleinigkeiten*, the latter term Beethoven used in his sketches for the bagatelles op. 126. Over the course of his lifetime Beethoven published three sets of bagatelles, of which only the last was conceived as an integral set. The seven bagatelles published in 1803 as op. 33 were assembled from a group of pieces, at least one of which apparently can be traced to his earliest years as a composer in Bonn. The final group of six bagatelles, composed in 1824 and published in 1825 as op. 126, was Beethoven's last published piano work. Two years earlier Beethoven assembled eleven pieces eventually published as op. 119. Numbers 7–11 from this set were composed in 1820 and published in a book of pieces for use by piano teachers in 1821. Shortly afterward Beethoven collected another five short pieces begun in the 1790s through the early 1800s, some of which most likely were abandoned movements to larger works. He then wrote a new bagatelle that fit the revisions to the earlier ones to produce a unified set. The five earlier reworked bagatelles eventually became op. 119, nos. 1–5, the new baga- telle op. 119, no. 6. Although the eleven pieces in op. 119 were original- ly published together, Barry Cooper argues persuasively that this opus more accurately represents two sets, each of which, especially the latter set, nos. 1–6, was revised in 1822, and that each set demonstrates its own careful planning and musical integrity (1986–1987).

At the time that Beethoven was selecting and reworking the first five pieces and composing from scratch the sixth piece of the future op. 119, he was also considering assembling thirteen or fourteen other pieces from his inventory of musical bagatelles, trifles short in length perhaps, but often abundant in invention, for future publication. Unfortunately, none of these bagatelles seemed appropriate for inclusion in op. 119, and Beethoven was unable to find a way to assemble or reconfigure a group of these remaining pieces into a publishable set. Apparently he did not pursue the idea of publishing the pieces separately or in a less unified group. In the end it proved easier to compose an entirely new set of six, op. 126, than to organize the leftover bagatelles into publishable form.

One abandoned bagatelle eventually became one of the most famous piano compositions, not only by Beethoven, but also by anyone, the little piece known today as *Für Elise* (*For Elise* or *Eliza*). After he abandoned it in 1822, the piece was not heard from again until forty years after Beethoven's death when it was published for the first time by the scholar Ludwig Nohl in 1867. The score Nohl used to prepare his edition was an autograph score, now lost, that Beethoven inscribed "For Elise, on 27th April as a remembrance from L. v. Bthvn." Since Beethoven did not provide a year, scholars have based their conjectures on two manuscripts, a short but well-developed sketch probably from 1808 and a draft that is nearly complete (and closely resembles Nohl's 1867 edition) that may either be concurrent with the 1808 sketch or drafted as late as 1810.

Nohl had no idea that in 1822, when Beethoven was reworking the first five pieces and composing a new sixth piece for the future op. 119, that one of the bagatelles he had revisited on a new sketch page for potential publication was the same piece Beethoven had earlier inscribed "Für Elise." Since Beethoven had relinquished the original autograph gift in 1810, he relied on the sketches from that time as well as his memory when he returned to the work in 1822.

A consensus of scholars have concluded that *Für Elise* was originally intended as a gift for Therese Malfatti and that Nohl misread Beethoven's Therese as Elise (or alternatively that Elise was a pet name for Therese). Therese, we may recall, was the young woman of Italian descent who was the intended recipient of *Dimmi, ben mio* and perhaps a marriage prospect in 1810. We do not know why Beethoven's presumed plans to marry Therese did not work out, but knowing Beethoven's romantic history, we should not be surprised.

Nohl's 1867 version of the *Für Elise* of 1810, the only one regularly published, performed, and recorded, is in rondo form:

A   8 measures   Main theme in A minor

A   8 measures   Main theme repeated

| B- | 14 measures | Contrasting middle section and return to the main |
| A | | theme in A minor |

| B- | 14 measures | Repeat of B-A |
| A | | |

| C | 15 measures | New theme in F and C major, ending on the |
| | | dominant of A minor |

A-	22 measures	Main theme, contrasting middle section, and main
B-		theme in A minor
A		

| D | 17 measures | D minor and Bb major |

| E | 5 measures | Transition in triplets in A minor |

A-	22 measures	Main theme, contrasting middle section, and main
B-		theme in A minor
A		

The revised bagatelle WoO 59 (*Für Elise*), edited and published by Barry Cooper in 1991, can be heard in an online midi version, if not on commercial recordings. When he returned to the bagatelle in 1822, Beethoven made a few noticeable as well as several less conspicuous changes. Formally, he added four additional measures between the second ending of the first BA section and the new C section, a type of addition that can be found in other reworked bagatelles at the time. He also added four transition measures before inserting an extra statement of A-B-A (without repeats). In the E transition section Beethoven removed one measure of the triplets. Finally, he added one new measure in the final A one measure from the end.

Perhaps the most noticeable changes occur in the opening A-B-A statement of the main theme itself. For example, it is clear from Beethoven's extant sketches that he wanted the final three notes of A to be D–C–B–A rather than Nohl's transcription of E–C–B–A. This may seem like a minor change, but since the final three notes of the main melody appear five times in Nohl's edition, the seemingly small difference would be audible to most listeners. In addition to this likely misreading of the earlier version, Beethoven's revisions offer a significantly new version of the left hand that invariably accompanies the main theme. In Nohl's version (Beethoven's earlier version), still the only version generally known, the accompaniment figure of three sixteenth notes in every measure invariably begins on the downbeat of each measure. In the 1822 revisions Beethoven added a sixteenth-note *rest* before each group of three sixteenths. So now instead of DUM-dum-dum we hear REST-dum-dum-dum. Pianists and listeners can debate the relative merits of this departure from the familiar, but from my perspective it is unfortunate that Beethoven never got around to publishing his final word on the revised *Für Therese*.

8

DAIKU: THE BIG NINTH (1824)

The conductor, instrumentalists, chorus members, soloists, and audiences all participate equally in the performance. And therein lies, it seems to me, the secret of the intimacy and harmony between the music of Beethoven and the spiritual life of the Japanese.
—Yano Junichi writing on the meaning of Beethoven's Ninth, known in Japan simply as "Daiku." *Japan Quarterly* (1982, 477)

We live in the valley of the Ninth Symphony.
—Joseph Kerman, *The Beethoven Quartets* (1967, 194)

GRAND MUSICAL ACADEMY [CONCERT] BY HERR L. V. BEETHOVEN

Grand Musical Academy [Concert] by Herr L. v. Beethoven which will take place Tomorrow, May 7, 1824 in the Royal Imperial Theater beside the Kärtnerthor. The musical pieces to be performed are the latest works of Herr Ludwig van Beethoven.

First: A Grand Overture

This was the overture to *The Consecration of the House*, op. 124, which Beethoven had composed in September 1822 to open the newly rebuilt Theater in der Josefstadt one month later. The overture was published in 1825.

Second: Three Grand Hymns with Solo and Choral Voices

This was the Kyrie, Credo, and Agnus Dei from the *Missa solemnis*, Beethoven's largest choral work. It was composed between 1819 and 1823 and originally intended to honor the installation of Beethoven's great patron, the Archduke Rudolf, as an archbishop in 1820. Beethoven missed this deadline, became sidetracked with other compositions, and consequently was unable to complete his mass and present it to the archduke until March 1823. The absence of the correct title on the Academy program can be explained by the fact that works with a liturgical text were required to be advertised as hymns to satisfy the censors (the two movements of the Mass in C at the 1808 Academy were similarly described). Since Prince Galitzin had arranged for a complete performance of the new mass shortly before on April 7 in St. Petersburg, this Vienna performance of the three mass movements could not be considered as a premiere.

Third: A Grand Symphony with Solo and Chorus Voices Entering in the Finale on Schiller's "Ode to Joy"

[Ninth Symphony, op. 125]. The solos will be performed by the Demoiselles [Henriette] Sontag and [Karoline] Unger and the Herren [Anton] Haizinger and [Joseph] Seipelt. Herr [Ignaz] Schuppanzigh has undertaken the direction of the orchestra, Herr Kapellmeister [Michael] Umlauf the direction of the whole, and the Music Society the augmentation of the chorus and orchestra as a favor.

Herr Ludwig van Beethoven will himself participate in the general direction.
Prices of admission as usual.
Beginning at seven o'clock in the evening. (Forbes 1964, 907–8)

By May 1824 it had been a full decade since the concert at the Grand Redoutensaal in 1814 when Vienna audiences re-heard the Seventh Symphony and *Wellington's Victory* on the same concert that featured the premiere of Beethoven's Eighth. After composing eight symphonies between 1800 and 1812, the Ninth would be both his next and his last work in this genre. In 1815 the Philharmonic Society of London invited Beethoven to visit London and to compose two new symphonies. In

1822 the Society inspired Beethoven further when they sent an advance of fifty pounds.

Closer to home, despite the rich musical life in 1820s Vienna, public concerts featuring symphonies were rare events. In fact, not until the founding of the Vienna Philharmonic in 1842 could the city boast a professional orchestra dedicated to symphonic music. This institutional gap explains why the orchestra that Beethoven used for the 1824 Academy concert to debut the Ninth was composed mainly of members from the Imperial Royal Theater, a theater orchestra considered the best in Vienna, augmented by members of the Gesellschaft der Musikfreunde (the Society of the Friends of Music, the Music Society noted in the announcement). Chorus members were recruited from the Gesellschaft and local boy sopranos.

As with the Academies of 1800, 1803, 1808, and 1814, Beethoven was expected to execute the administrative duties customarily relegated in our time to hall managers and their staffs. In exchange he would be eligible to receive the bulk of any financial benefits. Persuaded by a petition instigated by Prince Lichnowsky to premiere the new symphony in Vienna rather than Berlin, Beethoven's next step was to select an appropriate and available venue. He then needed to secure four vocal soloists for the symphony finale and the personnel for the orchestra and chorus, professional and amateur. In the end the orchestra consisted of fifty-eight string players (twenty-four violins, ten violas, twelve cellos, and twelve basses), double winds, and a ninety-member chorus. Beethoven also had to set the price and performance time, schedule the rehearsals, and pay five different copyists to notate the orchestral and choral parts.

Despite a number of scheduling delays, the performance, which took place on May 7, enjoyed "an unusually large audience" (Levy 2003, 134). The Vienna correspondent for the Leipzig *Allgemeine musikalische Zeitung* offered valuable information about what was seen and heard: "Hr. [Herr] Schuppanzigh directed at the violin, Hr. Kapellmeister Umlauf directed with the baton, and the composer himself participated in the general direction of everything" (135). All agreed that Beethoven would not conduct the performers directly, a decision noted by the correspondent who wrote that the composer stood "by the side of the presiding marshal and indicated the beginning of each new tempo, following his original score, because due to his hearing deficiency, the higher enjoyment was sadly denied him" (135–36).

Despite his criticism of the performance quality, the correspondent/reviewer assessed the performance and the composition favorably overall: "And still the effect was indescribably great and magnificent, jubilant applause from full hearts was enthusiastically given the master, whose inexhaustible genius revealed a new world to us and unveiled never-before-heard, never-imagined magical secrets of the holy art!" (Levy 2003, 136). The *Theater Zeitung* (*Theater Newspaper*) also described the enthusiastic response: "The public received the tone-hero with the most respectful sympathy and listened to his wonderful, gigantic creations with the most intense attentiveness, and they broke out in jubilant applause—often during movements—but repeatedly after each of them" (133).

Several witnesses remember applause at the end of movements, a common occurrence in Beethoven's time. Readers might recall that the popular second movement of the Seventh Symphony was encored at its first and future performances. Before LP recordings, cassette tapes, CDs, DVDs, MP3s, streaming, Naxos, and Spotify, audiences were lucky to hear a movement twice at the premiere of a work or at a future performance. Today encores consist of a short piece or perhaps two at the end of solo and chamber recitals, more seldom for orchestral concerts. Applause at the end of a movement still occurs but is generally sporadic and associated with inexperienced or inattentive listeners, frowned upon, and quickly stifled.

The future piano virtuoso Sigismond Thalberg recalled attending the premiere of the Ninth when he was twelve years old. The recollection was recorded more than three decades later, in 1860, when Thalberg told Beethoven's biographer Alexander Wheelock Thayer he still remembered how at the end of the *scherzo* "B[eethoven] stood turning over the leaves of his score utterly deaf to the immense applause, and Unger pulled him by the sleeve, and then pointed to the audience when he turned and bowed" (Forbes 1964, 909). Accounts by Karoline Unger and Anton Schindler report that such an incident happened at the end of the *concert* rather than at the end of the *scherzo*, and it is this later, more dramatic version that remains the most often repeated. A conversation book mentions that audience members cried out "Vivat!" four times, an action that led to the police commissioner stepping in to demand silence. It is not possible to offer definitive proof, but (in my view) the youthful Thalberg's impressionable account rings truer than the more dramatic accounts by Unger and Schindler. Surely one would think even Beethoven would have noticed the conductor Umlauf turning around to acknowledge the cheers.

A few weeks later on May 23, the entire symphony was encored at the Redoutensaal at a concert that began at half past noon. The second concert also began with *The Consecration of the House* overture and included the Kyrie (and this time only the Kyrie) from the *Missa solemnis*. In addition, Beethoven and perhaps other concert planners added two new smaller works to this shorter concert, Beethoven's vocal trio, *Tremate, empi, Tremate*, op. 116, which had been heard in its revised state at the concert of 1814 (the concert that marked the debut of the Eighth Symphony), and a tenor aria by Rossini. Louis Duport, the manager of the Kärntnertor Theater, agreed to withhold Beethoven's expenses, perhaps as a conciliatory gesture in the light of the poor receipts for the first performance and Beethoven's accusations that he was cheated. Unfortunately, although Beethoven was guaranteed the sum of five hundred florins, confusion about the date of the concert and poor publicity led to an even lower financial return. The second performance served posterity, however, by providing new reviewers the opportunity to hear the work and publish their often perceptive observations and opinions.

The two May performances were the last public concerts in Vienna during Beethoven's lifetime, and they must be considered among the century's historic major public musical events. Perhaps not surprisingly given the size and difficulty of Beethoven's latest symphony, early reviewers, while largely positive, were not unanimous in their praise. What might surprise modern listeners is that the now-popular finale with its universally loved "Ode to Joy" was the least appreciated movement, a verdict more comprehensible if one considers that a symphony with a choral finale was unprecedented in 1824. Gottfried Weber, the same editor of *Cäcilia* who would soon provoke Beethoven's memorable (and scatological remark) in response to the negative response to *Wellington's Victory* (see chapter 5), felt quite differently about Beethoven's new work and considered the first performance of the Ninth one of the most significant dates in the history of classical music. Several decades later the influential Adolph Bernhard Marx, who had studied the score but had not yet heard the symphony, proclaimed the Ninth to be "the profoundest and most mature instrumental composition by the greatest genius and the most conscientious of living composers" (Levy 2003, 160). The predictions of Weber and Marx have been long fulfilled in a world where performances of the Ninth have become an annual Christmas ritual in Europe, America, and Asia, especially in Japan, and a piece marked for special occasions with unusually deep cultural resonances around ideas of freedom and art.

COMPOSITIONAL GENESIS

Beethoven expressed an interest in setting Friedrich Schiller's poem *An die Freude* (*To Joy*), eight years after its original publication in 1785. Beethoven may have set all or part of Schiller's poem in 1798, but only two brief sketches remain. Even in its present state, the opening of *Gegenliebe* (Love returned), the second part of *Seufzer eines ungeliebten* (Sigh of one who is unloved) from 1794–1795 WoO 118, clearly anticipates the future "Ode to Joy." With its two sets of variations, one for the orchestra alone and a second set with the addition of chorus, the *Choral Fantasy* of 1808 anticipates the finale of the Ninth structurally as well as melodically, the latter resemblance noted by Beethoven when he described the Ninth to his publisher as "in the style of my fantasia for piano with chorus but on a grander scale, with vocal solos and choruses based on the words of Schiller's immortal and famous song *An die Freude*" (Lockwood 2003, 424). Two years after the *Fantasy* Beethoven used the opening ten notes of the "Ode" to begin his setting of Goethe's *Mit einem gemalten Band* (With a decorated rhythm). The rapid conclusion of the *King Stephen* overture composed in 1812 also closely resembles the beginning of the "Ode" as it appears in the *prestissimo* that concludes the Ninth.

Thus for more than twenty years before he officially began to draft the "Ode" we know today, Beethoven had conceived the opening phrases of the melody that forms the center of the Ninth's finale and arguably the symphony as a whole. Meanwhile, the "Ode's" context and meaning had changed. By the time Beethoven began work on his last symphony, the aftermath of the Congress of Vienna had diminished the promise of the 1780s under Emperor Joseph, an era idealized, in

contrast to the repressive political atmosphere in Clemens von Metter-
nich's Vienna of the 1810s and 1820s. The "Ode to Joy" was a valentine
to an era now long passed (but not forgotten). As Lewis Lockwood
writes in *Beethoven: The Music and the Life* (2003), Beethoven's "decision to fashion a great work that would convey the poet's utopian vision
of human brotherhood is a statement of support for the principles of
democracy at a time when direct political action on behalf of such
principles was difficult and dangerous" (417).

The physical evidence reveals that Beethoven treated the "Ode"
with considerable seriousness and attention. The gold standard for a
tune of great folk-like simplicity and memorability was his former
teacher Haydn's so-called *Emperor's Hymn* from the late 1790s, a tune
that remains Germany's national anthem. Haydn, like Beethoven, also
based a theme-and-variations movement around his famous hymn in
one of his greatest instrumental compositions, the string quartet, op. 76,
no. 3, known as the *Emperor*. Although it was probably designed as a
fugue subject for a string quintet, by 1815 Beethoven had also sketched
a melody that anticipates the *scherzo* of his Ninth, and by 1818 he had
drafted much of the opening bars of the symphony and settled on the
idea of a symphony with voices. Despite this promising start, it wasn't
until after May 1823 that Beethoven decided how to complete his
"Ode." By then he had composed at least nineteen drafts of the future
tune.

Scholars tend to concur that once Beethoven had conceived the idea
of a symphony with a vocal finale and enough of the future tune (one or
two phrases) that could be anticipated in early movements, he was
prepared to devote the vast majority of his compositional energies to
this single work. Most of Beethoven's significant large works fit this
compositional approach, in which he began with preliminary sketches
or drafts while working on other pieces before concentrating on one
work in particular. Consequently, despite a seemingly long gestation
and a series of scattered sketches with material that ended up in the
Ninth between 1815 and 1822, some of which now seem to have been
originally conceived for other compositions or left unused, the real work
on the Ninth began about May 1823. By the following February the
symphony was nearly complete.

The focus on the Ninth beginning in the spring of 1823 corresponds
to the fact that Beethoven had recently completed two major works

begun in 1819, the *Missa solemnis*, which he presented to the archduke, now also the archbishop, in March, and the *Diabelli* Variations, published in June. During the past three years Beethoven had also completed the final three piano sonatas and eleven bagatelles, but little more than the groundwork on his Ninth Symphony. Once he had begun his focused labor, work on the Ninth led to the birth of a (virtually completed) healthy symphony nine months later.

THE MUSIC

First Movement: *Allegro ma Non Troppo e un Poco Maestoso*

The distinctive and idiosyncratic opening of the Ninth would echo throughout the remaining decades of the nineteenth century. We can hear it as late as Bruckner's Third Symphony in the 1870s and Mahler's First in the 1880s. The first sounds we hear are prolonged hollow perfect fifths in the horns and sixteenth-note sextuplets, also *pianissimo* and a fifth apart on the second violins and cellos. Beethoven is careful to notate the rhythm precisely, but many conductors prefer to convert the sextuplets into rapid, unmeasured *tremolos* (rapid reiterations). The two notes now sounding simultaneously (A and E) are the root and the fifth of the dominant harmony, but without a third to suggest either major or minor. Soon we hear the same fifth, now descending successively in the first violins against the A–E drones. The two notes are then reversed, A–E, then E–A in the violas and basses, and the pattern repeated. Soon the descending fourths and fifths fill in the silences, as the fourths and fifths go from octave to octave. The music continues to *crescendo* on the dominant until the opening rhythm turns into a short but distinct tune, clearly on the D minor tonic, with the full orchestra playing *fortissimo*. Listeners should savor this forceful resolution to the tonic. They will not hear another tonic resolution for more than four hundred measures. By then, the music has completed its exposition (163 measures), development (137 measures), and recapitulation (117 measures) and will soon embark on a substantial coda (120 measures).

Instead of lingering after the first tonic resolution, Beethoven returns to the mysterious and suspenseful opening. This time the harmonic starting point is the tonic itself, but instead of reestablishing the tonic the music swerves unexpectedly to a harmony six steps away, a chord (the submediant) on the sixth degree of D minor. We have landed in Bb major, the same secondary key area of the C Minor Piano Sonata op. 111 where the sixth degree is Ab. After hearing the main theme in this new key, the music travels to a secondary group that includes six brief but distinctive themes, all in Bb. From here to the end of the symphony these two opening keys, D minor and Bb major, will serve as harmonic poles guiding the musical direction. Only the second movement *scherzo* avoids this polar orbit, alternating between D minor and D major instead. The third movement alternates between two distinct lyrical themes, the first in Bb major and the second in D major, and the finale, which finally confirms D major, contains a significant amount of music in the key of Bb in the so-called Turkish section and the fugue that follows. Although these key changes may be difficult to perceive, it is hoped that readers will nonetheless appreciate the underlying tonal unity of the symphony.

We will have more to say later about what the symphony "means," but for now, at the risk of oversimplification, we might summarize this meaning as Beethoven's attempt to move from despair to joy, an idea embodied in the eventual introduction and triumph of the melody known as the "Ode to Joy," and of course Schiller's text. But even in the absence of the text and without being able to equate a specific tune with an extra-musical concept, it is possible to discern, at least in retrospect, that the snippet of a theme that directly precedes the first of the six secondary themes in Bb stands to the listener as out of the ordinary. We sense this snippet of melody means *something*, even if we do not know yet just what it means. The passage stands out as the first moment in the symphony to feature the winds, mainly oboes and horns in thirds, *piano* and *dolce* (sweetly), but also flutes, clarinets, and bassoons, with only the barest rumbling in the strings. At the risk of giving away the plot, I will note that we have just heard the first foreshadowing of joy. It will not be the last.

In contrast to his earlier symphonies, in the Ninth Beethoven does not include a repeat sign for the exposition. As observed in the first *Razumovksy* Quartet, Beethoven begins the development with the same material that opened the exposition. Also, as in the string quartet, Beethoven soon reaches a place where the music departs from the exposition. Since we are so accustomed to expect the exposition to repeat, we notice belatedly we have entered a new realm. The clue is the unexpected touch of D major in the double bass.

Many scholars have noted that the development of the Ninth is for the most part more leisurely and less turbulent than we would expect a development to be. It also sticks quite closely to the main theme for its material, including a fugato based on this theme. Beethoven prepares carefully for the return of the tonic in the retransition to the recapitulation, but when the main theme returns, along with the tonic, what we hear is not the main theme but the introduction to the main theme. With the full orchestra playing *fortissimo* and the timpani playing a drum roll, mainly on the note D for thirty-eight measures, it is hard to miss this dramatic moment.

This seemingly violent return of the opening of the recapitulation is one of the most discussed passages of the symphony. What seems to frighten those who comment on this striking musical moment is the ferocity that contradicts the purpose of a recapitulation, which is to offer stability after an unstable and disruptive development. Beethoven reverses these expectations and purposes by following a relatively subdued development with a decidedly unstable recapitulation. Ironically, perhaps the chief disruptive element in what follows is Beethoven's decision to begin the recapitulation in D *major*, the future key and mode of the "Ode to Joy." By placing the third of D major (the F#) in the lowest sounding part (i.e., a first inversion triad), Beethoven further destabilizes the sense of an arrival on D, whether major or minor. While the timpani are rolling their Ds, the harmony changes momentarily to Bb major before eventually settling on D minor, which is where we *should* be in a D minor movement.

Since the music did not state the first theme properly in the tonic minor in the opening of the recapitulation, and in fact, failed to resolve clearly to D minor, the task of accomplishing this objective falls to the coda, which we noted is the first such resolution in over four hundred measures. At last, the melodic material of the resolution is the main theme itself, not the introduction to the main theme. In the final moments of the coda Beethoven introduces a new distinctive march-like theme in the tonic, *piano*, a theme regularly described as a funeral march. Underneath this somber new tune the bassoons and lower strings (and later the upper strings as well) play a recurring spooky chromatic figure *pianissimo* that heightens the funereal gloom. The movement that began with heightened expectations ends with violence and despair with one last *fortissimo* statement of the main theme.

Second Movement: *Molto Vivace*

During the golden years of network television the most consistently popular nightly news broadcast was the *Huntley-Brinkley Report*. This news juggernaut ran from 1956 to 1970 on the National Broadcasting Company, after which Chet Huntley retired to Montana and David Brinkley became the program's sole news reader. In the dark ages before remote control devices, viewers who chose not to leave their chairs and couches to manually change the channel to one of the other two major networks heard a substantial excerpt of Beethoven's Ninth Symphony *scherzo* during the closing credits. On Huntley's farewell broadcast, easily accessible on YouTube, those interested can hear the first forty seconds (seventy-seven measures), ending shortly after the full orchestra plays the main theme for the first time. Since this was an NBC broadcast and since Arturo Toscanini's 1952 recording was perhaps the most popular of the era, Toscanini's famous studio band, the NBC Symphony Orchestra, provided the soundtrack. Eventually the network replaced Beethoven with other theme songs, including John Williams's catchy tune *The Mission*, between 1985 and 2004. Beethoven did make a comeback on *Countdown with Keith Olbermann* where, from 2003 to 2011, viewers with shorter attention spans heard the first six notes of the *scherzo* against a visual collage backdrop that included a photo of Huntley and Brinkley. After two seconds of Beethoven the music shifted to a jazz version that preserved bare remnants of the opening rhythm played with snare drum brushes.

The Ninth is the only Beethoven symphony in which a *scherzo* appears as the second movement, a placement that follows Beethoven's choice for the first *Razumovsky* string quartet, the piano sonatas op. 101 and op. 106, and several chamber works by Haydn and Mozart. The Ninth *scherzo* begins with a memorable three-note rhythm on a descending octave that is heard four times in succession, each time separated by a dramatic measure of silence, twice in the strings, once in the timpani tuned to two Fs an octave apart, and once with the full orchestra minus the timpani. This opening three-note gesture not only begins the main theme and its fugal treatment in the strings with a new entrance every fourth measure but also serves as an independent motive. Although formally a *scherzo* in two repeated parts followed by a trio in two repeated sections, Beethoven expands the scope of the form to include a fully worked-out development and coda to create a sonata-form movement within the *scherzo* structure. The recapitulation begins with four vigorous statements of the opening three-note motive *fortissimo* in the full orchestra. When the fourth statement returns with the main theme mostly in the winds and strings, Beethoven retains the motive's rhythm and octave as an accompaniment in the brass and lower strings.

A vigorously, almost violently brief (two-measure), transition in duple time prepares for a tuneful trio in D major, a section rarely, if not unprecedentedly, in duple meter. For the first time in the symphony the music now unmistakably foretells the future, a future fully realized in the finale. We can no longer doubt that the symphony is a search for D, a search last thwarted in the turbulent D major opening of the recapitulation. Thanks to Schiller's text, we also know that the symphony is a search for joy, embodied in the tune "Ode to Joy." Like the slaves in Michelangelo's unfinished sculptures struggling to extricate themselves from their marble prisons, in the first movement we heard "Ode to Joy" struggling to get out of a D minor despair. In the first part of the trio of the *scherzo*, the oboes and clarinets play a melody that shares the same notes as the opening phrase of the future "Ode to Joy," albeit in an altered rhythm that partially obscures the melodic truth. And as with the early incomplete foreshadowing before the second theme in the first movement, this far larger glimpse of "Ode to Joy" features the oboes and clarinets supported by the bassoons playing *staccato* quarter notes of the D major scale.

The movement also displays a clever shifting pattern of metrical organization. In the development Beethoven replaces the four-measure units of the main theme in the exposition with three-measure units and calls attention to this change with the notation *Ritmo di tre battute* (rhythm of three measures). To highlight this grouping Beethoven places the message above each entering instrument. Here's the order in case you want to follow: bassoon I, oboe I, bassoon I (but not labeled), and flute I (six measures without the pattern). After this first round, Beethoven plays a subtle trick. He retains the *Ritmo di tre battute* designation but gives the first beat of each three-measure pattern to the timpani with its main octave motive. Although he only labels it once in the score, he repeats the pattern five times. After several other three-measure groupings without the timpani, by now playing a role usually reserved for a more traditional solo orchestral instrument, Beethoven returns to the early four-measure units (*Ritmo di quattro battute*) but now places the fugal entries only two measures apart rather than four.

At the end of the movement, nearly eighty pages long in the Bärenreiter study score and lasting roughly the same amount of time as the first movement, Beethoven reveals his final surprise. Once again, Beethoven repeats the short and agitated transition in duple meter that earlier led to the D major trio, but this time, after stating the theme based on "Ode to Joy" for seven measures, he asks the entire orchestra to observe a measure of abrupt silence. He then uses the material of the transition measures to conclude the movement with a bang, albeit a bang without timpani. According to the twelve-year-old Thalberg, it was here that Beethoven was caught still turning pages (who could blame him) and was gently turned around by Demoiselle Unger to recognize the applause, an encouragement that apparently did not lead to an encore of the movement.

Third Movement: *Adagio Molto e Cantabile*

The ravishingly lyrical slow third movement reveals an unfulfilled search for D major and in which the "Ode" remains understated and easy to miss. As in the Fifth Symphony's second movement, the form is a double set of variations, although the Ninth offers relatively little contrast in mood beyond an increased tempo from an *Adagio* in Bb in the first section (the key of the second theme in the first movement) to an *Andante* in D major in the second (the key of the *scherzo*'s trio and the finale). Again, in contrast with the Fifth, no cadence or formal closure separates the two sections of the Ninth's slow movement, and although Bb and D may seem far apart tonally, they do share a crucial common note, D, the third degree of Bb and the first degree in D major or minor, which makes it possible for the ear to move easily from one key to another. The first section returns in Bb with an active first violin musical line, but instead of returning to D major for the second part, Beethoven moves with seeming suddenness to G major, a key that will play a major role in the finale.

After the second statement (or variation) of the second part in G, instead of returning to the first theme Beethoven inserts an episode in Eb (the subdominant of Bb, just as G major was the subdominant of D). Although the opening of this episode is clearly based on the first part, after two measures it moves on to new territory. The episode is especially distinctive for its focus on the winds, starting with clarinets and continuing with the first bassoon and fourth horn first accompanied by sparse *pizzicato* string and later a counter melody for the flute. The variation in Bb that follows the episode parallels the first part more completely with the addition of a florid and seemingly improvisatory legato musical line in the first violins that floats above the *pizzicatos* of the other string parts.

The search for D, although apparent only in the first *Andante*, nonetheless leaves a strong impression. Although harmonically the music in this section reinforces the key of D, the *melody*, marked *espressivo* in the second violins and violas playing in unison, tends to avoid this central note. When D does arrive, the harmony below has moved on. In the first measure of this section the melody sounds like the opening of "Three Blind Mice," but without the "mice," that is, the tonic D. The second and third measures continue with nearly every note in the D major scale *except* D before the music lights on D on the weak part of the beat in the fourth measure. This brings the music back to "three blind" (but still without the mice). When the second violins and violas repeat the melody, the first violin joins above with a countermelody in which the note D appears in the second, fourth, and sixth measures of the tune. After the first *Andante*, D major will vanish for the rest of the movement, gone but not forgotten.

The Eb episode also features a much-discussed modulation to the remote key of Cb major. This key is enharmonic with B major, another tonal area that has appeared in significant places in the first movement and will return in the finale. The relationship between the Eb that begins the episode and the Cb that concludes it is the same as what we found in the recapitulation of the Piano Sonata op. 110, where the music went from the tonic Ab to E major. In both cases the relationship is the flat sixth degree or flat submediant, the same as the relationship between D major and Bb major. To emphasize the unusual key of Cb, Beethoven gives the fourth horn player a prominent part that culminates with a one-measure solo, a solo that would have greatly taxed the player required to move his mouth and hands to execute this tricky passage in the absence of valves. After the solo that floats above *pizzicato* arpeggios in the strings (minus the bass), the Gb dominant of Cb moves down a half step to the F dominant of Bb. This paves the way for the return to Bb the original tonic, a half step lower than Cb/B. It is one of the most magical moments of the symphony.

The coda opens with an orchestral fanfare, followed by a final foreshadowing of "Ode to Joy" marked *cantabile*, the first eight notes played by the first flute and first oboe. The latter instrument has now played a part in all three foreshadowings of joy in this symphony, much as it played a symbolic role representing Leonore in *Fidelio*.

Fourth Movement: *Presto* (Followed by Many Changes of Tempo)

Beethoven follows the Bb major serenity of the third movement with a rude awakening, a loud and ferocious chord (a D minor trial with an added Bb) indelibly described by Wagner as the *Schreckensfanfare*—in English, "horror fanfare" (think of the character Shrek, although the scary-looking Shrek we know today is actually sweet and green). Unison cellos and basses answer this outburst with a passage that sounds much like a sung recitative in an opera, a phenomenon Beethoven introduced in his *Tempest* and again in the op. 110 piano sonatas. Many conductors, starting with Wagner, have chosen to disregard Beethoven's performance direction for this passage, which he designated in French: "Selon le charactère d'un Récitatif, mais in Tempo" (In the manner of a recitative but in tempo). Since the recitative does not contain words, it is not easy to understand what the cellos and basses are saying without a program, but in contrast to the earlier examples of instrumental recitative, Beethoven will soon offer a serviceable translation.

Before this occurs Beethoven immediately unleashes a *fortissimo* and dissonant intensification of the "horror fanfare," this time harmonized with an ominous diminished-seventh triad on C (C–Eb–F#–A) over a sustained D pedal point roll in the timpani. Following this second outburst of the intensified "horror" chord Beethoven turns to a series of thematic reminiscences that recall fragments of the earlier movements in close succession. In looking at the Fifth Symphony we observed that Beethoven thematically recalled the *scherzo* movement midway through the finale. Now for the first time he brings back portions of *all* the previous movements, albeit briefly. Interestingly, instead of stating the opening of these movements, he presents the main themes as heard in their developments or other internal sections.

The rapid rejection by the cellos and basses of these fleeting recollections is analogous to a baseball pitcher shaking off the sign from the catcher. No fast ball here. How about a changeup? Eventually the catcher, in this case the orchestra, signals for the welcome and recognizable fragment of "Ode to Joy," a theme that, as we have noted, has appeared in some form in each of the first three movements. Hearing what they want to hear, the cellos and basses now answer "yes" (actually two syllables, more like "Jawohl") and soon offer a complete statement of "Ode to Joy" for the first time in the symphony, after which the orchestra joins in for three variations and a generous coda.

The variations concluded, Beethoven interrupts the instrumental celebration of joy with the third and the most dissonant version of the "horror fanfare" (this time a diminished seventh on C#, C#–E–G–Bb against the dominant pedal A of the tonic D minor) to prepare listeners for a historic moment in the history of the classical symphony: the appearance of a voice, a baritone, who echoes the *timbre* or tone color (the distinguishing quality of a sound), style, and at the start, the identical melody we heard in the instrumental recitative played by the cellos and basses. After an opening phrase, delivered as a vocal recitative, the remaining text is derived from Schiller's "Ode to Joy." The first words belong to Beethoven, his sole addition to Schiller's text: "O Freunde, nicht diese Töne! Sondern last uns angenehmere anstimmen, und freudenvollere!" (Oh friends, not these tones! Let us instead tune our voices more pleasantly and joyfully!). The vocal component of the first choral symphony has now begun.

Beethoven scholars and enthusiasts have long contemplated the meaning of Beethoven's opening salvo. In particular, what does he mean by "tones"? While some conclude that Beethoven was referring only to the "horror fanfare," the prevailing (and I believe most persuasive) interpretation is that Beethoven's statement parallels the cellos and basses successive rejection of the first three movements and their embrace of the theme that represents and embodies the concept of joy. Wagner went even further when he interpreted the rejection of the earlier movements with a broader rejection of *all instrumental music.*

During the sketching process Beethoven contemplated but eventually rejected the idea of direct verbal statements that address the meaning of the thematic reminiscences. Beethoven's discarded notes clearly support the interpretation offered here. Over a draft of the cello-bass recitative in connection with the reminiscence of the first movement he wrote, "No . . . this would remind us too much of our despair" (Forbes 1964, 892). The notes that follow the glimpse of the *scherzo* reject that movement as "only a littler merrier," and the notes for the third movement describe that movement as "too tender" (893). Finally there is the punch line: "For something animated we must seek" (opening of "Ode to Joy"). "I shall see to it that I myself intone something then do you sing after me. This it is. Ha . . . now it is found. I myself will intone it" (893)—in other words, "not these tones." The implication is clear. The first three movements fall short. What we need is a movement full of joy, an "Ode to Joy." And this is what Beethoven intones. What follows is a descriptive outline of the movement's form:

PART I: THE SECULAR WORLD OF JOY

1. *Orchestral introduction and exposition.* Two "horror fanfares" separated by a passage of instrumental recitative played by cellos and basses (in the first a Bb is added to a D minor triad, and the second consists of a diminished-seventh chord on C against a D pedal). After the second more dissonant fanfare, the cellos and basses listen to thematic reminiscences of the first three movements and reject them ("not these tones") before the opening of the "Ode to Joy" affirms the desire for this melody that has been struggling to be heard.

2. *Theme.* A complete orchestral statement of "Ode to Joy" in D major (first part, two related four-measure phrases; second part, an eight-measure phrase repeated). As with the opening recitative, the tune is played alone by the cellos and basses. Three variations follow.

> Variation 1: The viola joins the cello with the melody to which Beethoven adds counterlines for the bassoons and basses.

Variation 2: The tune shifts to the first violins while the bassoon and bass lines continue alongside new melodic strands for the second violins and cellos.

Variation 3: A shift in dynamics from *piano* to *forte* for a full orchestra variation with the main tune in the winds and brass.

3. Vocal Introduction and Exposition (D major)

a. The third and most dissonant horror fanfare (D minor with an dominant A pedal tone and a diminished seventh on C#)
b. Baritone recitative, "O friends, not these tones"
c. Choral variations (D major). After the baritone utters Beethoven's sole addition to Schiller, the remaining text follows Schiller's words, albeit reorganized and reshaped by the composer, including the deletion of a significant amount of the poet's text published in 1803. Schiller organized his poem into verses and choruses from which Beethoven selected the first three verses and choruses 4, 1, and 3 (in this order).

Variation 4 (verse 1): First part and first statement of the second part for baritone; second statement of the second part answered by sopranos, altos, and tenors. Concludes with a four-measure coda.

Variation 5 (verse 2): First part and first statement of the second part for the four soloists; second statement of the second part for full choir followed by a four-measure coda.

Variation 6 (verse 3): A more ornamental variation of the "Ode," again the first part and first *statement of the second with soloists and second statement of the second part for full choir.*

d. Variation 7 (chorus 4): *Turkish* March. A short transition leads to a dramatic key change to Bb major, the alternate central key throughout the symphony. This is the *alla Marcia* section for tenor solo answered by a male choir. To capture the Turkish character Beethoven introduces a *timbre* that would have evoked a Janissary band in the 1820s as it did for Mozart in his opera *The Abduction from the Seraglio* in the 1780s. Turkey, the center of the Ottoman Empire, which almost scaled the walls and conquered the city of Vienna in 1683 and continued to be a military menace in Beethoven's time, also served as an exotic Other that was popular with composers and audiences. Beethoven's *Turkish* variation, however, is more joyful than menacing or exotic. At the beginning of the introduction we hear only the offbeat accents on the bassoons, contrabassoon, and *gran tamburo* (Italian for bass drum) in the score, the latter two instruments for the first time in the symphony. We then hear a variation based on the "Ode" in which the flutes, clarinets, and trumpets are joined by the pseudo-Turkish percussion, the triangle and cymbals (noted in Italian as the *triangolo* and *cinelli* in the score). If one accepts the slow tempo that Beethoven apparently gave to his publisher Schott, when it comes to the bassoons and contrabassoon, the introduction seems to evoke a comic and earthy quality that suggests a sound from the body one is expected to suppress in public. Before the tenor answers, the orchestra plays the pitches of the entire "Ode to Joy," although the rhythmic changes partially disguise and transform this familiar tune into something new and different. When the tenor enters he also sings a less literal but recognizable variation of the "Ode" that encourages Beethoven's brothers to "hurtle through the heavens as joyful as a hero on his way to triumph." Although the orchestral and vocal expositions are organized around theme-and-variation form, Beethoven has simultaneously imbued the form with elements that strongly suggest sonata form. Variation 7 is a case in point. If the melody of "Ode to Joy" constitutes a first theme, the *Turkish* March can be thought of as second theme, which like the second theme of the first movement, shares the key of Bb major.

e. Fugue: Orchestra transition from Bb major back to D major. This is a double fugue, a fugue with two subjects sounding simultaneously. One subject presents a rapid variation of "Ode to Joy"; the other, a continuation of the Turkish March rhythm. The first subject drops out, and the Turkish rhythms take the music back to the original key. The music begins to die down, and we hear the first three notes of "Ode to Joy" in B major, then back to the Turkish rhythms, then the first three notes of the "Ode" in B minor, then back to the Turkish rhythms, and finally the first three notes of "Ode to Joy" in D major. According to the film biography *Copying Beethoven* (2006), Beethoven's fictitious young female copyist gave the composer the idea of the shift to B minor. In the earlier Beethoven biopic *Immortal Beloved* (1994), the fugue provides an opportunity for the composer to imagine himself in flight from his brutal father, thus offering a literal visual interpretation of *fuga*, which means flight in Italian. If we wanted to think about this movement as a sonata form, the fugue, which lasts a full minute, functions as a credible development section.

  f. Variation 8 (verse 1). This is the first and only time we hear the full choir sing the complete "Ode to Joy." In sonata form this return would mark the beginning of the recapitulation.

PART 2: THE SACRED WORLD OF THE CREATOR (CHORUSES 1 AND 3)

Andante Maestoso—Adagio ma Non Troppo ma Divoto (Moderately Slow and Majestic—Slow but Not Too Much and with Religious Devotion)

If the first part of the movement is all about the secular world and promise of joy, the second part depicts the creator watching over humankind (i.e., our brothers and sisters) "überm Sternenzelt" (above the starry canopy). For this section Beethoven selects the texts of Schiller's first and third choruses beginning with the words "Seid umschlungen, Millionen!" (Be embraced, you millions!). The tempo changes to *Andante*, and the full choir, without soloists, sings a stately new melody in G major, the key of the second *Andante* of the third movement, beginning with the words "Seid umschlungen." It would be unusual in a sonata to have a new second theme in the recapitulation, especially one in the subdominant, but on the other hand a few years earlier in the recapitulation of the Piano Sonata op. 110 Beethoven stated what we called the "second" first theme in the subdominant as he does here. The dynamic level starts and remains at *fortissimo* until the tempo changes to *Adagio* for the words "Ihr stürzt nieder, Millionen?" (Do you fall to your knees, you millions?), the opening words of Schiller's chorus 3. The second section of this middle part is marked by strong and sometimes rapid dynamic contrasts, starting with *pianissimo* for the first phrase, a sudden *fortissimo* on the word Welt (world), a return to *pianissimo*, and a crescendo to *forte* on the words "Such' ihn überm Sternenzelt" (Seek him beyond the stars). The section ends with two statements of the final line of chorus 3, "Über Sternen muss er wohnen" (Beyond the stars he must dwell), the first *fortissimo*, the second *pianissimo*. In both, the sopranos stay fixed on a high F as they reach for the stars under a shimmering orchestra.

PART 3: "ODE TO JOY" AND *SEID UMSCHLUNGEN MILLIONEN!* (VERSE 1 AND CHORUS 1 COMBINED, THEN VERSE 1, LINES 1–2, 5–8, 5–8, AND FINALLY CHORUS 1 WITH STANZA 1, LINES 1–2)

Allegro Energico e Sempre ben Marcato (Fast, Energetic, and Always Well Marked)

For the third climactic section Beethoven combines the first stanza of Schiller's first verse and chorus 1 textually and thematically in a double fugue in which the main tune of the "Ode" and the music of "Seid umschlungen, Millionen!" sound together. In order to combine these two melodies successfully Beethoven had to alter the rhythm and used only the first twelve pitches of the "Ode," retaining the long-held rhythms and all fifteen of the melodic notes of "Seid umschlungen." After Beethoven makes the sopranos sing high As on the words "ganzen Welt!" (all the world!), he asks them to remain on this pitch, *fortissimo*, for nearly nine measures and then sing four more As for another repetition of "der ganzen Welt!" Next the music makes a sudden dynamic change to *piano* when the basses, tenors, and altos take turns with a jagged musical line on the repetition of the words "Ihr stürzt nieder, Millionen?" (basses), "Ahnest du den Schöpfer, Welt?" (World, do you sense your Maker?"; tenors), and "Such' ihn überm Sternenzelt" (altos), after which the entire chorus repeats the same jagged phrase on different starting notes. Leonard Bernstein points out that Beethoven's unconventional melody and harmonically nebulous passage presents eleven of the twelve tones available in the octave before returning to a conventional dominant triad beginning with the word "Brüder."

CODA

Beethoven concludes the finale with a coda mainly in D major that contains numerous thematic and tempo changes, nearly all based on recognizable snippets of the "Ode to Joy."

Allegro ma Non Tanto

After the orchestra plays a variation on the first part of the "Ode to Joy," the soloists trade material in pairs, first tenor and bass, then soprano and alto, then alto and soprano, and finally tenor and bass. The full choir concludes the section with material that is less closely related thematically to the "Ode."

Poco Adagio

On the famous words "Alle Menschen werden Brüder, Wo den sanfter Flügel weilt" (All men become brothers where your gentle wing rests), the soloists sing one of the most moving passages in the symphony. The supporting harmony is the remote B major, and each voice gets a chance to sing an elaborate melisma on the word sanfter (gentle). This marks the return of that special episode in the third movement when the valveless fourth horn takes the center stage on the enharmonic of B major, Cb major. At the end of the passage, on the final repetition of the word Welt (world), the mode shifts suddenly and dramatically from B major to B minor. While the upper three vocal parts stay on their pitches, the bass moves down from a B to an A and creates a D major triad. The music quickly accelerates to what might be called a second coda using the words of the first chorus ("Seid umschlungen") and the first two lines of the first verse. The tempo starts at *Presto*, interrupts with four measures of *Maestoso* in triple meter, and concludes with a final *Prestissimo sempre fortissimo* to bring the music to a rousing close.

A NOTE ON BEETHOVEN'S TEMPOS

Beethoven's Italian, and occasionally German, tempo indications used throughout his career offer a range of tempos from *adagio* to *allegro* and *prestissimo*, along with qualifiers such as *assai* or *molto* (very) or *non troppo* (not too much). During the years Beethoven composed his first eight symphonies, composers were unable to be more specific about this important musical component. The problem was solved in 1815, one year after the premiere of the Eighth Symphony, when Beethoven's acquaintance, Johann Nepomuk Mälzel, the man who developed a machine to play the battle music for *Wellington's Victory*, added a sliding scale of tempo markings to Dietrich Nikolaus Winkel's 1812 invention and patented it as a metronome. To this day the abbreviation M. M. above a musical score followed by a marking such as "one quarter note = 60" (i.e., one beat per second) stands for Mälzel's Metronome (not Metronome Marking, although that works too).

Beethoven quickly embraced this new invention and in 1817 published tempo markings for his first eight symphonies. When writing the Ninth he transmitted the specific tempo markings he had in mind in a letter copied by his nephew Karl (but signed by the composer) that he sent to the publisher Schott in 1826. The tempo markings were entered in time for the second edition in 1827. Although the markings offer one of the few starting points for the performance of the symphonies, from Beethoven's time to ours many conductors have found the tempos to be too fast. In short, prior to the recordings of Roger Norrington with the London Classical Players on historical instruments, conductors simply did not take Beethoven's marks seriously, even though the measurement of time has not changed since the 1820s, or for that matter since the beginning of measured time.

We know from recordings and live performances that as the twentieth century progressed conductors (with some exceptions) tended to adopt slower tempos in interpreting the works of revered classical composers. Until the historical performance movement of the late twentieth century, slow movements in particular seemed to be getting slower and slower. Thus it shouldn't be surprising that perhaps Beethoven's most controversial, and least followed, Ninth Symphony metronome marking is the one he assigned to the *Adagio* movement, in which the quartet note is given at sixty, that is, one beat per second. Before Norrington, who clocks in about fifty-eight, no major conductors went above forty-six. Most fall in the thirties or even below freezing in Farenheit (i.e., thirty-two). It is of course possible that Beethoven's notated tempos were a little faster than he intended. Nevertheless, to this day most conductors' tempos tend not even to approximate Beethoven's tempo marking for the third movement, although slow movement tempos for other symphonies have been gradually creeping up to Beethoven's stated markings

More controversial are two markings that have seemed too *slow*, in fact nearly half as fast as conductors have interpreted them. Although Beethoven signed off on these markings as well, conductors and scholars regularly attribute the seemingly excessively slow tempos for the trio of the *scherzo* and the *Turkish* March as errors of transmission. Since Norrington took these slow indications seriously, it is possible for listeners to judge for themselves whether the music for these passages is too slow. For most students of the symphonies the problem is that if one takes the tempo markings at the presumed tempos, which exactly double Beethoven's tempo, these passages would sound too fast, even out of control. John Eliot Gardiner's 1992 recording with the Orchestre Révolutionnaire et Romantique, as with Norrington's also played on historical instruments, demonstrates how these two passages sound at twice the tempo Beethoven marked. Since Beethoven's tempos seem too slow for most conductors and the presumed doubled tempos too fast, most conductors simply do what they want to do, which usually means a tempo somewhere between these extremes.

MEANINGS: A POSTSCRIPT

After some initial controversy, notably in England, within a decade after Beethoven's death the Ninth became a classic and has since retained its central place in the classical musical firmament throughout the world. On Christmas 1989, one month after the Berlin Wall came down, Leonard Bernstein contributed to the celebrations by conducting the symphony in the Schauspielhaus in the former East Berlin, again part of a reunited city attended by thousands. Video and audio recordings preserve the reality of this historic occasion. Several additional features make this performance stand out. It is the only recording to use boys as Beethoven did at the first performances in 1824. At seventy-eight minutes it is the slowest recording on record, four full minutes slower than the previous record of seventy-four minutes set by the German conductor Wilhelm Furtwängler in 1951. Finally, basing the decision on unsubstantiated historical assumptions, but mainly because he thought the occasion fit, Bernstein substituted the word Freiheit (freedom, as we know from *Fidelio*) every time Schiller's poem requests that the soloists and members of the choir sing the word Freude (joy). In fact, the new title *Ode to Freedom* is emblazoned on the covers of the CD and DVD in large capital letters. As we observed in *Fidelio*, the connections between Freiheit and Freude are profound. In fact, it is a hopeless challenge to envision the latter without the former.

The melody of "Ode to Joy" has lived a rich life of its own independent of the symphony. One could say without hyperbole that the "Ode," sung at every Olympic Games since 1956, has become one of the most universally recognized tunes. But the symphony as a whole has retained a strong presence. When the Sony Corporation in the early 1980s developed the technology needed to permit the optimal diameter for a CD, the chosen work was the Beethoven composition known as *Daiku* or the Big Ninth, and the specific length was set by Furtwängler's recorded performance, then the slowest available. Bernstein's recording would stretch the technology to accommodate another four minutes.

The idea that Beethoven's Ninth is about the search for joy, a search that also encompasses a search for D major, the key in which joy dwells, remains central to our understanding of the symphony. The seeds of joy are audibly planted when the winds take over briefly early in the first movement and nearly blooms in the trio of the *scherzo* before becoming more submerged in the third movement, which also contains a section in D, the first *Andante*. Interestingly, the critic Franz Joseph Fröhlich, writing from Mainz in the journal *Cäcilia* in 1828, interprets the overall absence of joy in the first three movements before joy fully blossoms in the finale to mean that Beethoven was trying to reveal in music how joy can overcome despair. For Fröhlich, other works by Beethoven may possess undisclosed meanings understood only to the composer but in the case of the Ninth, the text made the meaning clear. Robin Wallace in his survey *Beethoven's Critics* (1986), summarizes Fröhlich's interpretation:

> The theme is the transcendent power of joy to overcome both everyday sorrows and the larger issues which oppress mankind. In Beethoven's case, the larger issue was deafness, and, says Fröhlich, the composer had only realized the redeeming power of joy after great spiritual struggle. The symphony portrays this struggle and its resolu-

tion, beginning in D minor and ending in D major with the choral
tribute to joy's divine spark (Wallace 1986, 77–78).

Beethoven's addendum to the document generally known as the
Heiligenstadt Testament of 1802 may shed some light on what joy
meant to the composer, and its importance. The testament was an unsent letter to his brothers in which the composer raged against his
suffering caused by his deafness before dramatically expressing his resolve to live for art. In the addendum Beethoven implores Providence
to grant him "at last but one day of pure *joy*—it is so long since real joy
echoed in my heart" (Solomon 1998, 154). It is not unreasonable to
conclude that Beethoven had been searching for joy ever since. The
idea that suffering leads to joy turns up much later and in a somewhat
different context, in a letter Beethoven wrote to the Countess Erdödy
in 1815, the year he entered the first recognizable sketch for the Ninth
Symphony. Beethoven's remark may reflect only his response to the
countess's difficult coach journey, and we may be misguided in interpreting Beethoven's comment as a statement about a profound philo-
sophical quest. Still, Romain Rolland in his once phenomenally popular
book *Beethoven the Creator* published originally in French in 1927, but
soon widely influential in its German, English, and more surprisingly,
Japanese translations, concluded that Beethoven's remark to his dear
friend that "the best of us obtain joy through suffering" (Cook 1993, 96)
can be read as an explanation of what the Ninth Symphony was all
about. After listening to the optimistic close of Beethoven's final symphony, it is not too far a leap to think that Rolland might have been
right.

9

THE STRING QUARTET IN C-SHARP
MINOR, OP. 131 (1826)

The C sharp minor quartet, I must admit, was here revealed to me in its true form for the first time, as its melos had hitherto been unclear to me. Even if I had no other memories from my stay in Paris at that time, I would have to single that out as unforgettable and significant. —Richard Wagner after hearing a performance of op. 131 by the Maurin-Chevillard Quartet in Paris, October 1853. (Wagner, *My Life* [New York: Da Capo, 1992], 503)

BACKGROUND

We have earlier noted Richard Wagner's widely quoted epiphany on the Seventh Symphony as "the apotheosis of the dance" (chapter 5), his enthusiasm for Beethoven's melodic gifts in "Beethoven and Song" (chapter 6), and his lasting description of the *Schreckensfanfare*, the dissonant "horror fanfare" that opens the Ninth Symphony (chapter 8). Clearly Beethoven played an incalculable role in Wagner's musical development. It seems the acolyte never stopped thinking about the master, how to understand and talk about his music, and how to surpass the symphonic Beethoven in his own music dramas such as the *Ring*. Arguably Beethoven's most influential successor, Wagner also influenced Beethoven's reception and overall impact, an impact that goes beyond a few highly quotable descriptions. The historical and artistic connections between Beethoven and Wagner are definitely a two-way street worthy of at least a book of its own.

One year after the "unforgettable and significant" memory of hearing Beethoven's penultimate quartet, the C# Minor, op. 131, in Paris, Wagner offered a programmatic explanation for the work as he had done earlier with the *Eroica*, the Ninth Symphony, and the *Coriolan* Overture. Before too long Wagner became a major catalyst in disseminating the idea that Beethoven's deafness, rather than the cause of the difficulties and infelicities in the late music, was in fact the inspiration for a renewed and deeper spirituality. According to the Wagner scholar Klaus Kropfinger in *Wagner and Beethoven: Richard Wagner's Reception of Beethoven* (1991), the essence of Wagner's programmatic interpretation of the C# Minor Quartet parallels our interpretation of the Ninth, a work in which we can observe "Beethoven as a suffering human being, consumed by his longing for joy" (65).

In his symphony Beethoven conquers suffering, and the *Ode to Joy* finally triumphs. In contrast, the C# Minor Quartet, which also demonstrates a valiant search for D major, must in the end settle for C# major. As Kropfinger writes, "What finally awaits him, however, is not joy but painful resignation" (65). J. W. N. Sullivan in his influential and popular *Beethoven: His Spiritual Development* (1927) described the C# Minor Quartet as "a feat of concentration, of abstraction, of utter truthfulness, that is without equal" (160). For those who value organic unity in a musical work (i.e., interconnections of melody, harmony, rhythm, and form), the musical message of the C# Minor Quartet supports the spiritual, and in the opinion of many, allegedly including the composer, op. 131 stands as Beethoven's finest musical achievement. It is a work that inspires awe and inhibits speech, and it is definitely a tall order to explain in words how this daunting work can accomplish so much in craft and meaning. But since a guiding premise of this book is that words can potentially guide readers toward a greater understanding and appreciation of a musical work, even a complex work such as the C# Minor Quartet, I will make the attempt to do so. First, some background on the historical origins of the quartets.

On November 9, 1822, the Russian nobleman Prince Nicolai Galitzin commissioned Beethoven to write "one, two, or three quartets for which labor I will be glad to pay you what you think proper" (Solomon 1998, 412) in exchange for the dedication. Less than two years later,

Galitzin, an accomplished amateur cellist and chamber musician, would arrange the St. Petersburg premiere of the *Missa solemnis*, one month before the premiere of the Ninth Symphony. It was not until the May premiere of the Ninth that Beethoven could begin work on the Eb Major Quartet (op. 127), a work he completed in February 1825. From February to July he composed the second Galitzin Quartet in A Minor, op. 132. He then proceeded directly with the Bb Quartet, op. 130, finishing the third Galitzin quartet in November with its original finale, the *Grosse Fuge*, eventually published separately as op. 133. While Beethoven was working belatedly on the trio of works commonly known as the "Galitzin Quartets" (the quartets op. 127, op. 132, and op. 130), Galitzin kept busy by arranging a number of Beethoven's piano sonatas for various chamber combinations, several of which were published.

After completing the three commissioned Galitzin quartets, Beethoven decided to compose first one and then another quartet, both of which incorporated the overflow of unused ideas from the first trio of quartets. Op. 131 was conceived in December 1825, completed about July 1826, and delivered to the publisher Schott in August. The final, and briefest, quartet, the F Major, op. 135, was begun in July and completed in October. By now persuaded that he needed to sever the enormous *Grosse Fuge* from the rest of the Bb Quartet, Beethoven wrote a new finale in November. After working virtually exclusively on string quartets from mid-1824 to the end of 1826, the new finale turned out to be Beethoven's final completed composition, although he left some sketches for a planned Tenth Symphony. From November to his death the following March 27, Beethoven was too ill to start or finish any further compositions.

The commission of the quartets coincided with the return to Vienna of violinist Ignaz Schuppanzigh in April 1823 after a seven-year diaspora in St. Petersburg, in time to serve as the concertmaster for the debut of Beethoven's Ninth in May 1824. By this time Beethoven and the large man he affectionately referred to as "My Lord Falstaff" had been friends and musical associates for decades. Beginning in the 1790s Schuppanzigh had served in Prince Karl Lichnowsky's resident quartet, and over the years the quartet gave the premieres of Beethoven's first eleven quartets: the six op. 18 quartets of 1801, the three *Razumovsky* Quartets of 1806, and the quartets op. 74 and op. 95, the last of these in 1814, not long before the beginning of Schuppanzigh's Russian exodus in 1816. Without Schuppanzigh's indispensable encouragement and participation, it is unlikely that the quartets of the composer's last years would have been performed or even composed. The first Galitzin Quartet, op. 127, was performed in Schuppanzigh's recently formed subscription series in March 1825. The next Galitzin, the A Minor, was performed outside the series, at a concert for the benefit of Schuppanzigh's cellist Joseph Linke (November 1825). The Bb Major enjoyed two premieres, a special Schuppanzigh nonseries concert in March 1825 with the *Grosse Fuge* finale and another Linke benefit with the new finale in April 1827, one month after Beethoven's death. Op. 135 premiered at Linke's benefit concert in March 1828.

Only one of Beethoven's final quartets is thus bereft of a known premiere within a year after Beethoven's death: the C# Minor. The first documented performance of this quartet in Vienna occurred at a concert with Leopold Jansa and his quartet in November 1834. It is possible, however, that the "Last Quartet Entertainment by Mr. Schuppanzigh" (Gingerich 2010, 486), a mixed concert presented in March 1828 that included an aria, a set of piano variations, a duet for clarinet and horn—none of which were composed by Beethoven—and *An die ferne Geliebte*, may have contained the C# Minor, even though the program advertised a "new quartet by Beethoven, in A minor"(487), i.e., op. 132. The Schubert scholar John Gingerich considers the key a misprint, reasoning that a previously heard work would not be listed as new (2010). In any event, the A minor had already received two performances in addition to its 1826 premiere. The conversation books refer to a rehearsal of the C# Minor in August 1826, the month Beethoven sent his score to the publisher Schott, and in a letter to Schott Beethoven mentions a projected benefit performance for the violinist Joseph Böhm. Despite these signs of a possible performance, the C# Minor remains the only one of the five late quartets without a documented performance by Schuppanzigh and his associates.

Before we settle on 1834 as the most accurate date of a Vienna premiere, we should call another witness to testify: Karl Holz, the second violinist in the Schuppanzigh quartet. Holz became a central figure in Beethoven's life in 1825 when he replaced Anton Schindler as Beethoven's unpaid secretarial assistant. Schindler had resigned from this thankless position the previous year after being accused (falsely) of swindling the master of ticket receipts from the Ninth Symphony performances. From then until shortly before Beethoven's death, when he left the composer's service to marry, Holz was a central member of the composer's personal inner circle, as is evident in a paper trail of letters and frequent entries in the conversation books, and an important source of information about the performances of Beethoven's late quartets. We should also note that Holz was an acquaintance of Schubert and had played the second violin part at the first performances of Schubert's String Quartet in A Minor (D. 804) in 1824 and the Octet (D. 803) in 1827 under Schuppanzigh, and the first movement of either the D Minor (D. 810) or G Major (D. 887) Quartet at a Schubertiade memorial concert for Beethoven in March 1828. He was not involved in other major Schubert premieres during these years, such as Schuppanzigh's performance of the Piano Trio in Bb (D. 898). Holz is generally regarded as a reliable narrator by Beethoven scholars, especially when compared with Schindler, who resumed his unpaid duties during Beethoven's last months. It is also from Holz that we learn that Beethoven thought his C# Minor Quartet to be his greatest.

In preparing a book on Beethoven several decades after the composer's death, Ludwig Nohl, whom we met earlier as the man who rediscovered and published *Für Elise*, quotes a statement that Holz communicated to a third party a few months before he died in 1858. In the statement Holz reports a private performance that probably occurred on November 14, 1828 (Schubert died on the nineteenth). Here is the quote in full:

> Franz Schubert wanted very much to hear the master's C sharp minor Quartet (Op. 131, composed in the spring of 1826, this is a year before Beethoven's death). Messrs. Holz, Karl Gross [violinist] and Baron König [cellist] played it for him, Doleschalek, the piano teacher, being the only other person present [presumably a violist was present as well]. Schubert was sent into such transports of delight and enthusiasm and was so overcome that they all feared for him. A slight indisposition, from which he had been suffering and from which he had not completely recovered, grew enormously worse, developed into typhoid fever and in five days Schubert was dead. The C sharp minor Quartet was the last music that he heard! The King of Harmony had sent the King of Song a friendly bidding to the crossing! They both reached the kingdom of the Blessed penniless![1]

The conversation books, which became a necessity early in 1818, document a lot of talk, usually one-sided talk (since Beethoven mainly replied orally or used a slate), about the late quartets. From the conversation books, among other sources, we learn, perhaps to the surprise of more decorous modern audiences, that audiences at Schuppanzigh's concerts clapped at the end of movements and that performers were accustomed to audiences voicing their enthusiasms or appreciation of a solo turn, not unlike what happens at a jazz concert today. The conversation books also inform us that both the second and fourth movements were repeated at the premiere of op. 130. An audience protocol for chamber music that differs markedly from our own may help explain why op. 131 became the lone quartet not to receive a premiere at the Schuppanzigh concerts.

One of the many unique features of op. 131 is its overall structure. Not only does it contain an unprecedented seven movements, but also Beethoven was adamant that the movements be played without a break from one to the next. An entry in a conversation book reveals Holz balking at this request: "Does it have to be played through without stopping? But then we won't be able to repeat anything! When are we supposed to tune?" (Gingerich 2010, 468). Another factor inhibiting a performance of the C# Minor Quartet may be attributed to Beethoven's obsessive reluctance to relinquish his score so that its players would receive the much-needed opportunity to learn this difficult new work. Still, Beethoven's uncompromising instruction to play the nearly forty-minute quartet without allowing audiences the chance to express their enthusiasm may well have played the deciding role in delaying the public premiere until several years after the private performance for Schubert on his deathbed.

Although only op. 127 was published in Beethoven's lifetime, before he died the composer had negotiated high fees for the other four as well, above and beyond Galitzin's generous commission (although Galitzin's payment was delayed and proved difficult to collect). The final quartet was published in February 1828. As with the other late quartets, op. 135 was not only published in individual parts according to standard practice but also, as a study score, a new development that allowed works to be studied and appreciated by connoisseurs.

THE COMPOSITIONAL GENESIS

The conversation books rarely include musical notations, which were usually reserved for Beethoven's desktop sketchbooks for home use and pocket sketchbooks for his daily walks. But within a month after the completion of the Bb Major Quartet with the *Grosse Fuge* in November 1825, Beethoven entered a rare draft in late December for the fugue subject that opens the C# Minor Quartet. Remarkably, the first six notes (out of eight) are both melodically and rhythmically identical to the final version. These include the first part of the fugue subject consisting of four notes and the first two notes of the subject's second part. The rest would be worked out later when Beethoven added several new quarter notes but ended on the same final note as in the sketch. A draft of the variation theme, which became the fourth movement, followed in January, also, again unusually, in a conversation book. From then until the work's completion, a compositional process marked by considerable twists and turns and false starts, future plans invariably included the idea of beginning with a fugue and a middle *Andante* movement in two-fourths time.

When he was twenty-seven years old in 1798 Beethoven switched from entering his sketches on loose sheets to bound sketchbooks. In 1814 he added pocket sketchbooks to his creative arsenal without abandoning the primacy of the larger sketchbooks. Work on the late quartets led to another sketching activity, score sketches, a practice he would follow for his remaining creative years, 1824 to 1826. Score sketches include all four string parts rather than the single line sketches Beethoven used when he created his earlier quartets. During his approximately seven months of concentrated labor on op. 131, Beethoven managed to use up over 650 pages of sketches (mainly score sketches), more sketches than any other work in the composer's vast output. More than 130 of these pages are reserved for the finale alone.

Several of Haydn's op. 20 quartets and a number of compositions by Mozart include a fugal finale, but the idea of opening a quartet with a fugue was a radical and probably unprecedented departure from Beethoven's classical predecessors. In about seventy-five pages of sketches Beethoven demonstrated that the fugal opening was central to his C# Minor Quartet. He also decided early in the sketching to create and then continued to increase the rigorous continuity between the seven movements, which remained unnumbered until he sent the copyist's score to Schott. Beethoven's insistence on continuity might explain why he was so adamant in responding to Holz in stressing the importance of playing the seven movements without a break. Finally, during this first large patch of sketches, Beethoven worked to define the unusual tonal areas that set this quartet apart from its companions. The writings of Robert Winter on the compositional process of this quartet have proven especially helpful in what follows (1977 and 1982).

Beethoven considered no less than five separate movement plans for the quartet as a whole, all of which begin with a fugue and include a middle movement *Andante* in two-fourths time. Plan 1 presented the more traditional number of four movements: the Fugue in C# Minor is followed by a recitative that leads to an *Andante* in A major; the third movement was a *scherzo* in D major, and the finale in duple meter returns to the tonic. In future plans, the idea of a first and last movement in the tonic minor and other movements in A major and D major would be retained, albeit in a new ordering for these middle movements.

With plan 2 Beethoven returns still more emphatically to ideas present in his only previous work composed in the key of C# minor, the famous *Moonlight* Piano Sonata, op. 27, no. 2 (discussed in chapter 3). As with the C# Minor Quartet composed over twenty years later and unlike most sonatas, the *Moonlight* began with a slow movement that avoided first-movement sonata form and concluded, also in C# minor, with a fast movement in traditional first-movement form. By way of contrast, the *Moonlight* included a middle *scherzo* movement in the tonic major, spelled enharmonically as Db major. Plan 2 of the quartet followed the plan of the sonata, a three-movement work in which the beginning and final movements are in the tonic minor (the first a slow movement not in sonata form and the third a sonata-form fast movement) that serve as bookends to a fast middle movement in the tonic *major*, now spelled as C# major instead of Db major.

Plan 3 called for five movements. After the default opening fugue in C# minor, the second movement was to be an *Allegro* in F# minor (the minor subdominant) and six-eighths time. The choice of meter anticipates Beethoven's final choice for a second movement, an *Allegro* in six-eighths time (albeit in the key of D major). The third movement, a slow movement in A major, corresponds to the eventual *Andante* theme-

and-variations movement, also in A major; the fourth movement *scherzo* in F# minor corresponds to the eventual *scherzo* in E major; and the fifth movement in C# minor corresponds to the finale of the quartet that Beethoven sent to his publisher. Plan 3 also attached a codicil to the Quartet in Db Major with a melody that begins with the same melody (and key) Beethoven used for the slow movement of his next and final quartet in F major. Plans 4 and 5 also keep the opening fugue and the middle movement *Andante* in two-fourths but offer still other solutions that were eventually discarded.

THE QUARTET WE KNOW TODAY: THE MUSIC

In the end Beethoven took elements from all these compositional plans but added two short movements to create an unprecedented seven-movement string quartet, thus surpassing the A Minor Quartet (five movements) and the Bb Major Quartet (six movements) as well as the Eb and F Major Quartets that offer the traditional four movements. Table 9.1 shows an outline of the quartet we know today.

Table 9.1.

Form	Tempo	Key	App timing
1. Fugue	Adagio ma non troppo e molto espressivo	C# minor (i)	6:30 min.
2. Rondo	Allegro molto vivace	D major (bII)	3:00 min.
3. Recitative	Allegro moderato		1:00 min.
4. Theme and variations	Andante ma non troppo e molto cantabile	A major (VI)	15:00 min.
5. Scherzo	Presto	E major (III)	5:00 min.
6. Aria	Adagio quasi un poco andante	G# minor (v)	2:00 min.
7. Sonata	Allegro	C# minor/major	7:00 min.

The C# Minor Quartet exhibits several highly unusual and even unprecedented features. Here's a short list:

- The quartet is one of only two instrumental compositions in C# minor from Beethoven's entire career (the other is the *Moonlight* Sonata).

- The quartet is one of only two major Beethoven compositions in which all the movements are connected to the next (the other is the song cycle *An die ferne Geliebte*).
- The quartet is the only seven-movement instrumental work by Beethoven in a standard genre (two movements, nos. 3 and 6, however, are brief).
- The quartet is Beethoven's only multimovement work in six *different* keys. The only repeated key is the tonic minor, C#, the first degree of the scale (i) used for the first and final movements.
- The quartet is the first major instrumental work to begin with a fugue.
- The first movement of the quartet concludes in the tonic major. This decision makes the C# Minor String Quartet one of only four major instrumental works by Beethoven in which a first movement in the minor mode concludes in the tonic major (the others are the Cello Sonata in G Minor, op. 5, no. 2; the Piano Sonata in G Minor, op. 49, no. 2; and the Piano Sonata in C Minor, op. 111).
- More than in any other large instrumental work, Beethoven preserves the extraordinary continuity in the C# Minor Quartet by delaying the *first* definitive cadence (V–i) until the beginning of the finale.

MOVEMENT-BY-MOVEMENT COMMENTARY

No. 1: *Adagio ma Non Troppo e Molto Espressivo*

Unlike the fugati in the *Eroica* (first, second, and fourth movements) or the development section of the Ninth Symphony finale, the fugue of the C# Minor Quartet is a fugue through and through, that is, a comprehensive contrapuntal working out of a melodic idea called the fugue subject with a set number of melodic lines known as voices (see Musical Forms: Fugue in the glossary). The models for the fugue in Beethoven's time, and until today for that matter, are the forty-eight fugues of the *Well-Tempered Clavier*, arranged in two books of twenty-four, each book presenting a prelude and fugue in each of the twelve major and twelve minor keys. This was the collection that Beethoven's teacher Christian Gottlob Neefe announced in a press release as a staple of his pupil's repertoire while still a teenager in Bonn. In discussing the piano quartet from Bonn in the unusual key of Eb minor (in the fast part of the first movement after the slow introduction in Eb major), we also noted that the opening harmonies as well as the key may have been inspired by Bach's prelude in that key. Beethoven scholars have detected other possible influences between certain fugues in the *WTC* and the C# Minor Fugue of op. 131.

All but three of the fugues in Bach's collection are for either three or four voices. The fugue that opens Beethoven's C# quartet is appropriately enough in four voices, one for each instrument. When each player has stated the fugue subject in overlapping entries from top (violin 1) to bottom (cello), the music has concluded the first part found in all fugues, a statement of the subject in all the parts known as the fugue exposition. As with most four-voiced fugues, the first and third entries are stated in the tonic, but unlike the customary *answers* (the term that refers to the second and fourth entrances of the subject) in the dominant, the answers to this fugue are in the subdominant (F# minor). A subdominant answer is so rare (and for reasons difficult to explain surprisingly difficult to detect) that some Bach scholars doubt that the fugue meister *ever* offered an answer in this key, although others contend he employed a subdominant answer as many as three times among his hundreds of fugues. The manuscripts reveal that the idea to state the answer in the subdominant did not occur to Beethoven until he had settled on most of the other key areas and especially after he had abandoned the idea of including an entire movement in the subdominant key area in plan 2. Significantly, in the final version, the subdominant is the *only* key area (out of seven possible key areas) that does not receive a movement of its own.

Although Beethoven introduces the fugue subject as a complete melody, throughout much of the movement he divides its melody into two separable parts. The first part corresponds exactly to the jotting in the conversation book of December 1825. It includes a quarter-note upbeat on the fifth degree of the C# minor scale, two half notes respectively on the seventh and eighth (same as the first) degree and an accented (*sforzando*) dotted half note, with the longest note of the subject on an A. This note A will later serve as a key area both in the fugue and as a movement in its own right, the fourth, the central theme and variations. Had Beethoven stated the answer on the dominant instead of the subdominant, the long dotted half-note would have been an E, the relative major of C# minor or III, another focal key area in both the fugue and the fifth movement *scherzo*. But by placing the answer in the subdominant, the accented note falls on the note D, the eventual destination of the fugue and the key of the second movement. D is also a special key in C# minor known as the Neapolitan or bII, a key we noted Beethoven turned to often in the *Appassionata* Sonata and a tonal area favored by later romantic composers when writing in the minor mode, starting with Schubert.

If we look at the opening fugue as a slow introduction to a movement in D, as several scholars have done, we are closer to Wagner's explanation that the subtext of the quartet, as it was for the Ninth Symphony, was a "longing for joy" (Kropfinger 1991, 65). For Wagner, the C# Minor Quartet, unlike the Ninth, expresses a joy that never arrives, despite its attempt to emerge out of the marble of the fugue, the second movement, and valiantly in the finale as well.

Beethoven's fugue is also striking with its absence of a countersubject, a counter melody almost invariably heard in the first voice accompanying the statement of the subject as the second voice plays the subject and in future statements of most fugue subjects. Alternating with the opening four statements in the fugue exposition and subsequent expositions, most fugues interject sections called episodes as well, in which the subject drops out in its original form. After the fugue exposition of the C# minor, Beethoven's first episode offers a slight variant of the first four notes in two voices (violin 1 and cello), but not the subject itself. At other places in the fugue he states only the second part of the fugue subject, either in quarter notes as in the original subject or in eighth notes, the fugal technique we have identified as diminution in op. 110. Near the end of the fugue we hear the entire subject in the first violin in its original note values while the cello simultaneously states the subject in doubled note values (augmentation, also in op. 110) at the same time the inner voices (violin II and viola) play a diminution of the second part of the fugue.

Sometimes Beethoven states the second part of the fugue subject in more than one voice in exact imitation (canon). At other times one or the other parts appear in overlapping entrances (stretto). Fugues are complicated, and in some ways Beethoven's fugue in this quartet is more complicated than most, but one hopes that gradually listeners will realize that for the entire six to seven minutes of this slow and melancholy first movement, virtually everything they hear is a direct statement or a direct outgrowth of the original fugue subject either as a whole or as one of its two parts.

Over the course of the fugue Beethoven lights on every possible scale degree in the C# minor scale in the order i–iv–III–v–VII–VI–bII. To demonstrate the extraordinary unity of the quartet, with one exception, iv, the subdominant answer, each of these keys will also serve as a central key for one of the future movements, albeit in a different ordering, i–bII–vii–VI–III–v. In other differences the third movement is in B minor (vii) instead of B major (VII); and the sixth movement, in G# minor (v) instead of G# major as it appears in the fugue. The last key area in the fugue, the bII or Neapolitan, prepares for the second movement, the jig-like rondo whose root is the Neapolitan, or D major. Beethoven sets this up in the final minute or so of the fugue when he states the subdominant answer instead of the tonic subject twice in succession in the most audible voices, first the cello in its low range overlapped with a statement in the first violin in its high range. As with the first answer in the subdominant at the beginning of the fugue, the accented note in the answer is the D, the Neapolitan key that will become the tonic of the next movement. The cello on D is only a half note, but the first violin D, also with a *sforzando* accent, is held for a whole note (i.e., one full measure). When the first violin descends a half step from the held D to the tonic C#, Beethoven celebrates this arrival by harmonizing the tonic in the major for the first time. This is followed by yet another D, on the fourth beat with a *sforzando* accent held for five whole beats. The violin 1 descends yet again back to the C# tonic, a resolution that paves the way for the second part of the fugue subject in a clear C# major.

The dynamic level lowers to *piano*, then *più* (more) *piano*, and finally *pianissimo*. On the last note, instead of retaining the powerful major mode, Beethoven removes all the harmony, leaving the players unanimously sounding the single note C# spread out over three octaves and held by a fermata. Without stopping for breath, everyone moves up to a D (the Neapolitan) and then up an octave to another D. So begins a new theme and a new movement fused to the old. For the first time the music has firmly found its joy in the key of D major.

No. 2: *Allegro Molto Vivace*

Having found D, the brief second movement will be full of pleasing and joyful dance-like sounds. It is the kind of movement we might expect as the *finale* in an earlier classical quartet, and although the form is not binary, the rhythm and tone suggest that of a gigue (French for jig, a lively dance, often in six-eighths time, that usually concluded a baroque dance suite). The movement also contains recognizable sonata-form elements, but the tune's rondo-like refrain, the rondo theme's return before the "second theme," the absence of a full development, and a recapitulation that states the second theme before the first contradict rather than support a sonata interpretation. On the other hand, the movement fits all of the necessary qualifications of a rondo, including the nature of its main theme, its frequent repetitions (three), and its three contrasting episodes, one of which offers some development of earlier materials. Here is a brief outline of the eight sections.

[1] Refrain (A)	Main theme	D major
[2] Episode 1 (B)	Transition E major	From D to E major
[3] Refrain (A)	Main theme	E major
[4] Episode 2 (C)	Second theme	A major
[5] Refrain (A)	Main theme	D major
[6] Episode 3 (B and C)	Varying themes to second theme	Varying keys to D major
[7] Refrain (A)	Main theme	G to D major
[8] Coda	Based on the second theme	D major

From the first notes of the main theme that moves from D down a half step to C#, the reverse of how the movement's introduction moved from C# up to D, Beethoven inserts the C#s from the first movement in several prominent places. They are most audible in the measures that precede the first return of the main theme, where the jig-like motive C#–D–C# appears four times in succession in the cello part in rising octaves against a held C# major chord in the violins and viola. Although the movement is mainly about D major, it seems to be watching the first movement's C# minor in the rear-view mirror. The joy is fragile and fleeting (about three minutes long).

No. 3: *Allegro Moderato*

The third movement enters without warning and within a few seconds vanishes. Although Beethoven clearly designated it in the score as an independent movement, its function is clearly as a transition from one place to another. It also serves a harmonic purpose. Without this transition, it is likely that the following expansive fourth movement in A major might be heard as the dominant of the second movement. Instead, the recitative-like third movement, a bridge from the remote key of B minor (remote in C# minor but the relative minor of the second movement's D major), has the effect of cleansing the palate between the pseudo finale that is the second movement and the more typical, expected slow third movement, albeit technically the fourth movement in this instance. Even within its brief span (less than a minute), Beethoven gives each player a chance to participate in a recitative formula from top to bottom. Beethoven follows this with a brief change of tempo to *adagio*, a short but virtuosic "vocal" cadenza for the first violin, and finally a passage in which all the quartet members come together. The first and second movements ended in suspended animation—a long-held note in the first and two *pianissimo* notes in the second. The third movement concludes on a short, expectant E major triad, the dominant of the central fourth movement in A major.

No. 4: *Andante ma non Troppo e Molto Cantabile*

The fourth movement offers a leisurely theme-and-variation movement that at approximately fifteen minutes occupies more time than most performances of the next two longest movements, nos. 1 and 7, put together. Just as each movement elides into the next, so does the theme lead directly into the first variation, and each of the remaining variations connects to the one that follows. After the sixth variation the movement concludes with a substantial coda.

The hallmark of the main theme, which consists of two long phrases each sixteen measures long, is a descending or ascending half step, the same interval Beethoven emphasized at the end of the fugue (and to a lesser extent the fugue subject itself) and the beginning of the second movement. Underneath a more elaborate melody, half steps with various starting points pervade the theme in the first violin and its answer in the second violin: A–G# (violin 1) and G#–A (violin 2) in the first two measures, followed by a return of the half-step sequence, D–C# (violin 1) and C#–D (violin 2) in the second two measures. The dialogue between the two violins continues with some slight modification throughout the theme while the viola for the most part sounds out long-held single notes or double stops and the cello a simple *pizzicato* accompaniment of three eighth notes preceded by an eighth-note rest.

Each of the variations is scored with a rich variety of string textures, rhythms, and imitation among the parts, the latter especially in the third variation that is imitative throughout and culminates with a brief four-part fugato. As with the *Diabelli* and the op. 111 variations, in each variation of the op. 131 quartet Beethoven usually manages to preserve a recognizable thematic feature of the central theme. After the fifth variation, which begins as though the instruments are tuning, the sixth and final variation moves the furthest afield from the original harmonies of the theme. Variation 6 also offers a meter of 9/4 time, unique in Beethoven (three groups of three quarter notes), and a textural and dynamic uniformity in which the instruments are asked to sound *sotto voce* (in an undertone), never rising above a *piano* dynamic.

In the second half of the first section of the theme and more frequently in the second the cello departs from the uniform quarter-note rhythms in the upper instrumental parts by interjecting four-sixteenth-note figures on the weak third beats. Each time the figure appears it oscillates between two notes a half step away, the defining interval of the theme of this movement and a recurring presence in the first two movements. Instead of coming to a closing cadence, Beethoven moves directly to a coda that begins with each instrument stating a cadenza, each beginning with a long note followed by eighth-note triplets (violin 1, viola, cello, violin 2, and violin 1). After its second cadenza the first violin trills first softly, and then still more softly for the next four measures, while the other players take turns with three quarter notes, each starting on an offbeat.

A brief and brisk return based on the main theme in the remote key of C major leads to a restatement of the original theme and key in the second violin and viola against a counter line in the first violin and an arpeggiated accompaniment in the cello. After a return of the C major material in F major and a violin cadenza, the music returns to A major for a codetta that emphasizes the dactyl rhythm (LONG-short-short) that will persistently mark the quartet's finale movement.

No. 5: *Presto*

After a soft and inconclusive *pizzicato* tonal landing and a fermata over a rest, the cello interrupts with a four-note motive using the notes of an E-major triad. The one measure of silence that follows turns out to be the first measure of the *scherzo* theme in E major in duple meter. While Beethoven had offered *scherzo* in duple rather than the expected triple meter in several works from his later years (the Piano Sonata op. 110, the trio of the Ninth Symphony *scherzo*, and the String Quartet op. 130) and one earlier work (the Piano Sonata op. 31, no. 3), the practice is certainly rare. The *Presto*, about five minutes long, is characterized by the continuous presence of two rhythmic motives upon which Beethoven bases nearly all the thematic material of *both* the *scherzo* and the trio sections: (1) four quarter notes and two half notes; and (2) five quarter notes. In the first section the two motives invariably appear one after the other, while in the second section Beethoven follows three statements of the first motive with a slightly altered repetition of the second measure of the first motive. He also adapts the pitches and rhythms from the two motives, starting with four half notes and followed by the first motive.

The overall form of the movement is *scherzo* 1–trio 1–*scherzo* 2–trio 2–*scherzo* 3–trio 3 (abbreviated)–*scherzo* 4 (abbreviated). Particularly memorable is the comical way Beethoven returns to the *scherzo* each time. After adhering with the *piano* and *pianissimo* dynamic, Beethoven concludes the first *scherzo* section with a *crescendo* to a *fortissimo* that ends with stark suddenness. After a measure of silence the next six measures present only one quarter note on the first beat of each measure *pizzicato*, still *fortissimo* (violin 2–violin 1–viola–cello–viola–violin 2). The cello returns to *arco* (bowed) with the same four-note outburst that began the movement, after which the music returns to its original soft dynamic level and *arco* in all the strings. The return to the third *scherzo* repeats the process, as does the abbreviated trio section with additional abrupt outbreaks of silence. Not only does the fourth and final *scherzo* section begin *pianissimo*, softer than the previous three, but also all four players are now asked to play *sul ponticello* (on the bridge) in rhythmic unison, a technique that creates a mysterious and haunting effect. After sixteen measures Beethoven instructs the players to return to their ordinary bowing as the music *crescendos* and all the players arrive on the original tonic E. Beethoven then, in a tonal surprise, repeats the closing rhythmic gestures on G#, the root of the next and penultimate movement, in G# minor.

It may be challenging to detect the presence of G# minor earlier in the movement, but this note should be somewhat audible in the dialogue that occurs among the four equal partners shortly before the conclusion of the *scherzo* sections. The *scherzo* key of E major already relates as the relative major to the central tonic C# minor, but since G# is the anticipated dominant of C# minor, its presence, even as a single (but emphatic pitch, not a full chord), serves as a crucial preparation for the eventual return of the tonic at the beginning of the finale.

No. 6: *Adagio Quasi un Poco Andante*

After an *attacca*, the instruction to move on without delay to the next movement, we hear the short (two minutes long) but passionate sixth movement, a movement that emphasizes the dominant and prepares for the C# minor tonic to follow in the finale. The *Adagio* sounds like an aria or song, first buried in the viola and then restated a few measures later in the first violin part where it will mostly remain. After a single introductory measure we hear three statements of the aria with varying continuations and at varying length (phrases of twelve, eight, and seven measures). Interestingly, the fourth measure of each phrase states a Neapolitan chord on the second degree of G# (bII or A major). This chord is known as the Neapolitan of the *dominant*. This choice of A major and its three repetitions not only recalls the central key of the theme and variations but also is reminiscent of this same chord relationship when it was the Neapolitan of the *tonic* (i.e., D) in the first movement and the tonal center of the second movement. Looking ahead, the move to the Neapolitan, although in this case the Neapolitan of the dominant, also serves as a premonition of the conspicuous return of the Neapolitan D major in the finale.

No. 7: *Allegro*

In the final measure of the sixth movement the mode shifts from G# minor to major (i.e., dominant minor to dominant major), which prepared for the first dominant-tonic cadence *in the entire work*. To mark this momentous event all four participants play a *fortissimo* C# on the first beat of the first movement of the *Allegro* spread out over three octaves.

The finale is the full-scale sonata-form movement, lasting about seven minutes that normally we would expect to hear as a first movement. Instead we have had to wait for more than half an hour for it to finally arrive. Here is its basic outline:

Exposition (77 measures)

> Main theme (C# minor, tonic minor or i)
> Transition (based on the opening rhythm and rearranged pitches of the fugue subject)
> Second theme (E major, relative major of C# minor or III)

Development (81 measures)

> Based primarily on the main theme
> Retransition (20 measures of dominant preparation)

Recapitulation (101 measures)

> Main theme (C# minor, tonic minor)
> Transition (based on the opening rhythm and rearranged pitches of the fugue subject)
> Second theme (D major, Neapolitan or bII)
> Second theme (C# major, tonic major or I)

Coda (126 measures)

> Main theme (C# minor tonic minor, i)
> Return of the fugue subject opening
> Main theme with interjections in the Neapolitan (or bII)
> Main theme inverted (C# minor, tonic minor, i)
> Codetta (18 measures) based on main theme in C# tonic major, I

If the main theme, heard in unison by all four instruments, sounds as though it might possess a family resemblance to the fugue, the reason is that they are musical cousins rearranged, if not musical cousins once or twice removed. In short, the opening of the main theme of the finale constitutes a reordering of the fugue's first four notes. The fugue subject started on the fifth degree of the C# minor scale (five up to seven up to one and down to six or G#–B#–C#–A). The main theme of the finale rearranges these pitches and uses an altered rhythm that significantly disguises the identity of the fugue's pitches. It begins with two six-note outbursts, further subdivided into 3 + 3 or short-short-LONG, short-short-LONG. The third through sixth notes (i.e., LONG-short-short-LONG) are identical to the fugue subject but rearranged: the first time we hear these four notes they start at five, then up to six, and then down to one and seven; the second and more resolved statement also starts at five, goes up to six, and down to seven, but goes up to one (leading tone to tonic). The continuation of the theme consists of a march-like melody in the first violin supported by a vigorous chordal accompaniment that matches the melody rhythmically.

The finale's main theme as melodic transformation of the fugue's first four notes occurs twice at the end of the first theme section, now rearranged in descending order 1–7–6–5 but now with the *rhythm* of the original fugue subject and the pitches rearranged from the fugue's 5–7–1–6 to clarify the connection. The transition theme itself brings us closer to the fugue since it contains the rhythm of the three notes of the fugue subject (quarter–half–half). Although Beethoven removes the fourth note and replaces the first note with a note one pitch lower, enough of the rhythm and pitch is present to make a clear and audible connection between the transition theme and the fugue subject.

Before arriving at the second main theme in the conventional second key of E major, the relative major and the key of the *scherzo*, Beethoven brings the first theme back once again. The second theme, a lyrical theme in the upper register of the first violin and the long-held double-stopped drone chords deep in the cello range, offers a dramatic contrast between the virulent opening unison rearrangement of the fugue subject and the march-like first theme. The respite is brief, and the exposition, the shortest of the four sections of the movement, is not repeated. Instead the music moves headlong into the development section.

The development begins as the movement began, with a unison *fortissimo* statement of the opening theme. This time, however, the key is F# minor, the subdominant; it is the key of the answer to the original fugue subject in the first movement and the only degree of the C# minor scale not to be given a key of its own in the first six movements of the quartet. After the initial unison outburst and completion of the first finale theme, the next portion of the development focuses on the march-like component of the theme while at the same time another melodic strand offers a double fugato on long-held notes. After that, the main finale theme returns, this time with harmonic moves to B minor (the key of the third movement) and D major (the Neapolitan key of the second movement).

This leads to what I would argue is one of the most powerful and exciting retransitions to a recapitulation in all of Beethoven. It contains four main features: (1) extraordinary length (twenty measures); (2) harmonic insistence on the dominant G# (the key of the sixth movement); (3) starting in the ninth measure, a relentless written-out trill in eight notes that oscillates between G# and A (the first and last notes of the fugue subject); and (4) an exciting rapid *crescendo* from *pianissimo* to *fortissimo* in the last four bars before the recapitulation. Supporting the eighth-note oscillation is a rhythmically augmented oscillation in the cello part starting on G# and moving one note below to F#, first in half notes and then in quarters (G#–F#–G#–F#, etc.).

The recapitulation arrives on C#, the long-awaited tonic minor—a climactic, *fortissimo* moment. Somehow Beethoven manages to make this powerful moment still more powerful. Instead of simply having all the instruments play the main theme in unison as he did to open the exposition and the development, he combines no less than three recognizable musical strands. The first is the continuation of the written-out eighth-note trill, the oscillation between G# and A in the first violin. This goes on for the first four measures of the recapitulation. The second strand is the return of the first four notes of the main theme in its original key. This happens first in the cello, and then in the first violin, after which the latter entrance launches the return of the march-like main theme. The third strand is the appearance of the march-like rhythms, mainly in the second violin part, stated *simultaneously* with the main theme and trill before it gradually assumes its role as an accompaniment to the march-like core of the main theme.

After the transition with its audible references to the fugue subject and main final theme, Beethoven startles with his next major surprise when he places the lyrical second theme in the Neapolitan, D major (bII). The Neapolitan D major is of course the key that has served as a major source of contrast with the tonic C# from the outset of the quartet. But the rediscovery of the key of joy is ultimately short lived. Instead Beethoven discovers what he has been searching for since the end of the first movement (before being interrupted by D major in the second movement). For the first time since the first movement so long ago, Beethoven basks in a lyrical and peaceful moment of C# *major*. It may not be joy, but without exaggeration one might call it bliss.

Beethoven could easily have ended his quartet in the tonic major. Instead he offers a coda that at 126 measures proportionally dwarfs the exposition and development and even surpasses the expanded recapitulation with its additional statement of the second theme. In earlier chapters we marveled at the fact that Beethoven's codas grew to be equal in size and scope to the other parts of the sonata. In several finales his codas actually *surpassed* the lengths of other sections, sometimes by large margins. Examples include the 150-measure coda of the Fifth Symphony finale (close to double the length of the exposition or recapitulation, both eighty-six measures), the coda of the Fourth Piano Concerto finale (one-third the length of the entire movement), and the coda to the finale of the Eighth Symphony (only thirty measures shorter than all the other sections *put together*). The enormous coda to the C# Minor String Quartet follows suit. It begins with portions of the main theme in the Neapolitan and then continues with portions of the transition theme and second theme, both containing audible portions of the fugue subject. After forty measures of what amounts to a second recapitulation, Beethoven returns to the main theme in unison and *sempre* (always) *forte* but resolving to a new final note. Instead of reaffirming the tonic minor, however, Beethoven interjects two potent *pianissimo* returns of the Neapolitan.

With forty measures to go and after more dominant preparation Beethoven reestablishes C# minor with portions of the main and transition themes. With eighteen measures to go, he arrives unobtrusively on C# major, which prepares for the movement's dramatic close on three *fortissimo* C# major triads. Although the chords contain only twelve notes, they sound as though someone decided to add a full-string or-chestra for the occasion.

BEETHOVEN'S GREATEST STRING QUARTET?

Beethoven's final five-string quartets composed between 1824 and 1826 constitute nearly all the music he managed to complete before his death at fifty-six in March 26, 1827. For decades these quartets were consid-ered proof that the composer's by-then near complete deafness and possible madness had seriously undermined his ability to create coher-ent music. While the quartets have remained a musical challenge even for present-day listeners, their musical stature has grown to astonishing proportions. The quartets are now widely regarded as among Beetho-ven's greatest compositions, for some, the most profound music of any composer. The quartets continue to merit our attention and study. They are complex, saturated with contrasts and new sonorities, and demon-strate new levels of unity designed for musical connoisseurs. With a little guidance less experienced listeners often come to understand and appreciate what Beethoven was trying to accomplish and in the end develop a connoisseur's passion for these works. Students of Beethoven also often eventually discover that, despite innovations so appealing to modern sensibilities, these last quartets retain a strong sense of continu-ity with the classical style of Haydn, and Beethoven's earlier music.

In Beethoven's penultimate quartet the composer may not have found the joyful key of D major as he did in the Ninth Symphony, a joy that after four movements emerges from the despair of D minor. Re-cent Beethoven scholars have concluded that the triumphant culmina-tion exhibited in the heroic C Major finale of the Fifth Symphony in C minor was no longer possible by the time that Beethoven entered his final years as composer. But to my ears Beethoven achieved music comparably heroic in the finale of his C# Minor Quartet finale with its triumphant return of the main theme in the recapitulation in the minor mode, the establishment of the parallel major in the second theme, and finally the three overwhelming, immense, and powerful C# major chords that conclude the work.

Wagner in his work *Beethoven* (1870) described the trajectory of the C# Minor Quartet as a journey from the introductory fugue, "the most melancholy ever to have been expressed in music" to a finale that captures "the inner aspect of the world."

> He awakes and coaxes from the strings dance music such as the world has never heard (Allegro Finale). It is the dance of the world itself: wild pleasure, painful lament, the delights of love, highest bliss, woe, rage, ecstasy and sorrow; lightning flashes and thunder rolls: and over it all stands the tremendous bandmaster controlling and captivating, proudly and surely guiding us through whirlpools to the abyss: he is smiling at himself for this magic was after all only a game. Night beckons him—his day is done. (Wagner 2014, 125)

According to Holz, the greatest quartet of the three Galitzins was the Bb Major, perhaps because of its profound, original finale, the *Grosse Fuge*, but perhaps also for its intensely lyrical and expressive cavatina with its striking modulation from Eb to Cb (as in the *Adagio* to the Ninth Symphony) and its intense violin melody marked *beklemmt* (anguished). In responding to Holz, Beethoven did not single out a particular quartet. Instead he made the following diplomatic statement: "Each in its own way. Art demands of us that we shall not stand still. You will find a new manner of voice treatment (part writing), and thank God there *is less lack of fancy than ever before*" (Forbes 1964, 983). After completing the C# Minor, however, he allegedly told Holz, without explanation, that he felt the C# Minor was his greatest. Perhaps this is why Schubert on his deathbed asked Holz to arrange a private performance of this quartet.

On the copy of op. 131 he submitted to Schott on August 12, Beethoven gave his publishers a scare by writing that the quartet was "put together from pilferings" (Forbes 1964, 983). Apparently the publisher misunderstood Beethoven's humorous intentions, which prompted the composer to write to Schott a week letter: "You wrote me that the quartet must be an original one. I felt rather hurt, so as a joke I wrote on the copy that it was put together from pilferings. Nevertheless, it is *brand new*."

During the course of this discussion on the C# String Quartet, the conversation books have come in handy. They have given us the first-known musical fragments that would eventually emerge as the fugue and theme-and-variations movement of this quartet. The conversations they record have provided insight into the importance of continuity for this quartet from Beethoven's perspective.

On occasion Beethoven also used his conversation books to jot down quotes he did not want to forget. Perhaps the most well-known example of this practice appeared in February 1820, a few years before he began these quartets, when Beethoven famously inscribed a phrase from the philosopher Immanuel Kant's *Critique of Pure Reason* (1781): "The moral law in us, and the starry sky above us—Kant!!!" The following month, on March 11, he copied a passage from the recent tragedy *Herostratos* by Franz Maria von Nell published in 1821.

> The world is a king and desires flattery in return for favor; but true art is obstinate and will not yield to the fashions of flattery. . . .
>
> They say art is long, life is short—only life is long and art is short; may its breath lift us to the Gods—That is an instant's grace. (Solomon 2003, 100)

One can readily grasp why these words held special meaning for Beethoven, a man who strove unceasingly to grow as an artist and to create an obstinate and sometimes unfashionable art, and an artist who realized the fragile potential for true art to bring humans closer to a divine grace.

NOTES

INTRODUCTION

1. WoO is the abbreviation of Werke ohne Opuszahl, in English, works (*Werke*) published without (*ohne*) opus number (*Opuszahl*); works published *with* opus numbers are designated op.

I. "THE SPIRIT OF MOZART" (1770–1792)

1. All recurring musical terms are located alphabetically in the glossary. To save readers from referring to the glossary unnecessarily, the first appearance of a glossary term in the text will also be accompanied with a brief explanation taken from the glossary or guide readers to the appropriate place in the glossary itself.

2. In Beethoven's era, tempo descriptions were for the most part indicated in Italian. The main categories, arranged from slow to fast are *adagio* (slow), *andante* (moderately slow), *allegretto* (somewhat fast), *allegro* (fast), *vivace* (lively), and *presto* (very fast), with many additional qualifiers such as *con brio* (with spirit), *con moto* (with motion), *assai* or *molto* (very), *mezzo* (medium), *poco* (a little), and *non troppo* (not too much). Much more rarely, Beethoven would indicate a tempo in German, for instance, *Ein wenig geschwinder*, the same as *poco allegretto*, or a little faster). All Beethoven tempo descriptions found in a work that is discussed in the main text are arranged alphabetically at the end of the glossary along with the work or works that used this expression marking. The text itself will indicate the tempo description in the original Italian (or much less commonly, German).

5. SYMPHONIC ALTERNATIVES TO THE HEROIC STYLE (1808–1814)

1. See *Marlbrough s'en va-t-en guerre*, *Wikipedia*, last updated September 27, 2015, https://en.wikipedia.org/wiki/Marlbrough_s%27en_va-t-en_guerre.

6. BEETHOVEN AND SONG

1. Quoted in *Cosima Wagner's Diaries, Vol. 2: 1878–1883*, ed. Martin Gregor-Dellin and Dietrich Mak (New York: Harcourt Brace Jovanovich, 1977), 427–28.

9. THE STRING QUARTET IN C-SHARP MINOR, OP. 131 (1826)

1. Quoted in Otto Erich Deutsch, ed., *Schubert: Memoirs by His Friends* (New York: MacMillan, 1958), 299.

GLOSSARY

MUSICAL TERMS

answer. *See* Musical Forms: Fugue.

arco. An instruction for string instruments to resume bowing after a passage marked *pizzicato*.

aria. The Italian word for song, especially those found in opera.

arioso. The Italian word that connotes a heightened recitative but falling short of a full-scaled aria. Beethoven labeled the third movement of the piano sonata op. 110 an arioso.

arpeggio. Sounding a chord successively rather than simultaneously; from the Italian word *arpa* or harp; an instrument especially prone to playing arpeggios or arpeggiated chords.

attacca. Attack; an instruction that asks performers to begin the next movement or section immediately.

authentic cadence. *See* functional harmony.

cadence. Melodic or harmonic points of arrival at the ends of phrases, sections, most movements, and in the classical period, invariably at the end of a composition. *See* authentic and deceptive cadence in functional harmony.

cadenza. A section late in a concerto's first movement where the soloist plays alone and can show off his or her improvisational skill and virtuosity. At the end of most cadenzas the soloist allows the orchestra to reenter, often with a trill, on an authentic or V–I cadence. Shorter cadenzas can also occur in other movements and places within a movement.

canon. Exact imitation of a melodic line at a fixed interval, such as canon at the fifth.

chromatic and chromaticism. *See* scales and modes.

coda. *See* Musical Forms: Sonata Form.

concerto-sonata form. *See* Musical Forms: Concerto-Sonata Form.

counterpoint (adjective contrapuntal; adverb contrapuntally). The technique of combining two or more independent (although often similar) melodic lines sounding simultaneously (i.e., contrapuntally). Contrapuntal is the adjective form of counterpoint as in a contrapuntal development section.

countersubject. *See* Musical Forms: Fugue.

crescendo. Getting louder.

deceptive cadence. *See* functional harmony.

development. *See* Musical Forms: Sonata Form.

diatonic and diatonicism. *See* scales and modes.

diminished seventh. A four-note chord in which each note is a minor third apart, thus creating a rootless, tense, and ambiguous sound.

diminuendo. Getting softer.

dominant. *See* tonality.

dominant seventh. *See* functional harmony.

dynamics. Levels of softness and loudness in music.

enharmonic. A musical homonym in which the same note receives an alternate spelling, for example, E# and F. With an enharmonic note, Einstein can be wrong. In music E = Fb, not as in physics $E = mc^2$.

episode. *See* Musical Forms: Fugue.

exposition. *See* Musical Forms: Sonata Form and Fugue.

fermata. A symbol with a curved line above a dot to indicate a hold of an indefinite length.

first and second endings. The notation of separate ways to end a section, usually the exposition in a sonata-allegro form movement, the first ending for the first time through the exposition and the second ending for the second time through.

forte. Loud (*f.*).

fortepiano. Loud followed immediately by soft (*fp*). When not a dynamic marking, fortepiano (literally, loud-soft) is the name given to early forms of the piano or pianoforte (soft-loud).

fortissimo. Very loud (*ff.*).

fortississimo. Very, very loud (*fff.*).

fugue, fugato, and fughetta. *See* Musical Forms: Fugue.

functional harmony. A central principle of tonality. In functional harmony each triad in the scale serves a hierarchical function in relation to a central tonal center or tonic. If tonality were like our solar system, the tonic would be the sun, and the other triads orbit around it with various gravitational pulls. The dominant chord (commonly with an added minor seventh, e.g., G–B–D–F), or *dominant seventh*, is the primary chord that pulls to the tonic, the center of the tonal hierarchy. The function of the supertonic (ii), the subdominant (IV), and the submediant (vi) is to prepare for a move *to* the dominant. The leading tone triad can function as a quasi-dominant and becomes a dominant seventh if a note is added a third below its root (e.g., adding a G a third below the diminished triad B–D–F). The move from a dominant to a tonic (V–I or V–i) is called an *authentic cadence*, the most conclusive cadence in tonal music. A cadence in which the dominant is followed by a chord other than the tonic, for example, the submediant (vi) or flat submediant (bVI), is called a *deceptive cadence*.

homophony (adjective homophonic). A melody supported by chords.

leading tone triad. *See* triads.

major and minor. *See* scales and modes; and triads.

mediant. *See* triads.

melisma. Many notes sung to a single syllable.

meter. The organization of musical time into units called measures. The principal metrical organizations are duple (two beats per measures) and triple (three beats per measure as in waltz time).

mezzo. Medium, as in *mezzo piano* (medium soft) or *mezzo forte* (medium loud).

minuet. *See* Musical Forms: Other Movements in a Multimovement Work.

modes. *See* scales and modes.

modulation. The process by which a composer moves from one tonal center to another. In most works in the major mode, this second key area will be the dominant of the original tonic. The way composers accomplish a modulation is to first move to what is known as the "secondary" dominant, or the dominant of the dominant (this movement normally occurs in the transition section of a sonata-form movement). For example, if the tonic is C and the dominant is G, five scale degrees above, the secondary dominant would be D, five degrees above G, and this secondary dominant will establish the new tonic. A parallel shift from major to minor or minor to major on the same tonic is not formally considered a modulation.

monothematicism. *See* Musical Forms: Sonata Form.

motive. A short melody or melodic fragment, often used as the major source for development.

Neapolitan. A chromatic chord built on the lowered second degree of a scale (bII) used prominently by Beethoven in his *Appassionata* Sonata and his C# Minor String Quartet and by Schubert and later romantic composers.

orchestration. The combining of instruments in orchestral writing to create a varied sound palette.

pedal tone. A tone held for several measures in one or more instruments while other instruments maintain their melody and harmonic activity. Most pedal tones appear in the bass, but they can also occur in an upper register. Pedal tones are especially frequent at the end of a movement.

phrase. A unit of musical syntax, analogous to a sentence in spoken or written language.

pianissimo. Very soft (*pp.*).

pianississimo. Very, very soft (*ppp.*).

piano. Soft (*p.*).

pizzicato. An indication to pluck rather than bow (*arco*) on string instruments.

plagal cadence. A harmonic cadence from IV to I. Since this cadence, far less definitive than an *authentic cadence* (*see* functional harmony), is frequently found at the end of hymns, it is often called an "amen" cadence.

polyphony (adjective polyphonic). The generic description for two or more melodies sounding simultaneously distinguished from the technique of composing polyphony, which is *counterpoint*.

recapitulation. *See* Musical Forms: Sonata Form.

recitative. Sung speech in Italian opera and other vocal music. German operas such as *Fidelio* used spoken dialogue rather than recitative, but Beethoven imitated the conventions of Italian recitative in a number of instrumental works, including the *Tempest* Sonata.

relative major. The key a minor third higher than the tonic with the same number of flats or sharps (e.g., C major up from A minor).

relative minor. The key a minor third lower than the tonic with the same number of flats or sharps (e.g., A minor down from C major).

rest. A notational symbol to indicate a particular duration of silence.

retransition. *See* Musical Forms: Sonata Form.

rhythm. General term that refers to all aspects of music that relate to time rather than sound.

ritornello. *See* Musical Forms: Concerto-Sonata Form.

rondo. *See* Musical Forms: Other Movements in a Multimovement Work.

scales and modes. The scale is the pool of pitches composers use in a given piece out of the twelve possible pitches within an octave. Most scales in the tonal system draw from a pool of seven different pitches known as the *diatonic* scale. If you start on a white note on a keyboard and move up its scale until you return to that note one octave (literally an eight-note span) higher, each note will give you a different arrangement of whole steps and half steps. These arrangements are called *modes*. In classical tonality most modes are either major or minor. A *major* mode uses the same seven-note diatonic scale Fraulein Maria teaches her young charges in the song "Do Re Mi" from *The Sound of Music*. If you ascend the scale, each note can be referred to as a scale degree from Do 1 to Ti 7, with 8 repeating 1 an octave higher. Each note in the scale also has a formal name (*see* triads). The *minor* mode exists in several arrangements from Do to Ti, but all have a lowered third and sixth degree from the major scale. The *chromatic* scale uses all twelve of the seven white and five black keys within an octave. In a chromatic scale the distance between any adjacent pitch is a half step. Music that primarily uses pitches belonging to a particular scale is referred to as diatonic or *diatonicism*; music that incorporates pitches outside of the scale is referred to as chromatic or *chromaticism*.

scherzo. *See* Musical Forms: Other Movements in a Multimovement Work.

semitone. A half step, the shortest distance between any two keys on the keyboard.

sforzando. With a sudden, strong emphasis (*sf*).

slow-movement form. *See* Musical Forms: Other Movements in a Multimovement Work.

sonata form. *See* Musical Forms: Sonata Form.

staccato. Detached; marked by a dot or stroke over a note.

stretto. Overlapping entrances of a musical line.

subdominant. *See* triads.

subito. Suddenly, as in *attacca subito* or *subito piano*.

submediant. *See* triads.

supertonic. *See* triads.

syncopation. Irregular accentuation (i.e., placing accents on offbeats rather than down-beats).

theme and variations. *See* Musical Forms: Theme and Variations.

timbre. Tone color or the quality of a sound that distinguishes one instrument from another.

tonality. Tonality is the practice of organizing the notes in a given scale around a tonal center, or key. The central key in tonal music is called the *tonic*. When we refer to Beethoven's Fifth Symphony in C Minor, it means that the tonic is C and the mode is minor (i.e., the C scale with a lowered or minor third between the first and third degrees). The most direct way to establish a tonic is to precede it by a triad five scalar notes (or degrees) above called the *dominant*. In the works of Haydn and Mozart and much of Beethoven, the initial theme in a movement also generally utilizes a dominant to establish the initial tonic. Larger forms almost invariably start by establishing a tonic before moving to the dominant for the second key area and eventually reestablishing the tonic to conclude a movement. If the work starts in a minor mode, the most common second tonal area will be the relative major (*see* relative major).

tonic. *See* tonality.

transition. *See* Musical Forms: Sonata Form.

triads. The most prevalent chordal units in tonal music. It consists of three pitches in its fundamental structural form, arranged in ascending thirds with the lowest note called the root; the middle note, the third; and the upper note, the fifth. If the distance between the root and the third encompasses two whole steps, the triad is *major* (C–E–G). If the third is lowered by one step, the result is a *minor* triad (C–Eb–G, with the lower third one and a half steps higher than the root). To understand the main building blocks in a given key, a good starting point is to create a triad on each note of the scale. In a major scale the resulting triads will be given the Roman numerals I, ii, iii, IV, V, vi, and vii° with large letters standing for major triads, small letters for minor, and an added circle signaling diminished. Each triad in the scale has a name: *tonic* (I), *subdominant* (IV), and dominant (V) triads are major triads, which means they contain a major third above the root; the *supertonic* (ii), *mediant* (iii), and *submediant* (vi) triads are minor triads, with a minor third above the root; the *leading tone* triad on the seventh degree (vii°) contains two minor thirds and is called a diminished triad.

trill. An ornament that consists of a rapid alternation between a note and the note above. In his late style Beethoven made great use of continuous trilling (e.g., the piano sonatas op. 109 and op. 111, the *Diabelli* Variations, and the string quartet in C# minor, op. 131).

tritone. An interval that consists of three (tri) whole steps (tones), for example, C to F# or C to Gb, an augmented fourth or diminished fifth.

MUSICAL FORMS

Sonata Form

Sonata form, or sonata-allegro form, is the principal form used by Haydn, Mozart, Beethoven, Schubert, and later nineteenth-century composers in large works such as symphonies, solo or duet sonatas, string quartets, piano trios, and even vocal genres. Nearly every multi-movement form in the classical period, those by Beethoven included, assigns sonata form to at least one movement. Since it is most often found in first movements, sonata form is also often referred to as first-movement form, and since the majority of first movements are in fast tempos, the form is also known as sonata-allegro form. Sonata form also appears either directly or in a modified state in the middle movements of multimovement works. The British musicologist, composer, and program annotator Donald Francis Tovey (1875–1940) offers a succinct explanation of sonata form in the following excerpt from an extended entry in the *Encyclopaedia Britannica*. Although written in 1929, and allowing for exceptions, Tovey's summary holds up well. The kibitzing in brackets and italicizing of terms are mine.

> The general scheme of the first-movement form or, *par excellence*, sonata form is as follows. There is a first group [of one or more themes or melodies] in the tonic, followed by a *transition* to another key [generally the dominant if the work is in a major key, e.g., G major in the key of C major, or the relative major if in a minor key, e.g., Eb major in the key of C minor], where there is a second group [or themes or melodies] that usually ends with a neat little cadence-theme [in the new key]. These groups constitute the *exposition*, which may be [is most often] repeated. Then follows the *development*, the function of which is to put the previous materials into new lights, regrouping the figures into new types of phrases, modulating freely, and settling, if at all, only in new keys. Eventually a return is made to the tonic [the *retransition*], and so to the *recapitulation*. This recapitulates the exposition, but it gives [states] the secondary group [of themes] in the tonic, and so completes the design. The development and recapitulation may be repeated [but seldom is, even in Haydn and Mozart]; a *coda* may follow the recapitulation [and usually does, often dramatically, in the works of Beethoven].

As related by Tovey, and in a later generation by Charles Rosen, among others, sonata form is a dramatic form rich in possibilities for variety and nuance. The two central dramatic moments in the form are the establishment of the second key area in the exposition and the return of the tonic (usually along with the original main theme) to mark the recapitulation. We see in *Experiencing Beethoven* that while Beethoven follows these norms most of the time he also departs from them, sometimes substantially. It is also worth noting that while Mozart almost invariably offers a contrasting theme when he reaches the second key, Beethoven, like his predecessor Haydn, often presents a recognizable variant of the first theme at the second key. This practice is often referred to as *monothematicism*.

Other Movements in a Multimovement Work

Slow-Movement Form

The second movement in a multimovement classical work is commonly, but not invariably, a slow movement. The term slow-movement form refers specifically to a slow movement, usually of a lyrical nature, that reduces tension by removing the development section from the first-movement form. Other frequently employed slow movement forms are A-B-A and *theme and variation* (the latter discussed separately below). In A-B-A form the composer presents a central theme, with or without subthemes; contrasts this with a B section in a different key, or keys; and then returns to A, with or without ornamentation or other variation.

Minuet/Scherzo and Trio-Sonata Form

Nearly all four-movement works (symphonies, string quartets, other chamber music genres, and some piano sonatas) contain a movement in minuet or *scherzo* form, usually, but not invariably, as the third movement. Minuets and *scherzi* (the latter the Italian word for jokes) employ the same triple meter (three beats per measures or waltz time) and form, although *scherzi* are faster (usually one beat per measure rather than the three beats per measure of minuets) and less sedate. The *scherzo*, invented by Haydn, soon outnumbered minuets in Beethoven's work, albeit often unlabeled. *Scherzi* are occasionally set in duple meter (two beats per measure), for example, the trio of the Ninth Symphony *scherzo* and the fifth movement of the C# string quartet.

The overall form of the minuet/*scherzo* is in three parts, A-B-A, each of which is also A-B-A. The first and third larger parts are simply referred to as the minuet or *scherzo* sections, the middle part, called the *trio*, is a section that is usually lighter with a reduced texture. Each section is in two parts (binary form), with each part repeated. The first part presents a main theme that ends with a cadence to the tonic, dominant, or if in minor, the relative major. The second part extends or establishes a new key before returning to the first key, usually in tandem with the main theme. The trio uses the same three-part form, albeit with contrasting material, often in a new key or mode. The minuet or *scherzo* section returns, usually performed without repeats. In a number of works (e.g., the Fourth, Seventh, and Ninth Symphonies, and the C# Minor String Quartet), Beethoven extends the form by adding a second and third *scherzo* section along with a return of the trio.

Sonata-Rondo Form

Finales can take a number of forms, including a full-scale sonata form or a theme and variations, but perhaps the most frequently used form is the rondo or the sonata-rondo.

Rondos are readily recognized by their tuneful and more regular themes and by their frequent occurrence. Most rondo forms are sectional forms such as A–B–A–C–A, in which the rondo theme is the A theme and the B theme a contrasting theme in a contrasting key, usually the dominant or relative major. The A and B themes are most often connected by a modulatory transition as in a sonata-allegro movement. The C section, usually beginning in its own key, can either introduce a new thematic episode or a development of the A or B themes (or both). Since sonata elements are present in a rondo, the sonata-rondo designation is usually assigned according to the degree in which the C section functions as a development.

Concerto-Sonata Form

The first movement of most classical concertos, including those by Beethoven, is a hybrid of the baroque concerto form, also known as ritornello form, and the classical sonata-allegro form. The baroque concerto component consists of a series of alternating orchestral statements (*tutti*) called *ritornellos* and solo sections (*soli*). After an initial ritornello in which the orchestra plays the main motives (short melodies in the central tonality), the soloist or soloists play a contrasting episode that takes the music back to all or a portion of the ritornello in various contrasting keys. The classical concerto begins with a large ritornello that presents a main theme, a second theme, and a closing theme, usually without modulation. The soloist then enters in the same original key, with either the original theme or a new theme to initiate an exposition that follows the first-movement sonata form model. Since both the orchestra and solo-with-orchestra regularly present the same themes, the opening orchestral section is often referred to as the double exposition, a term that unfortunately undermines a central purpose of an exposition, which is to modulate. As with sonata-allegro form, concerto-sonatas include sections analogous in function to expositions, developments, and recapitulations, with the addition of partial ritornellos. A central feature of classical concertos is a sense of dialogue and interplay between the orchestra and the soloist. At the point before the final ritornello, the soloist also gets the opportunity to improvise without the orchestra and to demonstrate his or her virtuosity (*see* cadenza).

Fugue

A fugue is a form based on a contrapuntal working out of a single main theme called the fugue subject or simply the subject. The contrapuntal parts, two or more, are called "voices," with three and four voices the most common. In the opening section of a fugue, the *exposition*, the subject is introduced once in each voice. After the subject is introduced alone in the first voice, a second entrance appears "at the fifth" (i.e., a fifth up or a fourth down). This is called the *answer*. While the second voice plays the answer, the first voice often introduces a *countersubject*, which will return in the fugue whenever the subject returns, either above or below the subject. Some fugues have a second countersubject as well. In the section that follows the exposition, the subject is withheld (at least in its original form). This section is called the *episode*. From this point until the end of the fugue, the piece alternates between fugal expositions (consisting either of a single entrance or multiple entrances) and episodes. In most fugues the episodes increase in length while the expositions stay the same.

In the baroque era, fugues were usually paired with a freer composition called a toccata or a prelude, whereas in the classical period fugues usually appear as separate movements within a multimovement work. In his late period Beethoven wrote several such movements, including the finales of the piano sonatas op. 106 and op. 110, the first movement of the C# Minor String Quartet (an unprecedented placement), Variation 32 of the *Diabelli* Variations, and several choruses of the *Missa solemnis*. A number of Beethoven works throughout his career also contain a fugato, a less-developed fugue within a movement that is not self-contained. Fugatos are most common in development-like sections. Examples include the development section of the *Eroica* funeral march and the double fugue (a fugue with two subjects) in the development of the Ninth Symphony, the latter occurring within a theme-and-variations and sonata-form hybrid. A *fughetta* is a short but self-contained fugue (e.g., Variation 24 of *Diabelli*). Although Beethoven knew and was inspired by Bach's *Well-Tempered Clavier*, his fugues often diverge considerably from those composed by the recognized master of the form.

Theme and Variations

Theme and variations can appear almost anywhere in a multimovement work, albeit less often as a first or middle movement. Many theme and variations are freestanding works that may contain a handful of variations or as many as *Righini*'s twenty-four and *Diabelli*'s thirty-three. The theme to be varied is a melody or a tune, borrowed or original, and often, but not necessarily, in two repeated binary parts. Most variations preserve the theme's formal structure and vary one or more musical elements inherent in the theme, while retaining other elements. Some variation sets preserve the harmony (with some modifications) and create new melodies, while others retain recognizable features of the original melody. Variations also can alter the original meter (e.g., from duple to triple or vice versa), the mode (from major to minor or vice versa), or the tempo. Most variation movements or freestanding sets in the classic period include a slow variation shortly before a lively coda.

TEMPO DESCRIPTIONS

Arranged by opus numbers (op.) and WoO numbers (Werke ohne Opuszahl, or works without opus numbers).

adagio (slow; op. 18/6, op. 31/2, op. 80)
adagio affettuoso ed appassionato (slow, tenderly, and passionately; op. 18/1)

adagio assai (very slow; op. 55)

adagio cantabile (slow and songlike; op. 13)

adagio ma non troppo (slow but not too much; op. 18/6)

adagio ma non troppo e molto espressivo (slow but not too much and very expressive; op. 131)

adagio molto (very slow; op. 21)

adagio molto e cantabile (very slow and songlike; op. 125)

adagio molto e mesto (very slow and sad; op. 59/1)

adagio molto semplice e cantabile (very slow, simple, and songlike; op. 111)

adagio quasi un poco andante (slow, almost a little moderately slow; op. 131)

adagio sostenuto (slow and sustained; op. 27/2)

allegretto (somewhat fast; op. 27/2, op. 31/2, op. 68, op. 92, WoO 65)

allegretto quasi allegro (somewhat fast, almost fast; op. 18/6)

allegretto scherzando (somewhat fast and playful; op. 93)

allegretto vivace e sempre scherzando (somewhat fast, lively, and always playful; op. 59/1)

allegro (fast; op. 13, op. 31/2, op. 18/1, op. 59/1, op. 67, op. 68, op. 72, op. 131)

allegro assai (very fast; op. 98/3, op. 125)

allegro assai vivace (very fast and lively; op. 125)

allegro con brio (fast with spirit; op. 15, op. 18/1, op. 18/6, op. 21, op. 55, op. 67, op. 92)

allegro con brio ed appassionata (fast and with spirit and passion; op. 111)

allegro di molto e con brio (very fast and with spirit; op. 13)

allegro energico, sempre ben marcato (fast, energetic, and always well marked; op. 125)

allegro ma non troppo, un poco maestoso (fast but not too much and a little majestic; op. 125)

allegro moderato (moderately fast; op. 58, op. 82/1, op. 131)

allegro molto (very fast; op. 18/1, op. 55)

allegro molto e vivace (very fast and lively; op. 21)

allegro molto vivace (very fast and lively; op. 131)

allegro scherzando (fast and playful; op. 15)

allegro vivace (fast and lively; op. 55, op. 93)

allegro vivace e con brio (fast, lively, and with spirit; op. 93) *andante cantabile con moto* (moderately slow, songlike; op. 21)

andante con moto (moderately slow with motion; op. 58, op. 67)

andante con moto, cantabile (moderately slow with motion and songlike; op. 98/6)

andante espressivo (moderately slow and expressive; op. 83/1)

andante ma non troppo e molto cantabile (moderately slow but not too much and very songlike; op. 131)

andante maestoso (moderately slow and majestic; op. 125)

andante moderato (moderately, moderately slow; op. 58)

andante molto moto (moderately slow with much motion; op. 68)

ein wenig geschwinder; poco allegretto (a little faster; op. 98/2)

grave (grave, solemn; op. 13)

largo (broad; op. 15, op. 31/2)

mit lebhaftigheit, jedoch nicht in geschwindem zeitmasse, und scherzend (lively, although not in a fast tempo, and playful; op. 128)

molto vivace (very lively; op. 125)

nicht zu geschwinde, angenehm und mit viel empfindung (not too fast, pleasing and with much feeling; op. 98/4)

poco adagio (a little slow; op. 32)

poco allegretto (a little fast; op. 75/3)

poco sostenuto (a little sustained; op. 92)

presto (very fast; op. 92, op. 125, op. 131)

presto agitato (very fast and agitated; op. 27/2)

vivace (lively; op. 58, op. 92, op. 98/5, op. 120)

ziemlich langsam und mit ausdruck (rather slowly and with expression; op. 98/1)

SELECTED BIBLIOGRAPHY

BOOKS

Reference

Albrecht, Theodore, ed. and trans. *Letters to Beethoven and Other Correspondence*. 3 vols. Lincoln: University of Nebraska Press, 1996.

Anderson, Emily, ed. and trans. *The Letters of Beethoven*. 3 vols. London: Macmillan, 1961; repr., 1985.

Beethoven Forum. Lincoln: University of Nebraska Press, 1992–.

Clive, Peter. *Beethoven and His World: A Biographical Dictionary*. New York: Oxford University Press, 2001.

Cooper, Barry, ed. *The Beethoven Compendium: A Guide to Beethoven's Life and Music*. Ann Arbor, MI: Borders, 1991; 2nd ed., 1996.

Dorfmüller, Kurt, Norbert Gertsch, and Julia Ronge, eds. *Ludwig van Beethoven: Thematisch-bibliographisches Werkverzeichnis*. 2 vols. Munich, Germany: G. Henle Verlag, 2014.

Forbes, Elliot, ed. *Thayer's Life of Beethoven*. Princeton, NJ: Princeton University Press, 1964.

Johnson, Douglas, Alan Tyson, and Robert Winter. *The Beethoven Sketchbooks: History, Reconstruction, Inventory*. Berkeley: University of California Press, 1985.

Kerman, Joseph, and Alan Tyson. *The New Grove Beethoven*. New York: Norton, 1983; updated as Joseph Kerman, et. al. "Beethoven, Ludwig van." Grove Music Online. Oxford Music Online. Oxford University Press. Web. 29 May 2016. http://www.oxfordmusiconline.com/subscriber/article/gorve/music/400267.

Reid, Paul. *The Beethoven Song Companion*. Manchester, UK: Manchester University Press, 2007.

Senner, Wayne M., ed. *The Critical Reception of Beethoven's Compositions by His German Contemporaries*. 2 vols. Lincoln: University of Nebraska Press, 1999, 2001.

Life and Works, Reception, and Miscellaneous

Bonds, Mark Evan. *After Beethoven: Imperatives of Originality in the Symphony*. Cambridge, MA: Harvard University Press, 1996.

Broyles, Michael. *Beethoven in America*. Bloomington: Indiana University Press, 2011.

Burnham, Scott, and Michael P. Steinberg, eds. *Beethoven and His World*. Princeton, NJ: Princeton University Press, 2000.

Cooper, Barry. *Beethoven*. New York: Oxford University Press, 2000; 2nd ed., 2008.

———. *Beethoven: An Extraordinary Life*. London: ABRSM, 2013.

———. *Beethoven and the Creative Process*. Oxford, UK: Clarendon, 1990.

Davies, Peter J. *Beethoven in Person: His Deafness, Illnesses, and Death*. Westport, CT: Greenwood, 2001.

———. *The Character of a Genius: Beethoven in Perspective*. Westport, CT: Greenwood, 2002.

DeNora, Tia. *Beethoven and the Construction of Genius: Musical Politics in Vienna, 1792–1803*. Berkeley: University of California Press, 1995.

Grove, George. *Beethoven, Schubert, Mendelssohn*. London: MacMillan, 1951; reprint of "Ludwig van Beethoven," ed. by Eric Blom. Originally published in *A Dictionary of Music and Musicians*, 4 vols. (1879, 1880, 1883, 1890), vol. I. London and New York: MacMillan, 1890.

Hanson, Alice M. *Musical Life in Biedermeier Vienna*. Cambridge: Cambridge University Press, 1985.

Heartz, Daniel. *Mozart, Haydn, and Early Beethoven, 1781–1802*. New York: Norton, 2009.

Kinderman, William. *Beethoven*. 2nd ed. New York: Oxford University Press, 1995, 2009.

Kivy, Peter. *The Possessor and the Possessed: Handel, Mozart, Beethoven, and the Idea of Musical Genius*. New Haven, CT: Yale University Press, 2001.

Kolodin, Irving. *The Interior Beethoven: A Biography of the Music*. New York: Knopf, 1975.

Kropfinger, Klaus. *Wagner and Beethoven: Richard Wagner's Reception of Beethoven*. Cambridge: Cambridge University Press, 1991.

Lockwood, Lewis. *Beethoven: Studies in the Creative Process*. Cambridge, MA: Harvard University Press, 1992.

———. *Beethoven: The Music and the Life*. New York: Norton, 2003.

Mai, François Martin. *Diagnosing Genius: The Life and Death of Beethoven*. Montreal: McGill-Queen's University Press, 2007.

Mathew, Nicholas. *Political Beethoven*. Cambridge: Cambridge University Press, 2013.

Schindler, Anton. *The Life of Beethoven*. Edited by Ignaz Moscheles. 2 vols. London, 1941, trans. of first ed., 1840; expanded and supplemented 3rd ed., 1860; repr. as *Beethoven as I Knew Him*, edited by Donald W. MacArdle. London: Norton, 1966.

Solomon, Maynard. *Beethoven*. New York: Schirmer, 1977; 2nd rev. ed., 1998.

———. *Beethoven Essays*. Cambridge, MA: Harvard University Press, 1988.

———. *Late Beethoven: Music, Thought, Imagination*. Berkeley: University of California Press, 2003.

Sonneck, O. G. *Beethoven: Impressions by His Contemporaries*. First published 1926. New York: Dover, 1967.

Stanley, Glenn, ed. *The Cambridge Companion to Beethoven*. Cambridge: Cambridge University Press, 2000.

Sullivan, J. W. N. *Beethoven: His Spiritual Development*. First published 1927. New York: Vintage, 1960.

Swafford, Jan. *Beethoven: Anguish and Triumph*. Boston: Houghton Mifflin Harcourt, 2014.

Tyson, Alan, ed. *Beethoven Studies*. New York: Norton, 1973.

———, ed. *Beethoven Studies*. Vol. 2. London: Oxford University Press, 1977.

———, ed. *Beethoven Studies*. Vol. 3. Cambridge: Cambridge University Press, 1982.

Wagner, Richard. *Beethoven*. 1870. Newly translated and with an introduction by Roger Allen. Woodbridge, UK: Boydell, 2014.

Wallace, Robin. *Beethoven's Critics: Aesthetic Dilemmas and Resolutions during the Composer's Lifetime*. Cambridge: Cambridge University Press, 1986.

Wegeler, Franz, and Ferdinand Ries. *Beethoven Remembered: The Biographical Notes of Franz Wegeler and Ferdinand Ries*. Originally published in German in 1838; 2nd ed., 1845. Arlington, Virginia: Great Ocean, 1987.

Winter, Robert, and Bruce Carr. *Beethoven, Performers, and Critics*. Detroit: Wayne State University Press, 1980.

Individual Works and Genre Studies

Albrecht, Theodore. "Beethoven's Tribute to Antonio Salieri in the Rondo of His Fortepiano Concerto in C Major, Opus 15 (and Beethoven's Hand-Copied Excerpts from *Les Danaïdes*)." *Beethoven Journal* 22, no. 1 (Summer 2007): 6–16.

Brown, A. Peter. *The Symphonic Repertoire. The First Golden Age of the Viennese Symphony: Haydn, Mozart, Beethoven, and Schubert*. Vol. 2. Bloomington: Indiana University Press, 2002.

Burnham, Scott. *Beethoven Hero*. Princeton, NJ: Princeton University Press, 1995.

Cook, Nicholas. *Beethoven: Symphony No. 9*. Cambridge: Cambridge University Press, 1993.

Cooper, Barry. "Commentaries." In *Beethoven: The 35 Piano Sonatas*, edited by Barry Cooper. 3 vols. London: Associated Board of the Royal School of Music, 2007; rev. 2013.

———. "Introductions." In *The Five Piano Concertos*, edited by Jonathan Del Mar. 5 vols. Kassel, Germany: Bärenreiter, 2015.

———. "Introductions." In *The Nine Symphonies*, edited by Jonathan Del Mar. 9 vols. Kassel, Germany: Bärenreiter, 1999.

Dahlhaus, Carl. *Nineteenth-Century Music*. Berkeley: University of California Press, 1989.

Drabkin, William. *Beethoven: "Missa solemnis."* Cambridge: Cambridge University Press, 1991.

Forbes, Elliot, ed. *Beethoven: Symphony No. 5 in C Minor*. New York: Norton, 1971.

Frohlich, Martha. *Beethoven's "Appassionata" Sonata*. Oxford, UK: Clarendon, 1991.

Grove, George. *Beethoven and His Nine Symphonies*. London: Constable, 1896; 3rd ed., London: Novello, Ewer, 1898; reprint of 3rd ed., New York: Dover, 1962.

Hopkins, Antony. *The Nine Symphonies of Beethoven*. London: Heinemann, 1981.

———. *The Seven Concertos of Beethoven*. Aldershot, UK: Ashgate, 1996.

Jander, Owen. *Beethoven's "Orpheus" Concerto: The Fourth Piano Concerto in Its Cultural Context*. Hillsdale, NY: Pendragon, 2009.

Johnson, Douglas. *Beethoven's Early Sketches in the "Fischhof Miscellany," Berlin Autograph 28*. Ann Arbor, MI: UMI, 1980.

Jones, Timothy. *Beethoven: The "Moonlight" and Other Sonatas, Op. 27 and Op. 31*. Cambridge: Cambridge University Press, 1999.

Kaufman, Moisés. *33 Variations*. New York: Dramatists Play Service, 2011.

Kerman, Joseph. *The Beethoven Quartets*. New York: Knopf, 1967.

———, ed. *Ludwig van Beethoven: Autograph Miscellany from circa 1786 to 1799* [the "Kafka" Sketchbook]. 2 vols. London: British Museum, 1970.

———. *Write All These Down: Essays on Music*. Berkeley: University of California Press, 1994 (includes reprints of "An die ferne Geliebte" [1973] and "Beethoven's Minority" [1998]).

Kinderman, William, ed. *Beethoven's Compositional Process*. Lincoln: University of Nebraska Press, 1991.

———. *Beethoven's Diabelli Variations*. New York: Oxford University Press, 1989.

Kivy, Peter. *The Possessor and the Possessed: Handel, Mozart, Beethoven, and the Idea of Musical Genius*. New Haven, CT: Yale University Press, 2001.

Korsyn, Kevin. "J. W. N. Sullivan and the *Heiliger Dankgesang*: Questions of Meaning in Late Beethoven." In *Beethoven Forum*, vol. 2, edited by Christopher Reynolds, 133–74. Lincoln: University of Nebraska Press, 1993.

Levy, David Benjamin. *Beethoven: The Ninth Symphony*. New York: Schirmer, 1995; rev. ed., New Haven, CT: Yale University Press, 2003.

Lockwood, Lewis, and Juilliard String Quartet. *Beethoven's Symphonies: An Artistic Vision*. New York: Norton, 2015.

———. *Inside Beethoven's Quartets: History, Interpretation, Performance*. Cambridge, MA: Harvard University Press, 2008.

Plantinga, Leon. *Beethoven's Concertos*. New York: Norton, 1999.

Robinson, Paul, ed. *Ludwig van Beethoven: "Fidelio."* Cambridge: Cambridge University Press, 1996.

Rosen, Charles. *Beethoven's Piano Sonatas: A Short Companion*. New Haven, CT: Yale University Press, 2002.

———. *The Classical Style: Haydn, Mozart, Beethoven*. New York: Norton, 1971; rev. 2nd ed., 1997.

———. *The Romantic Generation*. Cambridge, MA: Harvard University Press, 1995.

Sipe, Thomas. *Beethoven: "Eroica" Symphony*. Cambridge: Cambridge University Press, 1998.

Steinberg, Michael. *Choral Masterworks: A Listener's Guide*. New York: Oxford University Press, 2005.

———. *The Concerto: A Listener's Guide*. New York: Oxford University Press, 1998.

———. *The Symphony: A Listener's Guide*. New York: Oxford University Press, 1995.

Tovey, Donald Francis. *A Companion to Beethoven's Pianoforte Sonatas*. London: Associated Board of the Royal Schools of Music, 1931.

———. *Essays in Musical Analysis*. 6 vols. and supplementary volume: *Chamber Music*. London: Oxford University Press, 1944.

Winter, Robert. *Compositional Origins of Beethoven's Opus 131*. Ann Arbor, MI: UMI Research, 1982.

Winter, Robert, and Robert Martin, eds. *The Beethoven Quartet Companion*. Berkeley: University of California Press, 1994.

Wyn Jones, David. *Beethoven: "Pastoral Symphony."* Cambridge: Cambridge University Press, 1995.

———. *The Symphony in Beethoven's Vienna*. Cambridge: Cambridge University Press, 2006.

ARTICLES AND BOOK CHAPTERS

Albrecht, Theodore. "Anton Schindler as Destroyer and Forger of Beethoven's Conversation Books: A Case for Decriminalization." In *Music's Intellectual History*, edited by Zdravko Blažeković and Barbara Dobbs Mackenzie, 169–81. New York: Répertoire International de Littérature Musical, 2009.

Bernstein, Leonard. "Beethoven Symphony No. 3 in E Flat Major, Opus 55 ('Eroica')." In *The Infinite Variety of Music*, 195–227. New York: Simon and Schuster, 1966.

———. "Musical Semantics." In *The Unanswered Question: Six Talks at Harvard*, 119–89. Cambridge, MA: Harvard University Press, 1976.

———. "Why Beethoven?" In *The Joy of Music*, 21–29. New York: Simon and Schuster, 1959.

Block, Geoffrey. "Organic Relations in Beethoven's Early Piano Concerti and the 'The Spirit of Mozart.'" In *Beethoven's Compositional Press*, edited by William Kinderman, 55–81. Lincoln: University of Nebraska Press, 1991.

Brendel, Alfred. "Must Classical Music Be Entirely Serious? 2: Beethoven's Diabelli Variations." In *Music Sounded Out*, 37–53. New York: Noonday, 1990.

Cairns, David. "*Fidelio*." In *Responses*, 3–21. London: Secker and Warburg, 1973; repr., New York: Da Capo, 1980.

———. "*Fidelio*." In *The New Penguin Opera Guide*, edited by Amanda Holden, 43–46. London: Penguin, 2001.

Cook, Nicholas. "The Other Beethoven: Heroism, the Canon, and the Works of 1813–14." *19th Century Music* 27 (2003): 3–24.

Cooper, Barry. "Beethoven's Portfolio of Bagatelles." *Journal of the Royal Musical Association* 112, no. 2 (1986–1987): 208–28.

———. "Beethoven's Revisions to *Für Elise*." *Musical Times* 125 (October 1984): 561–63.

———. "Beethoven's Revisions to His Fourth Piano Concerto." In *Performing Beethoven*, ed. Robn Stowell, 23–48. Cambridge: Cambridge University Press, 1994.

Ferraguto, Mark. "Beethoven *à la Moujik*: Russianness and Learned Style in the 'Razumovsky' String Quartets." *Journal of the American Musicological Society* 67, no. 1 (Spring 2014): 77–124.

Forbes, Elliot. "Beethoven as a Choral Composer." *Proceedings of the Royal Musical Association* 97 (1970–1971): 69–82.

———. "A Neglected Work in Beethoven's Choral Music: The Funeral Cantata." In *Essays on Music in Honor of Archibald Davison by His Associates*, 253–61. Cambridge, MA: Department of Music, Harvard University, 1957.

Gingerich, John M. "Ignaz Schuppanzigh and Beethoven's Late Quartets." *Musical Quarterly* 93 (2010): 450–513.

———. "'If Love and Strength Are Wedded': The Meaning of the *Choral Fantasia*, Op. 80, and the Work's Narrative Significance as the Conclusion of the Beethoven's Concert of December 22, 1808." *Beethoven Journal* 30, no. 1 (Summer 2015): 4–24.

Johnson, Douglas. "1794–95: Decisive Years in Beethoven's Early Development." In *Beethoven Studies*, vol. 3, edited by Alan Tyson, 1–28. New York: Norton, 1973.

Kerman, Joseph. "An die ferne Geliebte." In *Beethoven Studies*, vol. 1, edited by Alan Tyson, 123–57. New York: Norton, 1973 (reprinted in Kerman, *Write All These Down*, 173–216; see "Individual Works and Genre Studies").

———. "The Beethoven Takeover." *New York Review of Books*, October 3, 1996, 23–25.

———. "Beethoven's Minority." In Kerman, *Write All These Down*, 217–37 (see "Individual Works and Genre Studies").

———. "Opus 131 and the Uncanny." In *The String Quartets of Beethoven*, edited by William Kinderman, 262–78. Urbana: University of Illinois Press, 1995.

Kinderman, William. "The Evolution and Structure of Beethoven's 'Diabelli' Variations." *Journal of the American Musicological Society* 35 (1982): 306–28.

———. "Transformational Processes in Beethoven's Op. 18 Quartets." In *The String Quartets of Beethoven*, edited by William Kinderman, 31–59. Urbana: University of Illinois Press, 2006.

Kirkendale, Warren. "New Roads to Old Ideas in Beethoven's Missa Solemnis." *Musical Quarterly* 56 (1970): 665–701; repr. in *The Creative World of Beethoven*, edited by Paul Henry Lang, 163–99. New York: Norton, 1971.

Knittel, K. M. "The Construction of Beethoven." In *The Cambridge History of Nineteenth-Century Music*, edited by Jim Samson, 118–50. Cambridge: Cambridge University Press, 2001.

———. "Wagner, Deafness, and the Reception of Beethoven's Late Style." *Journal of the American Musicological Society* 51 (1998): 49–82.

La Grange, Henry-Louis de. "Fidelio." In *Gustave Mahler, Vol. 3, Vienna: Triumph and Disillusion (1904-1907)*, 1–76. New York: Oxford University Press, 1999.

Lockwood, Lewis. "Beethoven before 1800: The Mozart Legacy." In *Beethoven Forum*, vol. 3, 39–52. Lincoln: University of Nebraska Press, 1994.

———. "Beethoven, Florestan, and the Varieties of Heroism." In *Beethoven and His World*, edited by Scott Burnham and Michael P. Steinberg, 27–50. Princeton, NJ: Princeton University Press, 2000.

———. "Beethoven's *Leonore* and *Fidelio*." *Journal of Interdisciplinary History* 36, no. 3, Opera and Society: Part 1 (Winter 2006): 473–82.

———. "On Beethoven's Sketches and Autographs: Some Problems of Definition and Interpretation." *Acta Musicologica* 42 (1970): 32–47.

Meredith, William. "The *Eroica* and Beethoven's Sexuality through a Feminist Lens: Susan McClary's Reading of Beethoven in *Queering the Pitch*." *Beethoven Newsletter* 8, no. 3; 9, no. 1 (Winter 1993–Spring 1994): 107–9.

Pederson, Sanna. "Beethoven and Masculinity." In *Beethoven and His World*, edited by Scott Burnham and Michael P. Steinberg, 323–31. Princeton, NJ: Princeton University Press, 2000.

Rosen, Charles. "Beethoven's Career." In *Critical Entertainments: Music Old and New*, 105–23. Cambridge, MA: Harvard University Press, 2000.

Schachter, Carl. "Mozart's Last and Beethoven's First: Echoes of K. 551 in the First Movement of Opus 21." In *Mozart Studies*, edited by Cliff Eisen, 227–51. Oxford, UK: Clarendon, 1991.

Solomon, Maynard. "Beethoven's Productivity at Bonn." *Music and Letters* 53, no. 2 (April 1972): 165–72.

———. "The Ninth Symphony: A Search for Order." In *Beethoven Essays*, 3–34. Cambridge, MA: Harvard University Press, 1988.

Spitzer, Michael. "Convergences: Criticism, Analysis and Beethoven Reception." *Musical Analysis* 16, no. 3 (October 1997): 369–91.

Stanley, Glenn. "The 'wirklich ganz neue Manier' to the Path to It: Beethoven's Variations for Piano, 1783–1802." *Beethoven Forum*, vol. 3, 53–80. Lincoln: University of Nebraska Press, 1994.

Steinberg, Michael. "Notes on the Quartets." In *The Beethoven Quartet Companion*, edited by Robert Winter and Robert Martin, 143–282. Berkeley: University of California Press, 1994.

Taruskin, Richard. "The First Romantics" and "The 'Struggle and Victory' Narrative and Its Relationship to Four C-Minor Works of Beethoven." In *The Oxford History of Western Music*, vol. 2: *The Seventeenth and Eighteenth Centuries*, 641–90. New York: Oxford University Press, 2005.

———. "Resisting the Ninth." *19th Century Music* 12, no. 3 (1988–1989): 241–56; repr. in *Text and Act: Essays on Music and Performance*, 235–61. New York: Oxford University Press, 1995.

Tyson, Alan. "Beethoven's Heroic Phase." *Musical Times* 110 (1969): 139–41.

———. "Beethoven's *Kafka Sketchbook*." *Musical Times* 111, Beethoven Bicentenary Issue (December 1970): 1194–95, 1197–98.

———. "The Problem of Beethoven's 'First' *Leonore* Overture." *Journal of the American Musicological Society* (Summer 1975): 292–334.

———. "The *Razumovsky* Quartets: Some Aspects of the Sources." *Beethoven Studies*, vol. 3, edited by Tyson, 107–40. Cambridge: Cambridge University Press, 1982.

Volek, Tomislav, and Jaroslav Macek. "Beethoven's Rehearsals at the Lobkowitz's." *Musical Times* 127 (February 1986): 75–80.

Webster, James. "The Concept of Beethoven's 'Early' Period in the Context of Periodizations in General." In *Beethoven Forum*, vol. 3, 1–28. Lincoln: University of Nebraska Press, 1994.

———. "The Form of the Finale of Beethoven's Ninth Symphony." In *Beethoven Forum*, vol. 1, 25–62. Lincoln: University of Nebraska Press, 1992.

Winter, Robert. "Plans for the Structure of the String Quartet in C Sharp Minor, Op. 131." In *Beethoven Studies*, vol. 2, edited by Alan Tyson, 106–37. London: Oxford University Press, 1977.

———. "The Sketches for the 'Ode to Joy.'" In *Beethoven, Performers, and Critics*, edited by Robert Winter and Bruce Carr, 176–214. Detroit: Wayne State University, 1980.

SELECTED DISCOGRAPHY

CHAMBER MUSIC

The Busch String Quartet: The Beethoven Late Quartets. Recorded 1933–1942: op. 59/1 (1942); op. 127 (1936); op. 130 (1941); op. 131 (1936); op. 132 (1937); op. 135 (1933). Pristine Classical PACM 093.

The Complete String Quartets. Belcea Quartet. Recorded 2011–2012. Outhere Music ZZT344. 8 CDs.

The Early String Quartets. Op. 18. Guarneri Quartet. Recorded 1966–1969. RCA 60456-2-RG. 3 CDs.

The Late String Quartets. Op. 127, 130, 131, 132, 133, 135. Guarneri Quartet. Recorded 1968–1969. RCA 60458-2-RG. 3 CDs.

The Late String Quartets. Budapest String Quartet in Concert at the Library of Congress. Recorded 1941–1945 and 1960. Op. 127 (1941); op. 130 (1960); op. 131 (1943); *Grosse Fuge,* op. 133 (1960); op. 132 (1945); op. 135 (1943). Bridge 9072 A/C. 3 CDs.

The Middle String Quartets. Op. 59, 74, 95. Guarneri Quartet. Recorded 1966–1968. RCA Victor 60457-2-RG. 3 CDs.

Piano Quartets. WoO 36. New Zealand Piano Quartet. Recorded 2005. Naxos 8.570998.

CHORAL AND OPERA

Cantata on the Death of Emperor Joseph II and Cantata on the Accession of Emperor Leopold II. Corydon Singers and Orchestra. Conducted by Matthew Best. Recorded 1996. Hyperion CDA 66880.

Choral Fantasy: Rudolf Serkin Plays Beethoven. New York Philharmonic. Conducted by Leonard Bernstein. Recorded 1962. Sony 988302. 11 CDs (CD 3).

Fidelio. Metropolitan Opera Orchestra and Chorus. Conducted by James Levine. Starring Karita Mattila (Leonore) and Ben Heppner (Florestan). Recorded 2000. DG 073052-9. DVD.

Fidelio. Philharmonia Chorus and Orchestra. Conducted by Otto Klemperer. Recorded 1962. EMI 7243 5 56211 2 2. 2 CDs (1814 version).

Leonore. Monteverdi Choir and Orchestre Révolutionnaire et Romantique. Conducted by John Eliot Gardiner. Recorded 1996. Archiv 453 461-2. 2 CDs (1805–1806 versions of *Fidelio*).

ORCHESTRAL (INCLUDING CONCERTOS)

Piano Concertos Nos. 1–2. Martha Argerich, piano. Philharmonia Orchestra. Conducted by Giuseppe Sinopoli. Recorded 1985. DG 415 682-1.

Piano Concertos Nos. 1–4. Leon Fleisher, piano. Cleveland Orchestra. Conducted by George Szell. Recorded 1959–1961: Nos. 1–3 (1961); No. 4 (1959). Sony SBK 47658 (Nos. 1 and 3). Sony SBK 48165 (Nos. 2 and 4).

Symphonies Nos. 1–9. NBC Symphony Orchestra and the Robert Shaw Chorale. Conducted by Arturo Toscanini. Recorded 1949 and 1951–1953. Reissued on RCA 55702. 5 CDs.

Symphonies Nos. 1–9. Orchestre Révolutionnaire et Romantique and the Monteverdi Choir. Conducted by John Eliot Gardiner. Recorded 1991–1994. Archiv 439 900-2. 5 CDs.

Symphonies Nos. 1–9: Overtures. London Classical Players and the Schütz Choir of London. Conducted by Roger Norrington. Recorded 1986–1988. Reissued on Virgin Classics 61943. 5 CDs.

Symphonies Nos. 5 and 7. Wiener Philharmoniker. Conducted by Carlos Kleiber. Recorded 1975–1976. DG 447 400-2.

Symphony No. 9: Ode to Freedom; Bernstein in Berlin. Bavarian Radio Symphony Orchestra, Bavarian Radio Chorus, Dresden Philharmonic Children's Chorus, and members of Dresden, Leningrad, London, New York, and Paris orchestras. Conducted by Leonard Bernstein. Recorded December 25, 1989. CD: DG 429 861-2; DVD: EuroArts EUA 2072039.

Wellington's Victory. Berliner Philharmoniker. Conducted by Herbert von Karajan. Recorded 1969. DG 419 624-2.

PIANO: SONATAS, VARIATIONS, AND BAGATELLES

Artur Schnabel Plays Beethoven Piano Sonatas Vol. 10. Op. 110, 111, *Eroica* Variations, op. 35. Recorded 1932 and 1938. Pristine Classical PAKM 048.

Bagatelles, Op. 33, 119, 126, Bagatelle in A Minor, WoO 59 (Für Elise). Alfred Brendel, piano. Recorded 1984 (*Für Elise*); 1996 (op. 33, 119, 126). Philips 456 031-2.

Diabelli Variations, Op. 120. Uri Caine and Concerto Köln. Recorded 2002. Winter & Winter WDR 910 086-2.

Diabelli Variations, Op. 120; Bagatelles Op. 119. Rudolf Serkin Plays Beethoven. Recorded 1957 (*Diabelli*); 1966 (op. 119). Sony 988302. 11 CDs (CD 10). Also available on CBS Records MPK 44837.

Diabelli Variations, Op. 120; Piano Sonatas, Op. 53, 109, 111; Piano Concerto No. 4. Great Pianists of the 20th Century: Artur Schnabel. Recorded 1933 (op. 53 and Piano Concerto No. 4); 1937 (*Diabelli*); 1942 (op. 109, 111). EMI 456 961-2. 2 CDs. Remastered Schnabel *Diabelli* is also available on Pristine Classical PAKM 047.

Piano Sonatas. Op. 2/1, op. 27/2 (*Moonlight*), op. 31/2 (*Tempest*), op. 101. Malcolm Bilson, fortepiano. Recorded 1994. Claves CD 50-9707/10.

Piano Sonatas Complete. Paul Lewis, piano. Recorded 2005–2007. Harmonia Mundi HMX 2901902.11. 10 CDs.

Piano Sonatas Vol. 10 (Elector Sonatas). WoO 47. Jenő Jandó, piano. Recorded 1989. Naxos 8.550255.

Variations and Vignettes for Piano. Righini Variations, WoO 65. Alfred Brendel, piano. Recorded 1964. VoxBox CD3X 3017. 3 CDs.

SONGS

Complete Beethoven Edition Vol. 16: "Lieder." Dietrich Fischer-Dieskau, baritone; Jörg
Demus, piano; Peter Schreier, tenor, Adele Stolte, soprano, Günther Leib, bass-baritone;
Walter Olbertz, piano. Recorded 1966–1970 and 1997. DG 453 782-2. 3 CDs.

INDEX

ABOUT THE AUTHOR

Geoffrey Block received his BA in music history and literature from the University of California at Los Angeles in 1970 and his MA (1973) and PhD (1979) in music history and theory from Harvard University. His dissertation on compositional process in Beethoven's first and second piano concertos was aided by manuscript research in Germany as a Fulbright Fellow (1975–1976). He joined the faculty of the University of Puget Sound in 1980 and was named distinguished professor of music history in 2008.

A prolific and wide-ranging scholar, Block has published most extensively on the music of Charles Ives and American musical theater, particularly the life and work of Richard Rodgers. His books include *Charles Ives: A Bio-Bibliography* (1988), *Charles Ives: "Concord" Sonata* (1996), *Charles Ives and the Classical Tradition*, coeditor (1996), *Enchanted Evenings: The Broadway Musical from "Show Boat" to Sondheim and Lloyd Webber* (1997; 2nd ed., 2009), *The Richard Rodgers Reader*, editor (2002), *Richard Rodgers* (2003), and *Schubert's Reputation from His Time to Ours* (2017). Block was also general editor of the Yale Broadway Masters Series between 1998 and 2010 and serves as series editor of Oxford's Broadway Legacies since 2008.

Block's Beethoven writings include essays in *Beethoven Essays: Studies in Honor of Elliot Forbes*, edited by Lewis Lockwood and Phyllis Benjamin (1984); *Beethoven's Composition Process*, edited by William Kinderman (1991); and *Beethoven Newsletter*.